OECD Tax Policy Studies

Inheritance Taxation in OECD Countries

No. 28

OECD
BETTER POLICIES FOR BETTER LIVES

Please cite this publication as:
OECD (2021), *Inheritance Taxation in OECD Countries*, OECD Tax Policy Studies, No. 28, OECD Publishing, Paris, https://doi.org/10.1787/e2879a7d-en.

ISBN 978-92-64-68329-7 (print)
ISBN 978-92-64-63428-2 (pdf)
ISBN 978-92-64-97750-1 (HTML)
ISBN 978-92-64-47067-5 (epub)

OECD Tax Policy Studies
ISSN 1990-0546 (print)
ISSN 1990-0538 (online)

Photo credits: Cover © selensergen/Thinkstock.

Corrigenda to publications may be found on line at: www.oecd.org/about/publishing/corrigenda.htm.

Foreword

Wealth inequality has become an increasingly prominent topic in recent years. Wealth is highly concentrated at the top of the distribution, much more so than income, and income and wealth inequalities can be mutually reinforcing. Moreover, household wealth inequality has remained persistently high and has even increased over time in some OECD countries, largely as a consequence of increases in asset prices and savings rates. In some OECD countries, wealth inequality is higher than it has been for several decades.

Trends in wealth transfers are also likely to reinforce wealth concentration. The share of inherited wealth in total private wealth has increased in some countries in recent decades. Inheritances are also expected to increase in number, with the baby-boom generation getting older, and in value, if trends in asset prices continue. In addition, wealth is expected to remain concentrated among older cohorts for longer periods of time and the age at which people inherit will likely continue to rise due to longer life expectancies.

The COVID-19 crisis will likely place countries under greater pressure to raise more revenues and address inequalities. The outbreak of COVID-19 has resulted in a health crisis and a drop in economic activity that are without precedent in recent history, and there remains considerable uncertainty around how events will unfold. As public spending has heavily increased during the crisis, governments will start looking to restore public finances as countries exit the crisis and economic recovery is underway. However, the crisis has exacerbated existing inequalities and hit many vulnerable households harder, and traditional revenue-raising approaches, such as raising taxes on labour income and consumption as was done in the wake of the 2008 global financial crisis, may be less desirable from an equity and growth perspective. The crisis will likely prompt reflection on the need to turn to new or under-utilised sources of revenue, which may also be compatible with inequality reduction objectives.

The report explores the role that inheritance taxation could play in raising revenues, addressing inequalities and improving efficiency in the future. While taxes on wealth transfers – including inheritance, estate, and gift taxes – are levied in 24 of the 36 OECD countries covered in the report,[1] they have typically played a limited role in raising revenues. In 2018, only 0.5% of total tax revenues were sourced from these taxes on average across the countries that levied them. A key question that the report examines is whether there might be a case for a greater use of inheritance taxation in OECD countries on equity, efficiency and administrative grounds.

The report also provides a comparative overview and assessment of inheritance, estate, and gift tax design across OECD countries and identifies a number of options for tax reform. Experiences with inheritance taxation have differed across countries, with significant cross-country variation in the design and implementation of inheritance, estate, and gift taxes. The report helps provide an understanding of how the design and implementation of inheritance, estate, and gift taxes have impacted their effectiveness and fairness in practice. Based on this comparative assessment, as well as findings from the literature, the report identifies a number of reform options that governments could consider to improve the design and functioning of their taxes on wealth transfers.

This project is part of a broader work stream on capital taxation at the OECD. In 2018, the OECD released two reports on *The Taxation of Household Savings* and *The Role and Design of Net Wealth Taxes*. This new report on inheritance taxation is a significant additional contribution in the area of personal capital taxation. The various projects that the OECD has undertaken on the taxation of personal capital income, net wealth and inheritances should be viewed as complementary given that these different taxes closely interact with each other.

The report contains four chapters. Chapter 1 looks at the distribution and the evolution of household wealth and wealth transfers. Chapter 2 examines the arguments for and against inheritance taxation based on equity, efficiency and administrative considerations. Chapter 3 examines how OECD countries currently tax wealth transfers, by providing a comparative overview of inheritance, estate, and gifts taxes across countries, and assesses the impact of their design features. Chapter 4 summarises the key messages of the report and identifies a number of options and recommendations for tax reform.

Acknowledgments

This study was produced by the Tax Policy and Statistics Division of the OECD Centre for Tax Policy and Administration, with the financial support of the Korea Institute of Public Finance (KIPF).

The report was led by Sarah Perret and written by Bethany Millar-Powell and Sarah Perret. The authors would like to thank Bert Brys and David Bradbury for their guidance and feedback throughout the project. The report also benefited from significant input from Michael Stemmer on the simulations included in Chapter 2 and from very helpful comments from Pierce O'Reilly and Alastair Thomas. The authors would also like to thank Carlotta Balestra for supplying the underlying data used in Chapter 1 based on the OECD Wealth Distribution Database and for providing feedback on Chapter 1, as well as Sebastian Königs for his review of Chapter 1. The authors are also very grateful to Carrie Tyler, Natalie Lagorce, Julien Dubuc, Hazel Healy and Karena Garnier for their support with communications and formatting, and to Violet Sochay for her assistance with administrative matters. In addition to OECD colleagues, the authors would like to acknowledge Emma Chamberlain (OBE CTA Barrister, Pump Court Tax Chambers) and Daniel Waldenström (Professor, Research Institute of Industrial Economics – IFN Stockholm) for their thorough review and comments on the first draft of the report. Ricardo Guerrero (PhD candidate, King's College London) provided some background research as input to Chapter 2.

The report would not have been possible without the significant involvement of the delegates of Working Party No.2 on Tax Policy Analysis and Tax Statistics (WP2) who replied to the "OECD Questionnaire on Inheritance, Estate, and Gift Taxes", upon which the analysis in the report is largely based, and provided feedback on the draft report at various stages.

This report was approved by WP2 delegates on 15 March 2021 and by the delegates of the Committee on Fiscal Affairs (CFA) on 14 April 2021. The report was prepared for publication by the OECD Secretariat.

Table of contents

FIGURES

TABLES

Executive summary

This report provides a comparative assessment of inheritance taxation across OECD countries and explores the role that inheritance, estate, and gift taxes could play in raising revenues, addressing inequalities and improving efficiency in the future. The report provides background on the distribution and evolution of household wealth and inheritances, assesses the case for and against inheritance taxation, and examines the design of inheritance, estate, and gift taxes in OECD countries. It concludes with a number of reform options that governments could consider to improve the design and functioning of taxes on wealth transfers.

Inheritance taxation could play a particularly important role in the current context. Wealth inequality has been persistently high and has increased in some countries over recent decades. Inheritances are also unequally distributed across households, with wealthier households reporting more and higher-value inheritances. In the future, inheritances are expected to grow in value if trends in asset prices continue, and in number as the baby-boom generation ages. Moreover, as a result of longer life expectancies, wealth concentration among older cohorts is expected to increase. These trends could further reinforce inequality. The COVID-19 crisis will also place countries under greater pressure to raise additional tax revenues and address inequalities, which have been exacerbated since the start of the pandemic.

Inheritance and estate taxes are levied in 24 OECD countries. Most countries levy recipient-based inheritance taxes. Denmark, Korea, the United Kingdom and the United States, on the other hand, levy estate taxes on donors' overall estates. Ireland levies a specific type of recipient-based inheritance and gift tax on lifetime wealth transfers. Among the OECD countries that do not levy inheritance or estate taxes, nine have abolished them since the early 1970s.

The design of inheritance, estate, and gift taxes varies widely across countries. Significant differences include the levels of wealth that can be passed on tax-free. Tax exemption thresholds tend to favour close relatives, but they vary considerably across countries, ranging for instance from close to USD 17 000 in Belgium (Brussels-capital) to more than USD 11 million in the United States for transfers to children. There is also significant variation in tax rates across countries. Most countries have progressive tax rates, but around one third apply flat tax rates, and tax rates differ widely. The tax treatment of gifts also varies depending on the country, even if in-life giving often benefits from preferential tax treatment compared to wealth transfers at death.

Across countries, however, numerous provisions have narrowed inheritance tax bases, reducing potential revenues, efficiency and fairness. Today, only 0.5% of total tax revenues are sourced from these taxes on average across the OECD countries that levy them. Low revenues largely reflect narrow inheritance tax bases and tax planning opportunities. A majority of estates go untaxed in a number of countries in large part due to the highly preferential tax treatment applying to transfers to close relatives and because of the relief provided for transfers of specific assets (e.g. main residence, business and farm assets, pension assets, and life insurance policies). In a number of countries, inheritance and estate taxes can also largely be avoided through in-life gifts, due to their more favourable tax treatment. Other tax planning opportunities (e.g. separating bare ownership from usufruct, use of preferential valuation rules) have also allowed taxpayers to minimise their inheritance or estate tax burdens. In addition to significantly reducing revenue collection, some of these relief provisions primarily benefit the wealthiest households, reducing the progressivity of inheritance and estate taxes.

The report finds that well-designed inheritance taxes can raise revenue and enhance equity, at lower efficiency and administrative costs than other alternatives. From an equity perspective, an inheritance tax, particularly one that targets relatively high levels of wealth transfers, can be an important tool to enhance equality of opportunity and reduce wealth concentration. The case for inheritance taxes might be strongest where the effective taxation of personal capital income and wealth tends to be low. From an efficiency perspective, while the number of studies is limited, the empirical literature generally suggests that inheritance taxes tend to have more limited effects on savings than other taxes levied on wealthy taxpayers, and confirms their positive effects on heirs' incentives to work and on donors' charitable giving. In addition, while inheritance taxes might negatively affect family business successions (depending on tax design), they might at the same time reduce risks of misallocating capital to less skilled heirs. Inheritance taxes also have a number of administrative advantages compared to other forms of wealth taxation, particularly those that are levied annually.

The report stresses that the way inheritance, estate, and gift taxes are designed is critical to ensuring that they achieve their objectives. It suggests a number of reform options that may be considered to enhance the revenue raising potential, efficiency, and equity of inheritance, estate, and gift taxes.

The report finds that a recipient-based inheritance tax may be more equitable than an estate tax on the total wealth transferred by donors. If the objective is to promote equality of opportunity, it is the amount of wealth received by each recipient and their personal circumstances that matter more than the overall amount of wealth left by the donor. A recipient-based inheritance tax allows for progressive tax rates to be levied on the amount of wealth received by beneficiaries. Another advantage of a recipient-based inheritance tax is that it may encourage the division of estates and further reduce concentrations of wealth, as splitting bequests among multiple beneficiaries reduces inheritance tax liabilities. In contrast to inheritance taxes, estate taxes are easier to collect because they are levied on overall estates and involve a smaller number of taxing points.

A particularly fair and efficient approach would consist of taxing beneficiaries on the gifts and bequests they receive over their life through a tax on lifetime wealth transfers. Under a tax on lifetime wealth transfers, the tax liability for each wealth transfer would be determined by taking into account the amount of wealth previously received by the beneficiary. Such a tax could be levied above a lifetime tax exemption threshold, i.e. above an amount of wealth that beneficiaries would be entitled to receive tax-free during the course of their life through both gifts and inheritances. Taking into account previous wealth received by beneficiaries would ensure that individuals who receive more wealth over their lifetime pay more inheritance tax than individuals who receive less, particularly if tax rates are progressive. It would also ensure that beneficiaries receiving the same amounts of wealth, regardless of whether it is through multiple small transfers or one large transfer, face similar tax labilities, which would enhance fairness and reduce avoidance opportunities. However, a tax on lifetime wealth transfers may increase administrative and compliance costs.

Regardless of the type of wealth transfer tax implemented, there are a range of reforms that countries could consider. Tax exemption thresholds should be designed to exempt small inheritances, allowing heirs to receive some amount of wealth tax-free. Where tax rates are flat, progressive tax rates could be considered to ensure that those who receive more wealth are taxed more. Where there are significant gaps between the tax treatment applying to direct descendants and that applying to more distant heirs, these could be narrowed. Applying higher tax rates to transfers to more distant family members provide even more incentives for donors to concentrate their wealth transfers among closer family members. Higher tax rates on wealth received from distantly related donors may also be questionable where recipients have not received much from their parents. Measures should also be put in place to help taxpayers overcome liquidity issues.

Opportunities for tax planning and avoidance should be minimised through better tax design, and efforts to combat tax evasion should be further strengthened. Maintaining broad tax bases is key, in particular by scaling back tax exemptions and relief for which there is no strong rationale and where such concessions tend to be regressive. Where there may be more justification for maintaining relief (e.g. main residences, business assets), countries should apply strict criteria, carefully monitor eligibility, and possibly cap available relief. The tax treatment of inheritances and gifts should be more closely aligned. In particular, if gift tax exemptions are renewed on a periodic basis, they should be carefully assessed and revised to ensure that they do not allow significant amounts of transferred wealth to go untaxed. More generally, measures should be put in place to prevent tax avoidance and evasion. With increasing digitalisation, strengthened reporting requirements, including for third party reporting, could significantly contribute to better monitoring and enforcement of inheritance taxes.

The report also suggests ways to help address the political obstacles often associated with inheritance tax reform. Evidence has shown that providing information on inherited wealth and inequality can play an important role in making inheritance taxes more acceptable for the public at large. Similarly, as people tend to overestimate the share of taxable wealth transfers and effective inheritance or estate tax rates, sometimes considerably so, providing information on the way inheritance and estate taxes work, and who they apply to, can significantly increase support for them. In addition, framing inheritance tax reforms around issues of fairness and equality of opportunity could play an important role, particularly if it goes hand-in-hand with changes to tax rules that address popular concerns, particularly in relation to tax avoidance.

The report highlights the importance of taking into account country-specific circumstances in assessing the need for and the appropriate design of inheritance, estate, and gift taxes. Important considerations include countries' levels of wealth inequality and administrative capacity, as well as the other taxes that are levied on capital income and assets.

The report also notes that inheritance taxation is not a silver bullet and should be complemented by other reforms. The report highlights in particular the role of well-designed taxes on personal capital income, including capital gains. The OECD will continue undertaking work on capital taxation, with a focus on the taxation of personal capital income and the taxation of high earners. This work is intended to further help countries identify reforms that could enhance the role of tax systems in reducing inequalities. It will support the major opportunity that countries have to revisit personal capital taxation, in light of the progress made on international tax transparency, in particular with the implementation of the Automatic Exchange of Financial Account Information for Tax Purposes.

Notes

[1] Colombia is not included as it became a member of the OECD after the data collection exercise was completed.

1 Household wealth and inheritances

Chapter 1 examines the level and the distribution of household wealth and inheritances. It provides an overview of the level, the composition and the trends in household wealth before discussing the distribution and the trends in inheritances and gifts. The characteristics of wealth inequality and inheritances and gifts are important in the context of taxing end-of-life wealth transfers.

This chapter provides an overview of the level and the distribution of household wealth and inheritances. The first sections look at the level, the composition and trends in household wealth. Examining the level of wealth inequality and patterns in its accumulation throughout the lifecycle is important in the context of taxing end-of-life wealth transfers. The composition of household wealth will also have implications for the revenue potential and administration of inheritance and estate taxes, and will be a significant determinant of their economic and distributional impact. The last section focuses on gift and inheritance trends and distribution. This is important as outcomes of inheritance taxation may be affected by the distribution of inheritances and gifts and their importance in private wealth.

This chapter shows that household wealth and inheritances are unevenly distributed, and that their levels are likely to rise in the future. While levels of household wealth vary across countries, they have grown substantially in recent years in a number of countries. The distribution of wealth partly reflects lifecycle behaviours, where people accumulate and consume wealth throughout their lives, but it remains highly concentrated at the top of the wealth distribution. The lowest-wealth households have low or negative net wealth. Real estate is the main component of wealth for most households but households in the top wealth quintile own the majority of real estate wealth. Financial assets are even more unevenly distributed and account for a larger share of household wealth at the top of the distribution. The chapter also shows that wealth transfers are unevenly distributed, as wealthy households report more and higher value gifts and inheritances. However, wealth transfers can have an equalising effect for poor households, where inheritances are large relative to households' wealth. Wealth held by the top 1% wealthiest households and the share of inherited wealth in private wealth have increased in some countries in recent decades. These trends are likely to continue and may be accentuated by ongoing asset price rises and ageing populations, and may have significant distributional implications.

1.1. The level of household wealth across OECD countries and over time

Mean gross household wealth amounts to USD 336,746[1] on average across 28 OECD countries, for which data are available. Figure 1.1 shows that mean gross household wealth is far from uniform in OECD countries, ranging from USD 83 449 in Latvia to USD 893 440 in Luxembourg. While gross wealth measures the household's total wealth, net wealth measures wealth that households have at their disposal once debt is deducted. On average across OECD countries, mean net wealth is USD 286 739, ranging from USD 70 280 in Latvia to USD 793 008 in Luxembourg. Mean liabilities range from USD 9 798 in the Slovak Republic to USD 129 005 in Norway, and are USD 50 007 on average across OECD countries. Countries with lower mean gross wealth tend to have lower mean liabilities, but this is not true of all countries. Mean gross wealth in Denmark is USD 222 333, but household debt is nearly half of that amount.[2]

Figure 1.1. Mean household wealth and liabilities, per household

2015 or latest available year

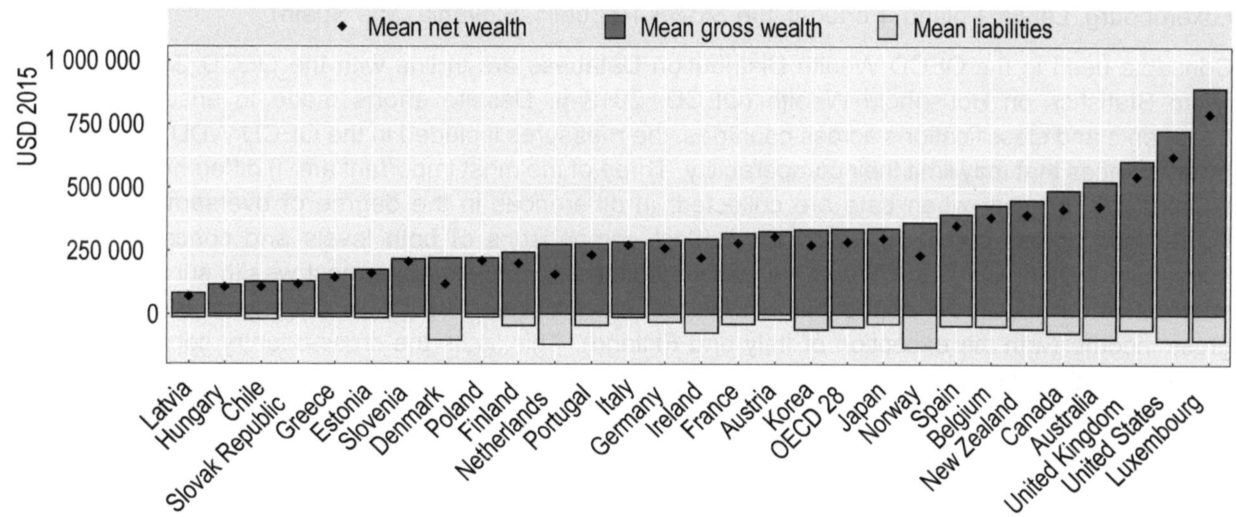

Note: Netherlands: Mean net wealth likely understates household wealth as it does not include occupational pensions, which are an important component of the wealth portfolio of many Dutch households.
Source: OECD Wealth Distribution Database, oe.cd/wealth.

StatLink https://stat.link/q31tel

Box 1.1. Measuring household wealth

This chapter draws extensively from the OECD Wealth Distribution Database (WDD, oe.cd/wdd). The WDD provides high quality and comparable micro-level data on household wealth across OECD countries, building on data provided by participating countries or computed in-house based on available microdata. The National Accounts household balance sheets, which provide high quality and comparable macro-level data on household assets across OECD countries, supplement the analysis.

Wealth Distribution Database

The WDD contains estimates for household wealth and its composition[3] for 28 OECD countries. For 11 countries, these estimates are compiled based on a questionnaire completed by national contact points in National Statistics Offices and central banks that regularly collect micro-level information on household wealth. Of these 11 countries, the information provided is based on tax and administrative records in 3 countries (Denmark, the Netherlands, and Norway) and on household surveys in 8 countries (Australia, Canada, Chile, Japan, Korea, New Zealand, the United Kingdom (limited to Great Britain), and the United States).

For the 17 countries that participate in the Euro-System Household Finance and Consumption Survey (HFCS), estimates are computed in-house from the public use file provided by the European Central Bank (Austria, Belgium, Estonia, Finland, France, Germany, Greece, Hungary, Ireland, Italy, Luxembourg, Latvia, Poland, Portugal, the Slovak Republic, Slovenia, and Spain).

Concepts used in the OECD Wealth Distribution Database are in line with the OECD Guidelines for Micro Statistics on Household Wealth (OECD, 2013[1]). Despite efforts made to ensure common treatments and classifications across countries, the measures included in the OECD WDD are affected by differences that may limit their comparability. Three of the most important are: i) differences between countries in the year when data are collected; ii) differences in the degree of oversampling of rich households across countries, which may affect comparisons of both levels and concentrations of household wealth; iii) differences in the income concept recorded; while most wealth surveys provide information on household disposable income, countries covered by the HFCS rely on the concept of gross income (with the exception of Italy and Finland). This limits the cross-country comparability of estimates of the joint distribution of income and wealth. Balestra and Tonkin (2018[2]) contains a detailed comparison on these differences, including country-year availability and degree of oversampling.

The WDD reports dollar values in national currency and current prices, while this chapter reports dollar values in USD 2015.

National Accounts household balance sheets

The National Accounts household balance sheets provide another source of data for measuring household wealth. The first element of household wealth is financial assets, which includes currency and deposits; debt securities; equity; investment fund shares/units; life insurance and annuity entitlements; and pension entitlements, claims of pension funds on pension managers and entitlements to non-pension benefits. Due to institutional differences in the way pensions systems are organised, countries with highly funded pensions systems will see more pension reserves assigned as household wealth and so care should be taken in making international comparisons.

The second element of household wealth is non-financial assets, which include land and dwellings, machinery and equipment, intellectual property, and other assets used in production, such as cars owned by taxi drivers. With the exception of dwellings, non-financial assets exclude assets that are not used for production, such as private vehicles. For some countries, data on non-financial assets are not available in National Accounts, but this chapter draws exclusively on countries for which data on financial and non-financial wealth are available. These indicators are compiled according to the 2008 System of National Accounts.

Comparing the Wealth Distribution Database and the National Accounts household balance sheets

Differences between the macro-level statistics in the National Accounts and the micro-level statistics in the WDD reflect several factors. Micro statistics are based on individual households and can be used to calculate distributional estimates, while macro statistics measure the household sector as a whole. As a result, the National Accounts data cover a broader population than the WDD, including wealth held by not-for-profits and individuals living in communal establishments, but cannot be used for distributional estimates. The National Accounts measure asset types for which data are more comprehensive at the macro level, such as occupational pensions, but do not measure wealth held in consumer durables, such as vehicles. These asset types, which are measured by the WDD, are typically a more important component of wealth for low-wealth households. Finally, the National Accounts data are available for more years and countries than the WDD. Evidence drawn from the National Accounts and the WDD are only broadly comparable.

Balestra and Tonkin (2018[2]) find that household assets per capita as measured by the National Accounts are systematically higher than average wealth per person, computed by the WDD. Work is ongoing to compare micro and macro statistics for household wealth and in the future more coherent statistics on household finances may be available. More information about the WDD, including comparison with the National Accounts, can be found in Balestra and Tonkin (2018[2]).

Tax administration taxpayer micro data

Recent analysis has highlighted the potential of individual tax record microdata for tax policy analysis (Kennedy, 2019[3]). Tax administration data has several advantages over survey data, as it records the entire population of taxpayers, does not have problems with non-response and respondents leaving longitudinal surveys, and results in a significantly larger sample size than is possible with surveys. This source of data is ideal for some types of analysis, including income dynamics and mobility. However, tax administration data on wealth and wealth transfers is less comprehensive than data on income in many countries. This can be due to high thresholds before gifts and inheritances should be reported, tax avoidance and evasion, or because a country does not levy taxes that require taxpayers to report to the tax administration, such as a net wealth tax or inheritance, estate, and gift taxes. Future work on wealth statistics can draw on combined data sources, exploiting the comparative advantages of survey data, national accounts data, and taxpayer microdata.

Average wealth can give an inflated picture of household wealth because of the large holdings by households at the top. Median wealth instead measures the wealth held by households in the middle of the wealth distribution, and is less affected by outliers. Figure 1.2 shows that in some countries, mean wealth is significantly higher than median wealth. The United States has the second highest mean net household wealth (USD 624 225), but the eighth lowest median household wealth (USD 76 436). Luxembourg has the highest mean and median net wealth of all countries in the sample, though like all countries in Figure 1.2, mean net wealth is greater than median net wealth.

Figure 1.2. Mean and median household net wealth

2015 or latest available year

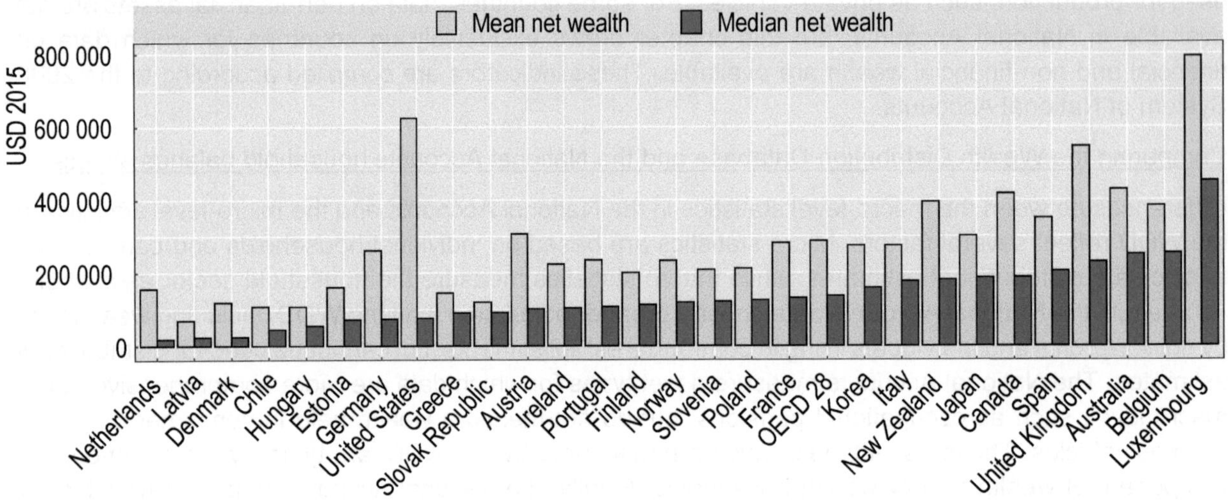

Note: Netherlands: Mean net wealth likely understates household wealth as it does not include occupational pensions, which are an important component of the wealth portfolio of many Dutch households.
Source: OECD Wealth Distribution Database, oe.cd/wealth, (Balestra and Tonkin, 2018[2]).

StatLink https://stat.link/yhbop6

Over time, wealth held by households has grown substantially in some countries. To complement figures exploring mean household wealth, Figure 1.3 shows household assets per capita, using data from National Accounts to measure wealth held by individuals (see Box 1.1). This figure tracks the evolution of household assets, which are set to 100 in the base year (1995 for all countries except Mexico (2003) and Korea (2008), as data for earlier years were not available). Household wealth rose in all countries in Figure 1.3 and grew significantly in some. Between 1995 and 2019, per capita wealth nearly tripled in France and more than doubled in Canada and the United Kingdom. Increases were smaller, though still notable, in countries for which fewer years of data were available, including Mexico (66 base points between 2003 and 2018) and Korea (27 base points between 2008 and 2018). Per capita wealth grew slowly in some countries, including Japan and the Czech Republic, which maintained a steady growth path during the 2008-09 financial crisis when per capita wealth decreased sharply for countries with higher per capita wealth.

Figure 1.3. Financial and non-financial assets held by households, per capita, 1995-2019, selected countries

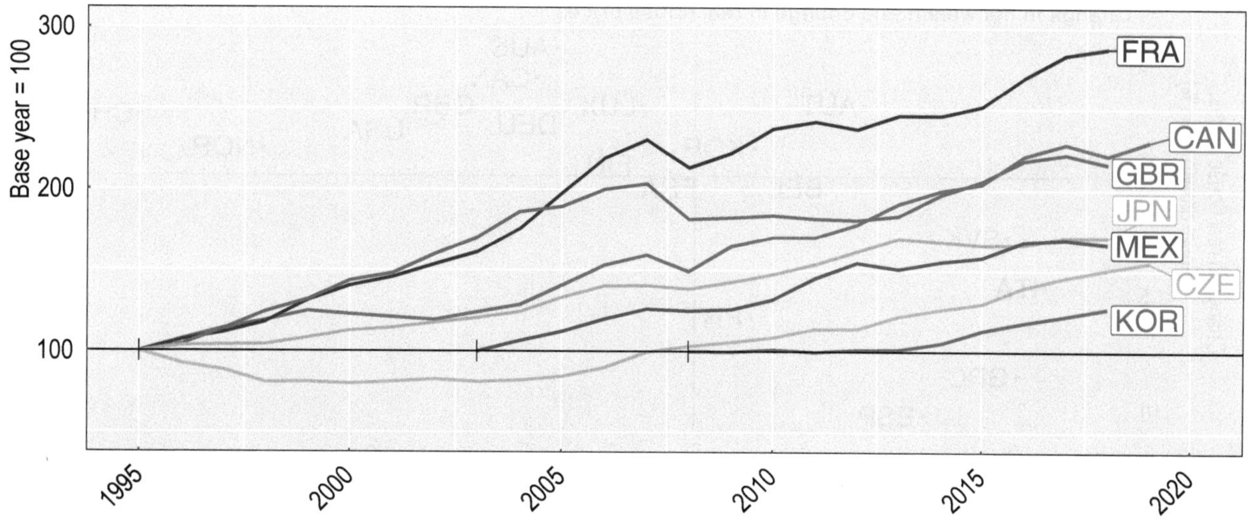

Note: The base year is 1995 for all countries except Mexico (2003) and Korea (2008), where the base year is the earliest year for which data are available. A vertical line marks the base year.
Source: OECD National Accounts

StatLink https://stat.link/mifh2w

Changes in savings rates and in the prices of housing and shares, which are widely held asset classes, can give insight into overall shifts in net wealth, as savings rates and variations in asset prices drive household wealth over time. Figure 1.4 compares changes in mean net wealth to three drivers: housing prices, share prices, and savings rates. These graphs illustrate relationships between household wealth and wider macroeconomic trends, but other variables, such as low interest rates, may also affect household wealth (Hviid and Kuchler, 2017[4]).

Figure 1.4 shows a clear relationship between changes in net wealth and changes in housing and share prices. Net wealth decreased in most countries where housing and share prices decreased, while net wealth grew in most countries with housing and share price growth. However, there are differences between growth in countries' net wealth for a given rate of housing and share price growth. For example, housing prices grew by around 1.2% in Korea and Norway, but net wealth decreased by 0.9% in the former and grew by 6.8% in the latter. In a minority of countries, housing or share price growth was associated with negative net wealth growth and vice versa. Housing prices increased in Austria and share prices increased in Belgium, but net wealth decreased. While no countries experienced net wealth growth without housing price growth, net wealth grew in Chile and Luxembourg even as share prices decreased.

Net wealth appears more weakly linked to gross household savings rates. Two countries had negative savings rates (Greece and Portugal), and both experienced decreases in net wealth, housing prices, and share prices. Three countries (Italy, Slovakia, and Spain) had savings rates below 5% and negative growth in housing and share prices. However, the strength of the relationship between higher savings rates and growing net wealth differs across countries, as the changes in net wealth varied substantially for a given rate of savings. For example, Australia and Austria had savings rates of 7.4% and 7.6%, respectively, but net wealth decreased by 2.7% in Austria while it grew 2.2% in Australia. It should be noted, however, that the link between wealth and savings rates may have been weakened during the period 2010-2015 due to significant asset price growth.

Figure 1.4. Change in net wealth and selected drivers of wealth accumulation

2010 to 2015 or closest available years

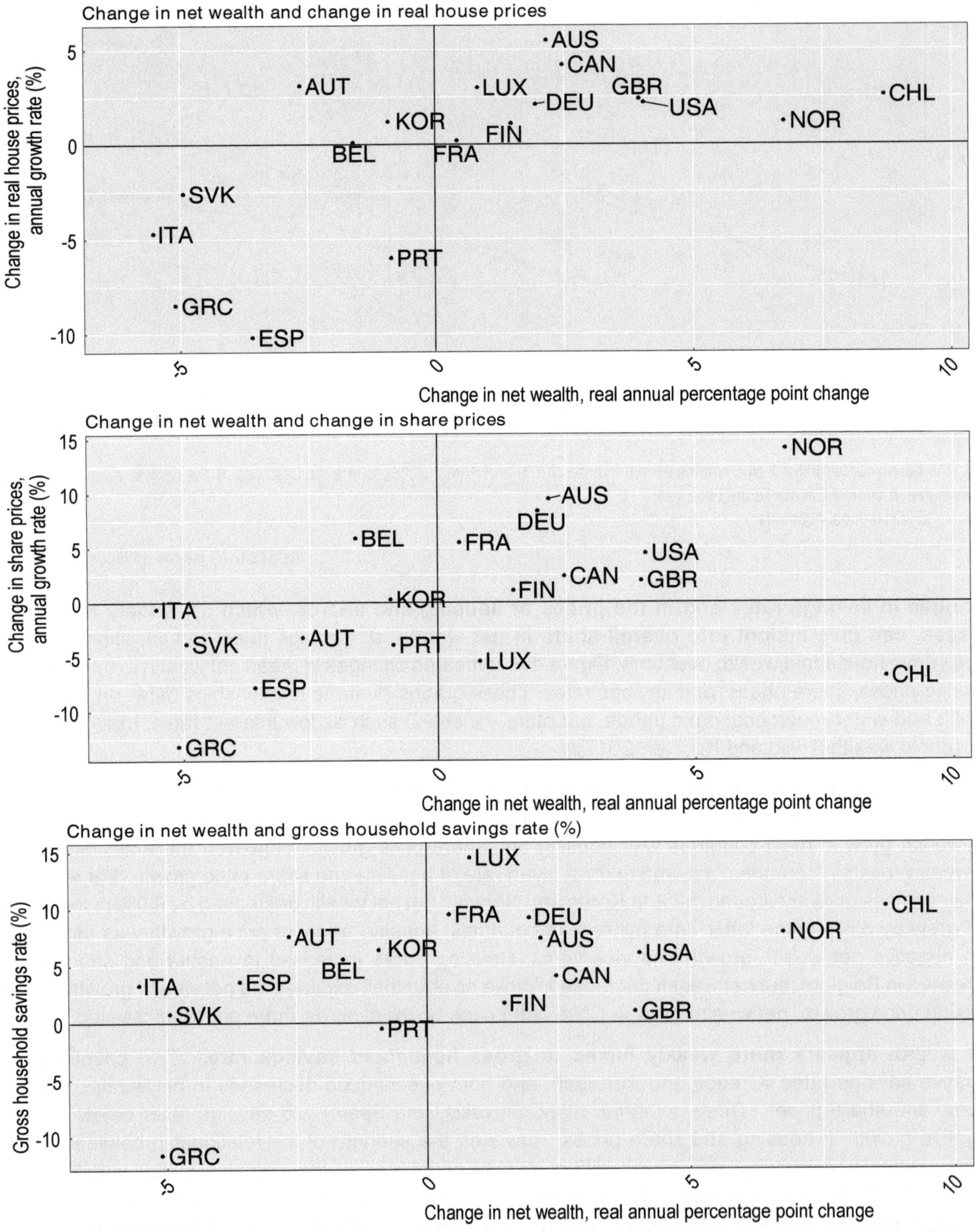

Note: The net household savings rate measures the total net savings, including in mandatory retirement savings, as a portion of net household disposable income.

Source: All indicators can be found in Balestra and Tonkin (2018[2]). Indicators excluding the change in net wealth can be found in the OECD National Accounts Database (http://stats.oecd.org/Index.aspx?DataSetCode=NAAG) and the Main Economic Indicators Database (http://stats.oecd.org/Index.aspx?DataSetCode=MEI).

StatLink https://stat.link/paewk4

1.2. The distribution of household wealth

Wealth is highly concentrated at the top of the distribution[4] in most countries. This is evidenced by a simple indicator of inequality, the ratio of median to mean wealth. Median wealth better represents the wealth held by a "typical" household in the middle of the wealth distribution, compared to mean wealth that is affected by high outliers, so mean wealth will be higher than median wealth when wealth is concentrated at the top. Mean wealth is higher than median wealth in every country in Figure 1.2. The figure shows that mean wealth is 1.3 to 4.7 times higher than median wealth in most OECD countries, but in the Netherlands and the United States, mean wealth is more than eight times higher than median wealth.

The wealthiest ten percent of households own half of all household wealth on average across 27 OECD countries (Figure 1.5). The share of wealth held by households in the top ten percent varies across countries, ranging from one third in the Slovak Republic to four-fifths in the United States. Furthermore, even within the top decile wealth levels are highly unequal. The share of total household wealth held by the 90th to 95th percentiles ranges from 11% (Slovenia) to 17% (Denmark) and the share of total household wealth held by the 96th to 99th percentiles ranges from 14% (Slovak Republic) to 28% (Latvia). On average, the top one percent of the wealth distribution own a striking 18% of household wealth. There is significant cross-country variation in the wealth shares held by the top one percent; ranging from 9% in Greece to 43% in the United States, which also has the highest top ten percent wealth share.

Figure 1.5. Share of total net household wealth held by the top ten percent of the wealth distribution

2015 or latest available year

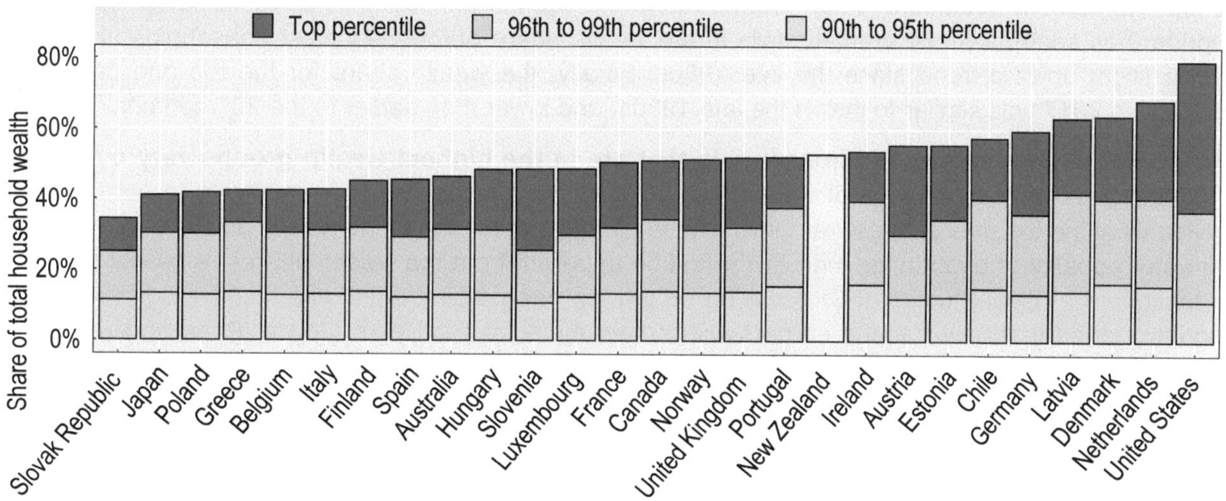

Note: Data were not available for Korea and a breakdown of wealth held by the top ten percent was not available for New Zealand. Netherlands: figure does not include occupational pensions, which are an important component of the wealth portfolio of many Dutch households.
Source: OECD Wealth Distribution Database, oe.cd/wealth.

StatLink https://stat.link/bhmd0i

Survey data may underestimate wealth inequality, due to the underrepresentation of the wealthiest households. Households at the top of the wealth distribution are underrepresented in typical household surveys, which surveys such as the HFCS seek to address through the oversampling of wealthy households. A recent study of the wealth distribution in Germany corrected the data gap through more targeted oversampling of wealthy households, for those with net assets worth EUR 3 million to 250 million, and through publicly available "rich lists" for the remainder of the wealth distribution (Schröder et al., 2020[5]). The authors found that when this data gap was closed, wealth was more concentrated at the top than previously found; the top one percent wealthiest households holds around 35% of total wealth, compared to 22% previously. Survey data may therefore be considered a lower bound estimate of wealth inequality, which can be complemented by sources like "rich lists" and individual tax record microdata.

Wealth inequality has experienced a secular decline over time and across countries. Long run analysis is helpful to show trends in wealth inequality as inequality is typically slow to change and policies to narrow wealth inequality, such as inheritance and estate taxes, take time to affect the wealth distribution. Unfortunately, long run data on wealth inequality are available for very few countries. Caution should be taken in generalising these countries' trends, as historic economic growth, and returns on investment, taxes and transfers and other factors that may affect long-run wealth inequality differ across countries. Figure 1.6 shows that in France, Germany, the United Kingdom, and the United States, the share of wealth held by households in the top one percent and top ten percent of the wealth distribution declined steadily throughout the 20th century. The most substantial drop was in the United Kingdom, where the share of wealth held by the top ten percent wealthiest households halved between 1914 and 1991, falling from 93% to 46%. Figure 1.6 also shows differences in wealth inequality trends across countries. The sharpest decreases in the top ten percent wealth share occurred in the 1910s in the United States, in the 1940s in France, and in the 1960s in the United Kingdom.

However, it appears that the long-run decrease in wealth inequality is reversing. Following a secular decline throughout the early and middle 20th century, top wealth shares increased during the latter part of the 20th century or the early 2000s, depending on the country. In France, the wealth share of the top one percent in 2000 was similar to the wealth share in the mid-1960s and mid-1940s and in the United States, the top one percent wealth share had returned to levels seen in the 1930s by 2014. Although the United Kingdom has seen the most dramatic falls in the wealth share of the wealthiest households, there has been a slight upward trend since the late 1980s. Finally, the wealth share for the top one percent in Germany in 2017 was similar to that in the late 1980s, and lower than earlier in the 20th century.

It is worth mentioning that the households that are in the highest wealth groups vary over time. While the growing concentration of wealth may be a cause for concern, it is important to note that the individuals at the top may change over time. These changes at the top of the wealth distribution may point to greater equality of opportunity than might first be apparent from top wealth shares. A recent study by the Institute for Fiscal Studies (IFS), focusing on the top one percent of income taxpayers in the United Kingdom, found that only half the earners will remain there for five years (Joyce, Pope and Roantree, 2019[6]). However, some earners drop in and out of the top one percent, indicating that they most likely remained very high earners even when not at the top. Changes in individuals in the top one percent of income may be more frequent than changes in top wealth shares, due for instance to non-recurring income from sale of assets.

Figure 1.6. Long run share of net wealth held by the top ten percent and top one percent wealthiest households, select countries

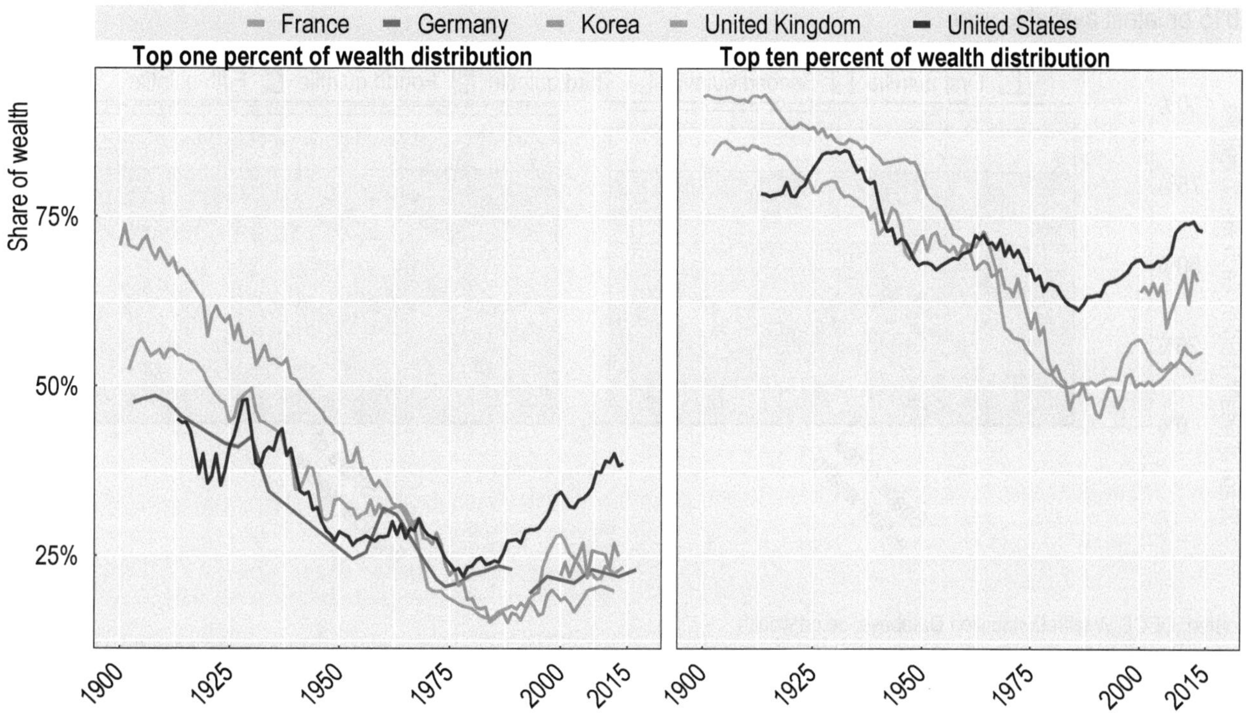

Note: While top wealth shares are broadly similar between the World Inequality Database, the source for all countries in this graph except Germany, and the WDD, used extensively in this chapter, these two sources rely on different methodological assumptions and are not strictly comparable. See Balestra and Tonkin (2018[2]) for a detailed comparison. Data are not annual for Germany.
Source: World Inequality Database, wid.world/data/, data for Germany in Albers, Bartels and Schularick (2020[7]).

StatLink https://stat.link/a0znop

Total financial and housing wealth are concentrated among the wealthiest households. On average across 28 OECD countries, households in the top wealth quintile own more than half of all real estate wealth and nearly 80% of all financial wealth (Figure 1.7). In contrast, households in the lowest wealth quintile own just 1% of financial wealth and 2% of real estate wealth. Real estate wealth is more evenly distributed than financial wealth; for example, the middle wealth quintiles (third and fourth quintiles) own over one third of real estate wealth, compared to just 17% of financial wealth. While housing wealth may have an equalising effect on the wealth distribution (Causa, Woloszko and Leite, 2019[8]), rising housing prices have contributed to rising wealth inequality in recent years, particularly along the divide between owner-occupier and renter households (OECD, 2019[9]).

Figure 1.7. Share of financial and real estate wealth held by each quintile, average for 28 OECD countries

2015 or latest available year

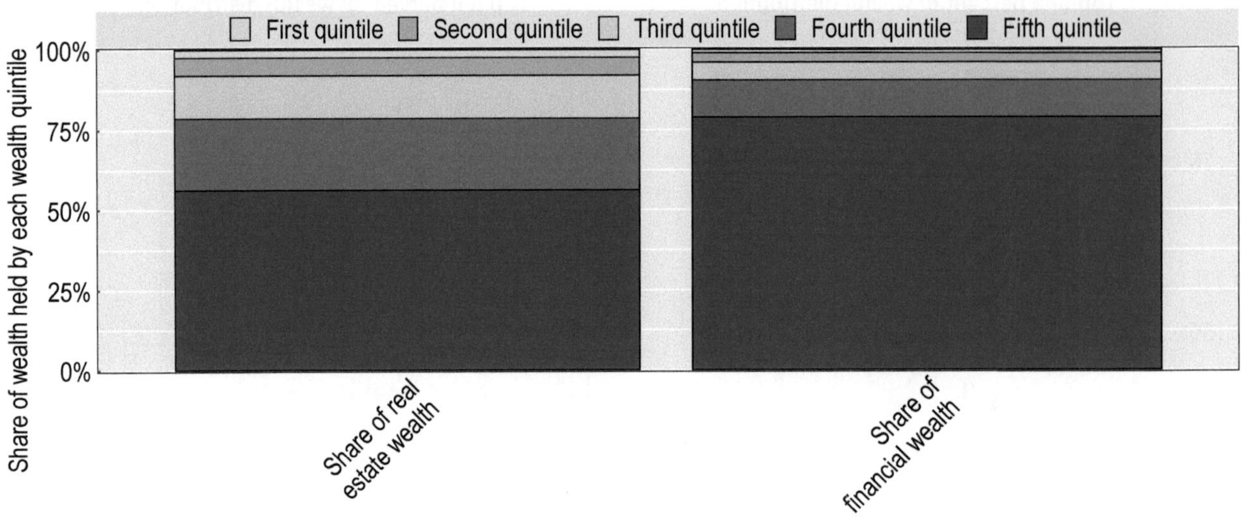

Source: OECD Wealth Distribution Database, oe.cd/wealth.

StatLink https://stat.link/swzy9t

Figure 1.8. Wealth distribution of each income quintile, average for 27 OECD countries

2015 or latest available year

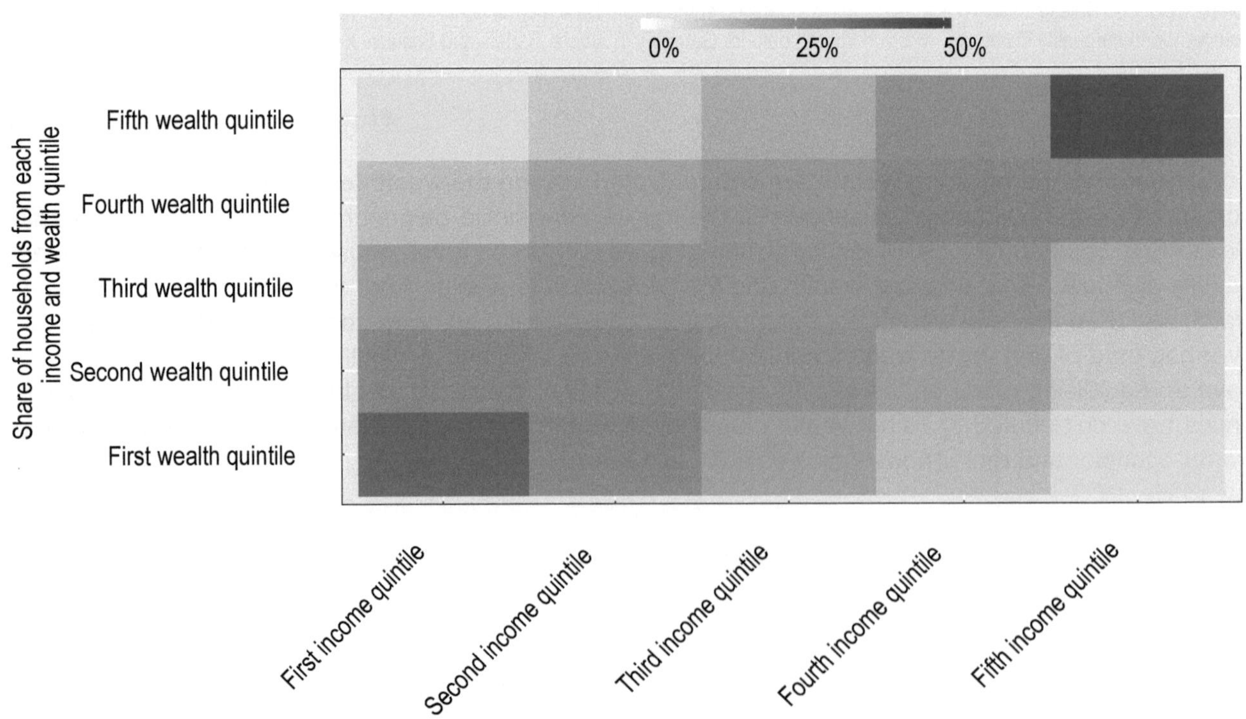

Note: Columns and rows each sum to 100% of households. Income shows gross income and is not equivalised across household types.
Source: OECD Wealth Distribution Database, oe.cd/wealth.

StatLink https://stat.link/7pdgk6

There is a strong relationship between income and wealth, particularly at the top of the distribution. While wealth is more unequally distributed than income, Figure 1.8 shows there is a clear relationship between the highest income and wealth quintiles and between the lowest income and wealth quintiles. The figure also shows that few households combine high wealth and low income, or high income and low wealth. However, the relationship between wealth and income is weaker in the middle of the wealth and income distributions. The relationship between income and wealth may be mutually reinforcing; high-income households can save more and then increase their income by, for example, earning a return on their savings or using seed capital to start a business. The inverse trend may apply at the bottom of the income distribution, where households have a lower propensity to save and may invest in low-risk, low-return assets (Campanale, 2007[10]).

1.3. The asset composition of household wealth

Households hold the largest share of their wealth in real estate. Evidence shows that for many households, the main form of savings is their own home (Causa, Woloszko and Leite, 2019[8]). Across the Eurozone countries that participate in the HFCS[5], the main residence accounts for 49.5% of total assets and is the largest asset type for 52.5% of households (Household Finance and Consumption and Network, 2016[11]). As owner-occupied housing has a dual role as a consumption good and an asset class, households may consume housing services while also building personal wealth. Households may view housing as a safe investment, due in part to sustained housing price increases in recent years, and may use mortgage repayments as a form of forced savings. Many OECD countries also provide favourable tax treatment for owner-occupied homes, which creates significant incentives to invest in housing (Fatica and Prammer, 2017[12]; OECD, 2018[13]; Rosen, 1985[14]). Homeownership may provide other benefits as, depending on rental regulations, homeownership can provide more stability relative to renting.

Housing is a larger share of assets for middle households than it is for wealthy and low-wealth households (Figure 1.9). While real estate is the dominant asset type across most households in most countries, this is especially notable for households in the middle wealth quintile. For these households, real estate comprises at least half their wealth in all 28 OECD countries and comprises more than three-quarters of wealth in 20 countries. For low-wealth households, assets such as valuables and vehicles are relatively more important than for middle and wealthy households. This reflects that low-wealth households hold more of their wealth in consumer durables and have low levels wealth overall. In five countries (Australia, Canada, Italy, New Zealand, and the United Kingdom), other forms of wealth outweigh housing wealth for low-wealth households, but across these countries, the relative importance of vehicles, valuables, and other non-financial assets is highly heterogeneous.

At the top of the wealth distribution, financial wealth is a large component of household wealth in most countries. This aligns with earlier findings that total financial wealth is concentrated in the hands of households at the top of the wealth distribution (Figure 1.7). For households in the top wealth quintile, more than half of total wealth is held in financial assets in the United States (67%), New Zealand (65%) and the United Kingdom (57%). On average across the 28 OECD countries, financial wealth accounts for 39% of net wealth for the top quintile, compared to 16% and 15% for the bottom and middle quintiles, respectively.

Figure 1.9. Composition of net wealth for bottom, middle and top wealth quintiles

2015 or latest available year

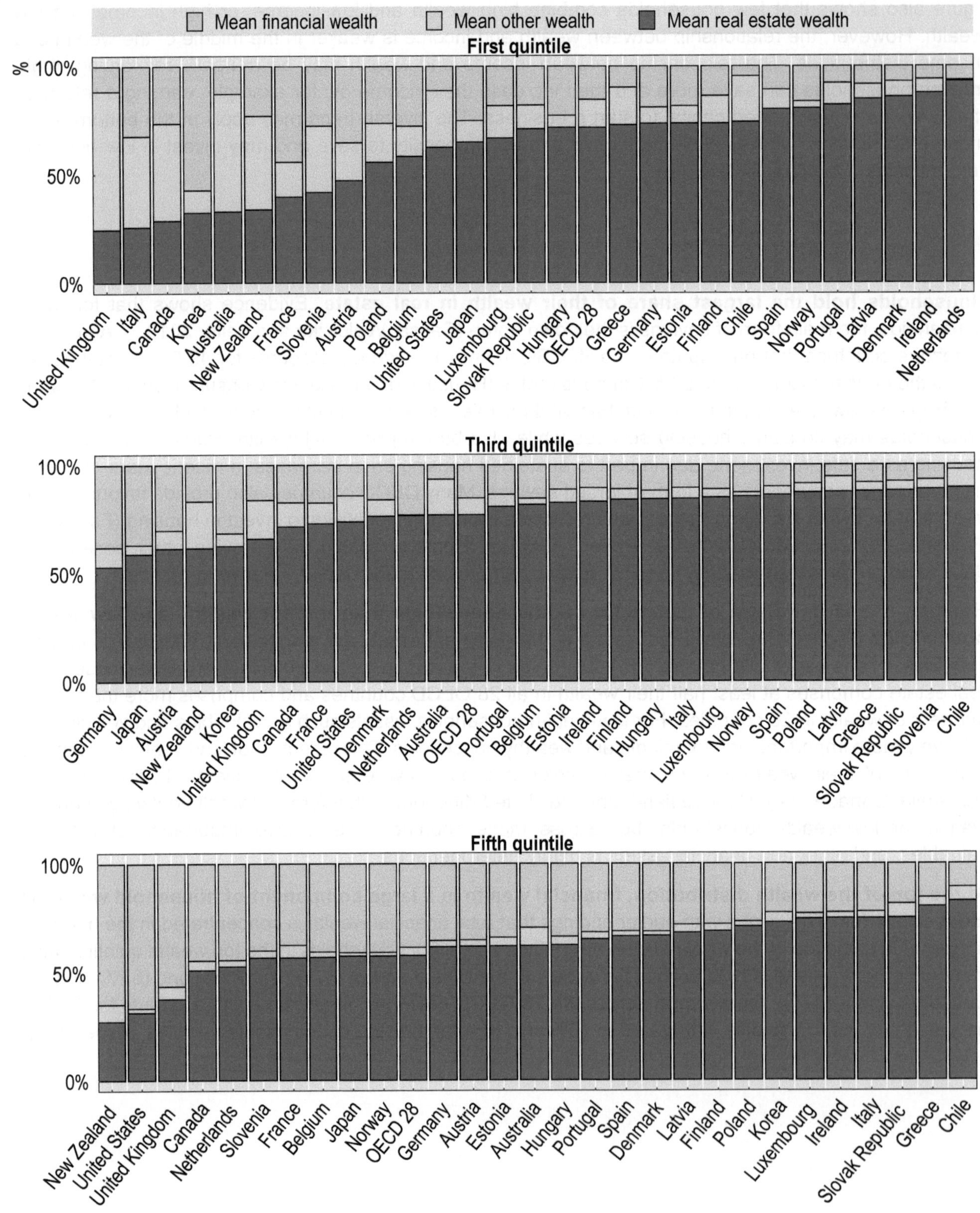

Source: OECD Wealth Distribution Database, oe.cd/wealth, (Balestra and Tonkin, 2018[2]).

StatLink https://stat.link/705cfh

Wealth held in occupational pensions is important in a minority of countries (Figure 1.10). The WDD includes voluntary private pensions in standard measures of household wealth, but excludes occupational and social security pensions as consistent data are not available across all participating countries. In contrast to the standard indicator, occupational pensions (for both private and public sector) are included in mean net extended wealth. This complements the standard indicator of household wealth, but the effect of moving from net wealth to extended net wealth is small for both wealth levels and inequality for most countries (Balestra and Tonkin, 2018[2]). Mean extended net wealth is notably higher in some countries with quasi-mandatory occupational pension schemes (Australia and Denmark) and in some countries where these schemes are voluntary (Canada, the United Kingdom, and the United States). While data on occupational pension schemes for the Netherlands are not currently included in the OECD Wealth Distribution Database, which was the basis for Figure 1.10, data published by Statistics Netherlands show they are a significant component of household wealth.[6] Public pension entitlements, referred to as state pension entitlements in some countries, accruing under government social security schemes are excluded from the standard and extended wealth indicators, as estimates of public pension wealth are not available at the household level in most countries. However, public pensions could affect savings behaviour as taxpayers may be entitled to income in retirement. The replacement rate[7], measured as pension entitlements as a share of pre-retirement earnings, is significant in some OECD countries; for an average-income worker, it is highest in Italy (79.5%), Luxembourg (78.8%), and Austria (76.5%) (OECD, 2019[15]).

Figure 1.10. Net wealth including and excluding occupational pensions

2015 or latest available year

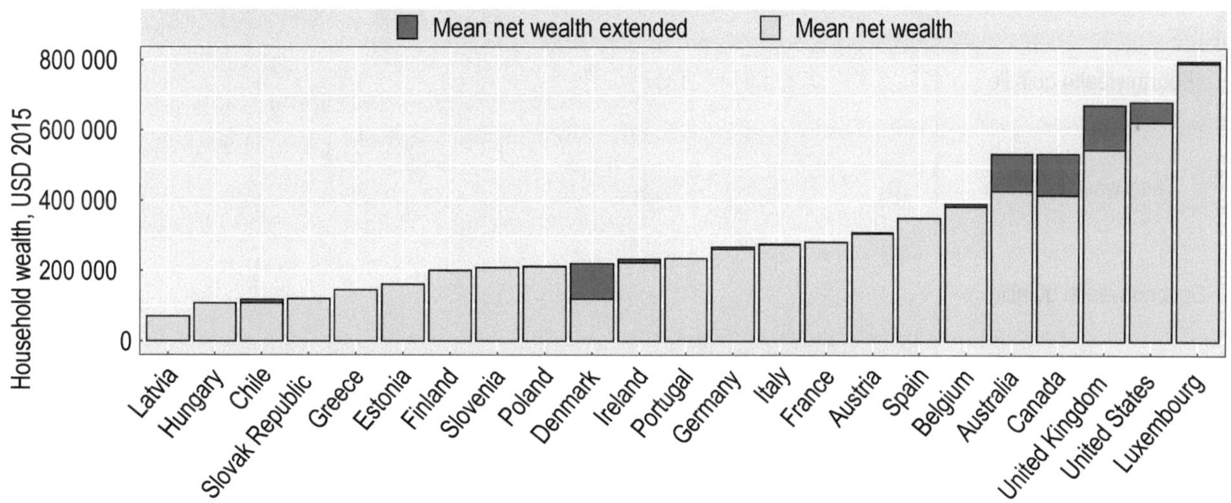

Note: Data were not available for Japan, Korea, the Netherlands, New Zealand, and Norway. Netherlands: while data on occupational pensions are not available in the Wealth Distribution Database, they are an important component of the wealth portfolio of many Dutch households.
Source: OECD Wealth Distribution Database, oe.cd/wealth, (Balestra and Tonkin, 2018[2]).

StatLink https://stat.link/bvkuot

1.4. Lifecycle patterns in household wealth

The distribution of wealth in many OECD countries partly reflects lifecycle behaviours. Young people typically have very little wealth but as people get older, they will have had more time to accumulate wealth and they are more likely to have received any inheritances. Workers in the later years of their career often have higher incomes, allowing them to save more (Dynan, Skinner and Zeldes, 2004[16]). As individuals move into retirement, their household's wealth may start to decline as their income falls and as they may rely on their wealth to finance consumption. Some households may downsize, opting for smaller housing to reduce maintenance costs and to access the equity they hold in their home, for example.

Young households are overrepresented at the bottom of the wealth distribution, while pre-retirement and retired households (55-74 years old) are most numerous at the top. Figure 1.11 shows that the wealth distribution across age groups follows an inverted U-shape pattern. Young households cluster at the bottom of the wealth distribution, where nearly 70% of households whose household head was aged under 35 are in the first two wealth quintiles. Between the ages of 35 and 44, households spread more evenly across the wealth distribution and by ages 45-54, they begin to concentrate toward the top. More than half of all households whose head is of pre-retirement and retirement age (55-74 years old) are in the top two wealth quintiles, including 28% of households in the top quintile. As household heads pass the age of 75, they become more numerous in the middle, where 47% of households are in the third and fourth wealth quintiles.

Figure 1.11. Share of each age group in wealth quintiles, average for 28 OECD countries

2015 or latest available year

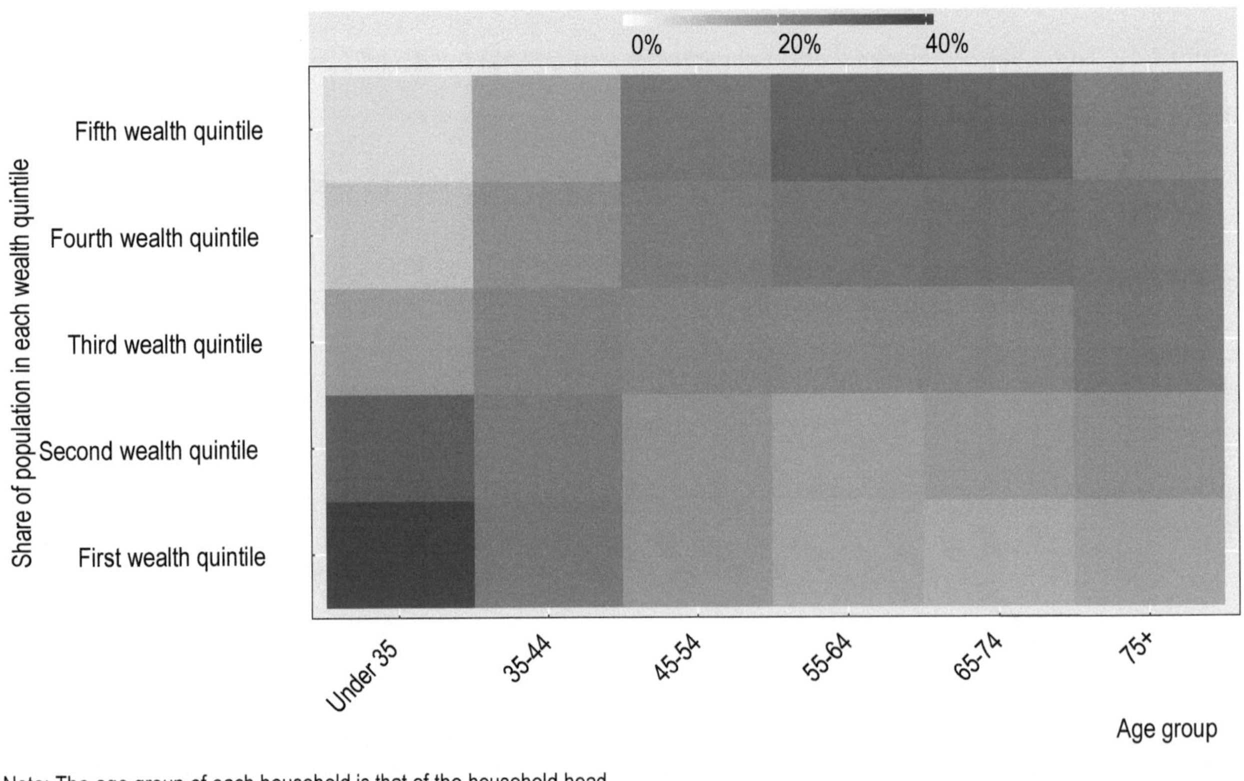

Note: The age group of each household is that of the household head
Source: OECD Wealth Distribution Database, oe.cd/wealth, (Balestra and Tonkin, 2018[2]).

StatLink https://stat.link/yahizv

Young households may find it harder to accumulate wealth than in the past. Comparing different age groups at a given point in time shows only a partial, static picture. A dynamic view could show younger households ageing and accumulating wealth over time, so young and low-wealth households will not necessarily remain in that position. However, there are concerns that traditional avenues for wealth accumulation may be less available to today's younger households. Research has shown that homeownership is associated with wealth accumulation (Causa, Woloszko and Leite, 2019[8]), but young households are finding it increasingly difficult to purchase a home as rising house prices decrease affordability (McKee, 2012[17]). The COVID-19 crisis, which has affected different demographic groups differently, may exacerbate difficulties for some households and increase the divide between older asset-owning households and younger households.

Households whose head is of pre-retirement or retirement age (55-64 years old) have the highest levels of housing and financial wealth on average across the 28 OECD countries. Figure 1.12 shows average net wealth and the composition of average gross wealth across the age distribution. Households headed by an individual aged 55-64 years hold gross wealth amounting to USD 451 413, of which about two-fifths is held in real estate and one-third is held in financial assets. Net wealth for 55-64 year olds amounts to USD 406 012, which is followed by USD 393 277 for households aged 65-74 and USD 324 391 for households aged 45-54. Young households whose head is aged under 35 have the lowest net wealth, at USD 93 127. While housing and financial wealth both increase as households age and net wealth increases, financial wealth becomes a larger component of wealth. This is consistent with patterns discussed above, where wealthier households tend to hold more wealth in the form of financial assets. Other types of wealth such as vehicles, artwork, and jewellery are a small part of total wealth for households of all ages.

The propensity to consume wealth in retirement is likely to vary across households, but evidence shows that wealth levels remain high among households whose head is over the age of 75. Lifecycle wealth accumulation suggests that households save at least in part to finance consumption in retirement, however, the extent to which households consume their wealth in retirement depends on several factors. Low-wealth households may need to consume their savings, while wealthier households may earn sufficient capital income to support themselves. Households intending to leave a bequest may also set aside wealth for this purpose (see Chapter 2) and as a result, some households will not fully consume their wealth in retirement. The broader tax and benefit context, including taxes on gifts and inheritances as well as means and asset testing for entitlements to public benefits and services (e.g. old-age care) may also influence households' decisions related to wealth accumulation, wealth transfers or consumption. The interactions between these different dimensions could be explored in future work. Figure 1.12 shows that households whose head is over the age of 75 hold substantial levels of wealth, more than a decade into retirement. Excess precautionary savings and a lower propensity to consume may contribute to high wealth levels for older households. This precautionary behaviour may include orienting savings towards safer assets, which can have broader economic consequences where safe assets are preferred over more productive but riskier assets. Higher wealth among older households increases their ability to leave a bequest, although rising life expectancy means that households may receive an inheritance later in life when they are themselves approaching retirement. Rising life expectancy may affect the age distribution of wealth; as households prepare for the possibility of a long retirement, older households may need to hold more wealth to finance consumption. Theoretical work has attempted to distinguish savings to finance retirement and savings to leave a bequest to heirs, but empirical work has not found clear evidence for the relative importance of each motive (see chapter 2).

Figure 1.12. Composition of wealth across age groups, average for 28 OECD countries

2015 or latest available year

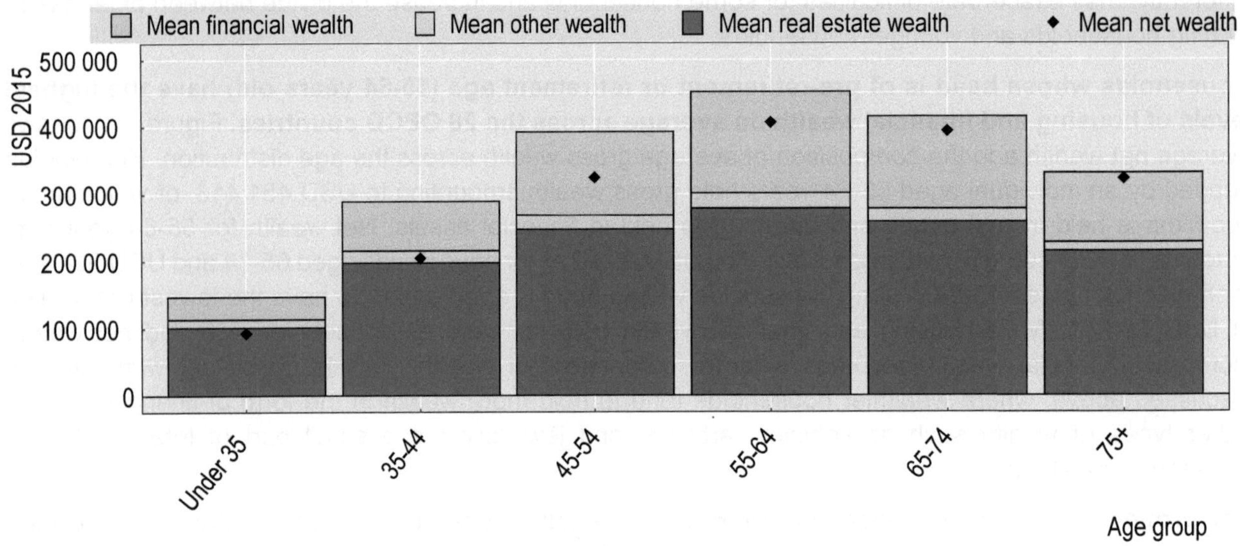

Note: The age group of each household is that of the household head
Source: OECD Wealth Distribution Database, oe.cd/wealth, (Balestra and Tonkin, 2018[2]).

StatLink https://stat.link/qjml0h

Financial wealth decreases faster in retirement than housing wealth. Figure 1.13 shows gross household wealth across the age distribution normalised to that of the 55-64 age group, separated into financial and real estate wealth. Note that while both real estate and financial wealth have a normalised value of one for the 55-64 age group, the level of financial wealth is lower than real estate wealth (see Figure 1.12). Figure 1.13 shows that housing and financial wealth grow throughout the lifecycle to reach their highest level for households aged 55-64 and then decrease for households aged over 65. After peaking for households aged 55-64 (normalised value of 1), real estate wealth declines steadily for households aged 65-74 (0.95) and households over 75 (0.82). Financial wealth, which also peaks for the 55-64 age group, drops more rapidly than housing wealth, to 0.75 and 0.63 for households aged 65-74 and over 75, respectively.

The trends in Figure 1.13 may reflect age and cohort effects, as well as the lower levels of financial wealth. Retired households draw down the wealth that they accumulate earlier in life; financial wealth may decrease more rapidly than housing wealth as financial wealth starts from a lower level and because households may choose to draw down liquid financial wealth before illiquid housing wealth. Figure 1.13 may also reflect the dual role of housing as an asset class and a consumption good providing housing services, with households preferring to retain housing rather than use it to finance consumption. Finally, the drop in financial wealth at retirement age may reflect the growing role of private pensions in household wealth[8], as retired households use the wealth they have saved for their retirement to finance consumption, rather than drawing on housing or other wealth. However, the trends may also reflect cohort effects. Recent research has found that households in the United Kingdom aged 80 years or older in 2012-13 held more wealth than households of the same age in 2002-03, principally due to increased housing wealth, tied to rising housing prices and higher rates of homeownership (Hood and Joyce, 2017[18]). The higher wealth of the 55-64 age group in Figure 1.13, relative to the 65 and above group, may therefore reflect steadily increasing levels of household wealth for younger generations.

Figure 1.13. Mean net financial and real estate wealth normalised to 55-64 year olds, OECD 28 average

2015 or latest available year

Note: The age group of each household is that of the household head
Source: OECD Wealth Distribution Database, oe.cd/wealth.

StatLink https://stat.link/6gjl9y

Debt held by retired households is small compared to their net wealth, while younger households have high debts compared to their net assets. Figure 1.14 shows how wealth accumulation and debt play out over the lifecycle. Young households hold liabilities worth nearly half of their net wealth. While the liabilities themselves are smaller in absolute terms than those held by older households, they are large compared to net wealth. As households get older and accumulate more wealth, their liabilities may grow in absolute value, but they become smaller as a portion of net wealth. As households move closer to retirement, debt becomes a very small portion of net wealth. Although not shown in the graph below, debt profiles may link to earning capacity and the ability to service a loan, and households may seek to reduce the risk associated with debt as they age.

Figure 1.14. Ratio of liabilities to net wealth across age groups, average 28 OECD countries

2015 or latest available year

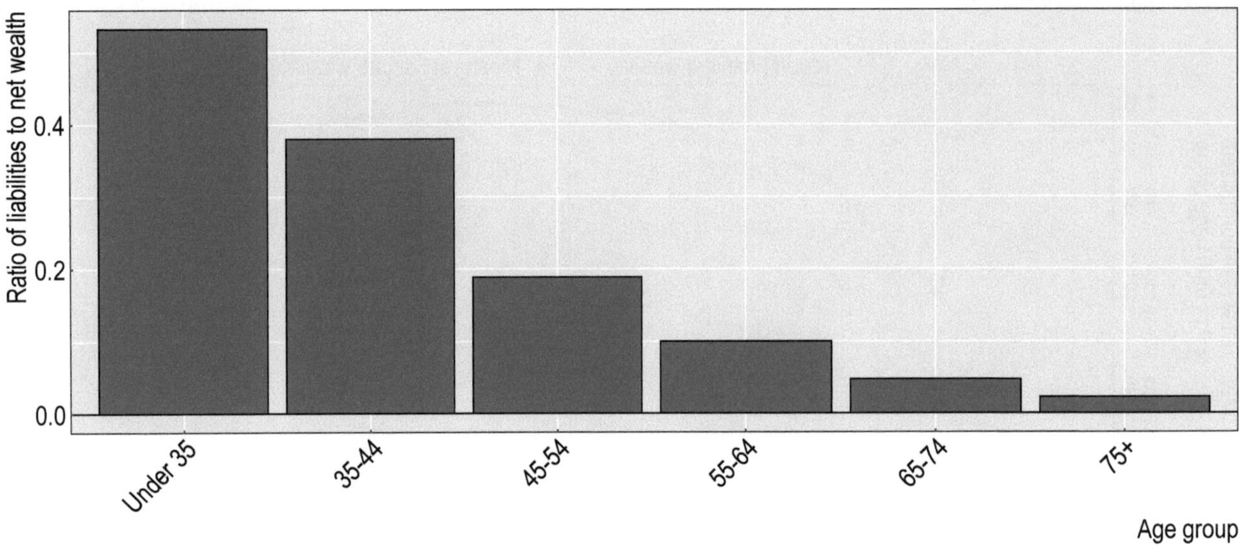

Source: OECD Wealth Distribution Database, oe.cd/wealth.

StatLink https://stat.link/d4y82j

1.5. Characteristics of wealth transfers

Inheritances are a significant source of household wealth and have important distributional consequences, as wealthy households receive more wealth than lower-wealth households. This section examines evidence on the size and prevalence of gifts and bequests and discusses their implications for the wealth distribution. Among the data sources that this section draws on, the WDD measures household wealth during the reference year and measures the value of gifts and inheritances over the lifetime, but does not measure wealth at the time that the household received the gift or inheritance.

Evidence on the size of wealth transmissions is sparse, but studies suggest that large amounts of wealth are transferred each year. The annual flow of bequests was estimated to be between 8-15% of Gross National Income (GNI) in some European countries in 2010 (Piketty and Zucman, 2015[19]). Over time, this figure has varied substantially in the few countries with available data. In France, Germany, and the United Kingdom, bequests have exhibited a U-shaped pattern since the beginning of the twentieth century. Inheritances amounted to around a quarter of national income at the turn of the century but steadily declined in the turbulence of the first half of the century, before returning to levels seen around the end of WWI by 2010.

There is evidence that the share of inheritances in private wealth is returning to the highs seen at the turn of the 20th century in some countries. Preliminary evidence of long-run trends in inherited wealth, and the methodology used to calculate them, are presented in Alvaredo, Garbinti and Piketty (2017[20]), drawing on Piketty (2011[21]). Figure 1.15 shows that in 1900, the majority of private wealth had been inherited; the share of inherited wealth in private wealth ranged from 55% in the United States to 78% in Sweden. This ratio peaked in the early 20th century for all countries in Figure 1.15, before declining steadily over the course of the 20th century. Beginning in the late 20th or early 21st century, inheritances began to rise as a share of private wealth in most countries. While the United Kingdom experienced a moderate but steady decline from 1900-1990 before rising slightly from 1990-2010, Germany experienced a sharp decline from 1950-1970 and a sharp increase from 1980-2010. The trends in France and the United States are similar to, but less accentuated than, the trend in Germany. If these trends continue, inherited wealth may once again reach the high levels of the early 1900s. However, the trend in Sweden is less suggestive of a return to early peaks, as the ratio of inherited to private wealth has remained stable since declining between 1900 and 1950.

Figure 1.15. Cumulated stock of inherited wealth as a fraction of private wealth, 1990-2010, selected countries

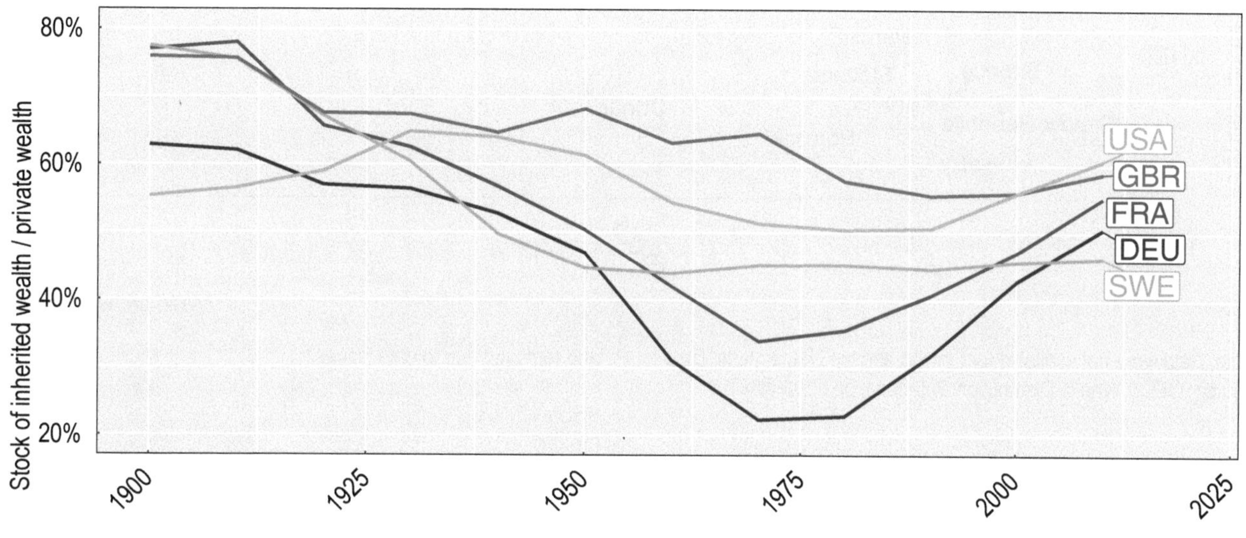

Note: Data for the United States are the unweighted average of benchmark and high-gift estimates.
Source: Alvaredo, Garbinti, and Piketty (2017), data for Sweden in Ohlsson, Roine, Waldenström (2020).

StatLink https://stat.link/7pyrwc

Countries with higher average household wealth tend to have higher average inheritances. Figure 1.16, which compares mean inheritances and gifts to mean net wealth for 16 countries for which data were available, shows that the average value of wealth transfers rises with average net wealth. Latvia, Hungary, and the Slovak Republic have low average inheritances and gifts and are among OECD countries with the lowest mean net wealth. Luxembourg and Spain are among the OECD countries with the highest mean net wealth and have the fourth and third highest average inheritances, respectively. However, Belgium and Canada have high mean net wealth yet relatively small average inheritances and several countries with mean net wealth close to the OECD average have relatively high average inheritances (Austria, France, Germany, and Italy). Italy and Portugal have similar average wealth, but average inheritances are significantly higher in Italy than in Portugal. Conversely, Canada and Greece have similar average inheritances, but mean net wealth is substantially higher in Canada.

Figure 1.16. Mean net wealth compared to mean inheritances and gifts

2015 or latest available year, USD 2015

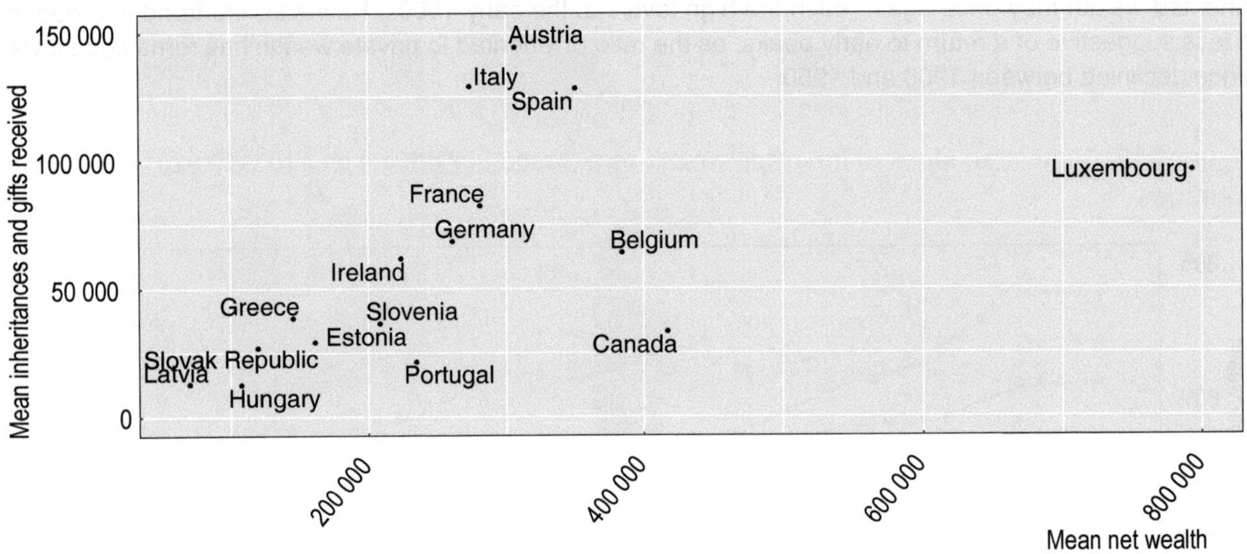

Note: Data were not available for Finland and the Netherlands. Data for Poland removed due to data issues.
Source: OECD Wealth Distribution Database, oe.cd/wealth.

StatLink https://stat.link/vbtkph

Survey data show that a large share of high-wealth households report receiving an inheritance or gift. On average across 18 OECD countries, 33% of households reported receiving an inheritance or a substantial gift[9], but these shares vary across countries, ranging from 25% (Latvia) to 47% (Finland). However, across all 18 OECD countries, a greater share of wealthy households received an inheritance or gift than low-wealth households. Figure 1.17 illustrates this link between current wealth and the chances of having received a wealth transfer. Among households in the top wealth quintile, the portion of households who have received an inheritance or gift ranges from 39% (Canada) to 66% (Finland), compared to between 3% (Italy) and 26% (Finland) among the poorest households. The difference between the top and bottom wealth quintiles is smallest in Hungary (24 percentage points), and largest for Ireland (51 percentage points).

Figure 1.17. Share of population that has received an inheritance or a substantial gift

2015 or latest available year

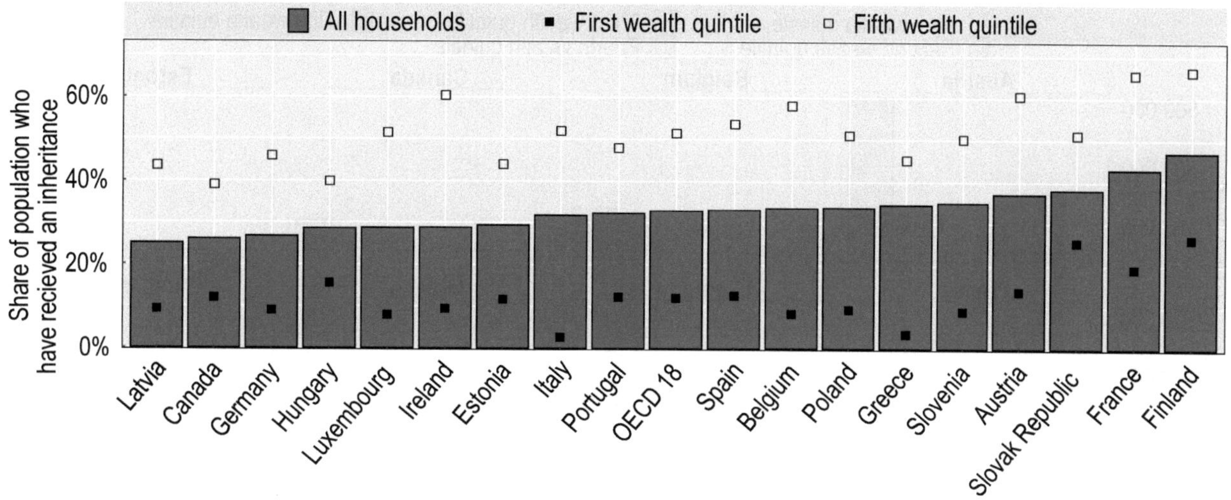

Source: OECD Wealth Distribution Database, oe.cd/wealth, (Balestra and Tonkin, 2018[2]).

StatLink https://stat.link/wschni

However, the survey data that inform this analysis should be interpreted with caution. The survey measured wealth at the time that the household responded to the questionnaire, but not at the time that the household received the inheritance or gift, This means, for example, that households may have received wealth when they were younger and less wealthy, but now report high net wealth. For this reason, caution should be taken in interpreting the relationship between wealth and inheritances.

The average value of inheritances and gifts varies across countries, but is consistently higher for wealthier households. Across 16 OECD countries for which data are available, the average inheritance or gift received by households in the bottom wealth quintile ranged from USD 295 (Latvia) to USD 11 052 (Belgium). For households in the top wealth quintile, the average inheritance or gift ranged from USD 30 441 in Hungary to USD 525 879 in Austria. Wealthier households consistently report receiving a larger inheritance or gift than poorer households, but it is possible to distinguish two groups of countries in Figure 1.18. In the first group, the value of inheritances and gifts increases steadily with household wealth (Belgium, Canada, Estonia, France, Greece, Hungary, Latvia, Portugal, Slovak Republic, and Slovenia). In the second group, the average value of inheritances also increases steadily with household wealth until the fourth quintile, and then jumps by more than USD 170 000 for the fifth quintile (Austria, Germany, Ireland, Italy, Luxembourg, and Spain). In every country, average inheritances and gifts for households in the bottom four wealth quintiles were less than USD 140 000, while households in the top wealth quintile inherited more than USD 140 000 on average in half of the countries in Figure 1.18.

Figure 1.18. Value of inheritances received across the wealth distribution

2015 or latest available year

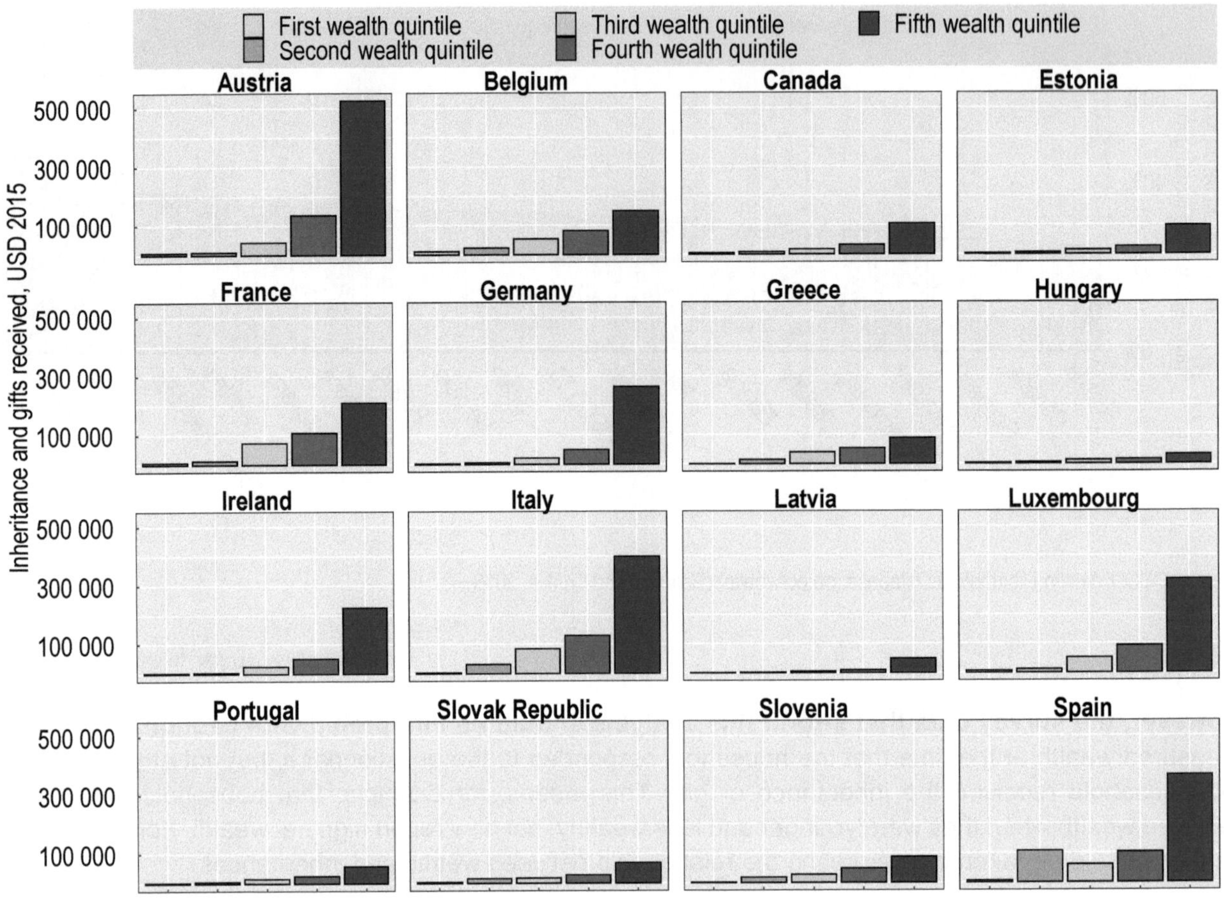

Note: Data were not available for Finland and the Netherlands. Data for Poland removed due to data issues. The value of past inheritances and gifts was converted to present values using an indicator that measures changes in asset prices between the year that the transfer took place and the survey year:

Capitalised (present) value of past transfers = Value at the time of the transfer × (Price index in present year ÷ Price index in year of transfer)

A share price index was derived from the OECD Macroeconomic Indicators Database for financial assets and a house price index was derived from the OECD Analytical Database or a comparable national source for non-financial assets. See (Balestra and Tonkin, 2018[2]) for more information.

Source: OECD Wealth Distribution Database, oe.cd/wealth, (Balestra and Tonkin, 2018[2]).

StatLink https://stat.link/fxbu62

There may be several reasons why wealthy households are more likely to receive an inheritance or gift and why those wealth transfers are of greater value. First, households may have already been wealthy when they received an inheritance. Wealthy parents may raise wealthy children and grandchildren; investing financial resources and social capital in their descendants, thereby giving them the tools to build their own wealth prior to receiving an inheritance or gift. Evidence suggests that as well as gifts and bequests, earnings and education explain a (smaller) portion of the parent-child wealth correlation (Adermon, Lindahl and Waldenström, 2018[22]). Second, non-wealthy households may have used an inheritance or gift to build their wealth. Households that were wealthy at the time that they responded to the survey may not have been wealthy in the past, but used the inheritance or gift to grow their wealth.

While Figure 1.17 shows a clear link between high wealth and having received a wealth transfer, identifying the extent to which these two factors drive that link is not possible with cross-sectional data.

While lower-wealth households receive smaller inheritances and gifts, these are typically large as a share of net wealth. Research has questioned the impact of inherited wealth on relative wealth inequality, because even a small inheritance can be substantial relative to pre-inheritance wealth (Boserup, Kopczuk and Kreiner, 2016[23]; Elinder, Erixson and Waldenström, 2018[24]). Although Figure 1.18 shows wealthier households receiving larger inheritances and gifts, Figure 1.19 shows that inherited wealth as a portion of net wealth was larger for lower-wealth households, compared to households in the top wealth quintile. In 12 countries, inherited wealth was relatively more important for households in the second wealth quintile than for households in the fifth wealth quintile. Inheritances were largest in relative terms for households in the second wealth quintile in Spain (95.6% of net wealth), Italy (52.4%), and in Austria (48.4%) and smallest in Luxembourg (7.4%), Portugal (15.4%), and Latvia (17.2%). This indicates that small inheritances and gifts can have an equalising effect on wealth shares, at least in the short run (see Chapter 2).

Figure 1.19. Ratio of inherited wealth to net wealth, second and fifth wealth quintiles

2015 or latest available year

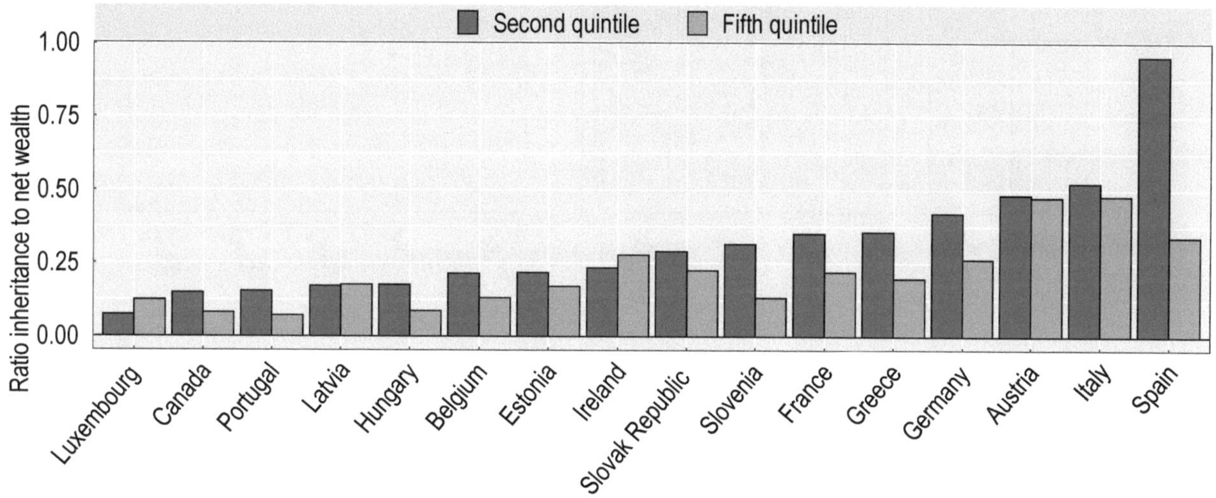

Note: Data were not available for Finland and the Netherlands. Data for Poland removed due to data issues. This graph shows the ratio of inherited wealth to net wealth for households in second and fifth quintiles, as households in the first quintile had negative wealth in several countries.
Source: OECD Wealth Distribution Database, oe.cd/wealth.

StatLink https://stat.link/tj5u34

People are generally older when they inherit. The right panel of Figure 1.20 shows that the share of the population that has received an inheritance or gift increases with age, with the exception of households over the age of 75. This may reflect cohort effects; people who are currently over 75 will mostly have been raised by a generation that lived through World War I and may not have had the same opportunities to accumulate wealth. The left panel tells a similar story; among households that have received an inheritance or gift, the average value of the wealth transfer increases with age. Elinder, Erixson and Waldenström (2018[24]) find that a slight majority of heirs in Sweden (56%) are between 50 and 70 years old. Younger households may receive smaller wealth transfers as they may be composed more of gifts than inheritances (e.g. help with a home deposit or education expenses) or because they may inherit from people who are also younger and have accumulated less wealth.

Figure 1.20. Value of inheritances and share of population that have received an inheritance, by age, average 28 OECD countries

2015 or latest available year

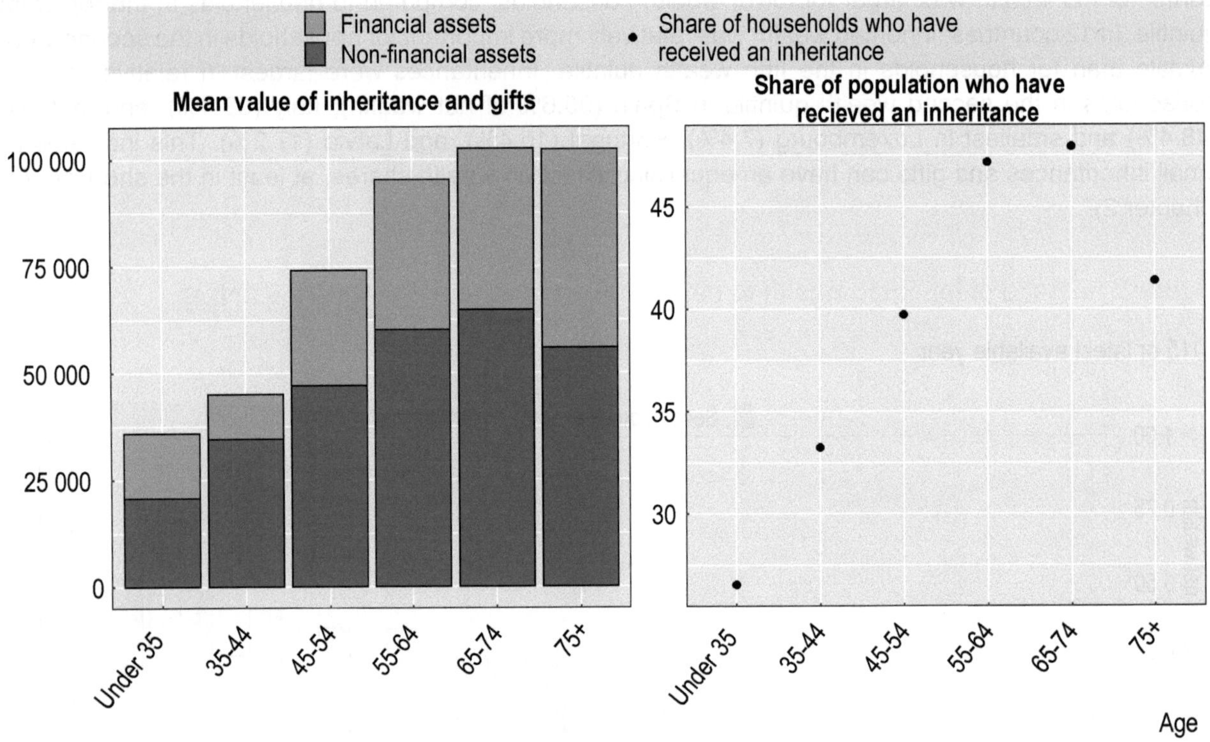

Source: OECD Wealth Distribution Database, oe.cd/wealth.

StatLink https://stat.link/fjh5p2

In the future, the impacts of wealth transfers on inequality are likely to become increasingly significant challenges. Wealth transfers may increase in value, if recent trends in asset prices continue, and in number, with the baby-boom generation getting older. Moreover, as a result of longer life expectancies, wealth concentration among older cohorts and the age at which people inherit are expected to rise. While older generations have benefited from rising asset prices since the post-war period, recent highly expansionary monetary policy may also contribute to upward pressure on asset prices. These trends could further increase wealth inequality and widen the gap between, for instance, the older asset-owning generations and younger generations, who might face increasingly high housing prices. This inter-generational inequality may increase in future, as people inherit later in life. Because wealth is increasingly concentrated and wealthy households tend to receive more and higher value inheritances, intra-generational inequality is also likely to increase. Low fertility rates and smaller families may also mean that there are fewer close family members amongst whom wealth may be divided, so heirs receive a larger share of the donor's estate.

References

Adermon, A., M. Lindahl and D. Waldenström (2018), "Intergenerational Wealth Mobility and the Role of Inheritance: Evidence from Multiple Generations", *The Economic Journal*, Vol. 128/612, pp. F482-F513, http://dx.doi.org/10.1111/ecoj.12535. [22]

Albers, T., C. Bartels and M. Schularick (2020), "The Distribution of Wealth in Germany, 1895-2018", ECONtribute. [7]

Alvaredo, F., B. Garbinti and T. Piketty (2017), "On the Share of Inheritance in Aggregate Wealth: Europe and the USA, 1900–2010", *Economica*, Vol. 84/334, pp. 239-260, http://dx.doi.org/10.1111/ecca.12233. [20]

Balestra, C. and R. Tonkin (2018), "Inequalities in household wealth across OECD countries: Evidence from the OECD Wealth Distribution Database", *OECD Statistics Working Papers*, No. 2018/01, OECD, Paris, https://doi.org/10.1787/18152031. [2]

Boserup, S., W. Kopczuk and C. Kreiner (2016), "The Role of Bequests in Shaping Wealth Inequality: Evidence from Danish Wealth Records", *American Economic Review*, Vol. 106/5, pp. 656–661, http://dx.doi.org/10.1257/aer.p20161036. [23]

Campanale, C. (2007), "Increasing returns to savings and wealth inequality", *Review of Economic Dynamics*, http://dx.doi.org/10.1016/j.red.2007.02.003. [10]

Causa, O., N. Woloszko and D. Leite (2019), "Housing, wealth accumulation and wealth distribution: Evidence and stylized facts", *OECD Economics Department Working Papers*, No. 1588, OECD Publishing, Paris, https://dx.doi.org/10.1787/86954c10-en. [8]

Dynan, K., J. Skinner and S. Zeldes (2004), "Do the Rich Save More?", *Journal of Political Economy*, Vol. 112/2. [16]

Elinder, M., O. Erixson and D. Waldenström (2018), "Inheritance and wealth inequality: Evidence from population registers", *Journal of Public Economics*, Vol. 165, pp. 17-30, http://dx.doi.org/10.1016/j.jpubeco.2018.06.012. [24]

Fatica, S. and D. Prammer (2017), "Working Paper Series Housing and the tax system: how large are the distortions in the euro area?", *Working Paper*, No. 2087, ECB, http://dx.doi.org/10.2866/456421. [12]

Hood, A. and R. Joyce (2017), *Inheritances and Inequality across and within Generations*, Institute for Fiscal Studies. [18]

Household Finance and Consumption and Network (2016), *The Household Finance and Consumption Survey: results from the second wave*, http://dx.doi.org/10.2866/177251. [11]

Hviid, S. and A. Kuchler (2017), "Consumption and savings in a low interest-rate environment", Danmarks Nationalbank, Copenhagen, http://hdl.handle.net/10419/171810www.econstor.eu. [4]

Joyce, R., T. Pope and B. Roantree (2019), *The characteristics and incomes of the top 1%.* [6]

Kennedy, S. (2019), "The potential of tax microdata for tax policy", *Taxation Working Papers*, No. 45, OECD Publishing, Paris. [3]

McKee, K. (2012), "Young People, Homeownership and Future Welfare", *Housing Studies*, Vol. 27/6, pp. 853-862, http://dx.doi.org/10.1080/02673037.2012.714463. [17]

OECD (2019), *Pensions at a Glance 2019: OECD and G20 Indicators*, OECD Publishing, Paris, https://dx.doi.org/10.1787/b6d3dcfc-en. [15]

OECD (2019), *Under Pressure: The Squeezed Middle Class*, OECD Publishing, Paris, https://dx.doi.org/10.1787/689afed1-en. [9]

OECD (2018), *Taxation of Household Savings*, OECD Tax Policy Studies, No. 25, OECD Publishing, Paris, https://dx.doi.org/10.1787/9789264289536-en. [13]

OECD (2013), *OECD Guidelines for Micro Statistics on Household Wealth*, OECD Publishing, Paris, https://dx.doi.org/10.1787/9789264194878-en. [1]

Piketty, T. (2011), "On the long run evolution of inheritance: France 1820–2050", *Quarterly Journal of Economics*, Vol. 126, pp. 1071-1131. [21]

Piketty, T. and G. Zucman (2015), "Wealth and Inheritance in the Long Run", in *Handbook of Income Distribution*, http://dx.doi.org/10.1016/B978-0-444-59429-7.00016-9. [19]

Rosen, H. (1985), "Housing Subsidies: Effects on Housing Decisions, Efficiency, and Equity", in Auerbach, A. and M. Feldstein (eds.), *Handbook of Public Economics*, Elsevier Science Publishers B. V., North-Holland. [14]

Schröder, C. et al. (2020), "Millionaires under the Microscope: Data Gap on Top Wealth Holders Closed; Wealth Concentration Higher than Presumed", *DIW Weekly Report*, Vol. 10, http://dx.doi.org/10.18723/diw_dwr:2020-30-1. [5]

Notes

[1] Dollar values are reported in 2015 USD. Data were obtained from Balestra and Tonkin (2018[2]) and from in-house calculations. Wealth values have first been expressed in a common year (2011) through consumer price indices and then converted into USD through the use of purchasing power parities for household consumption. The combined dataset was updated to 2015 terms.

[2] As in several OECD countries, the high ratio of mean liabilities to mean gross wealth may be linked to changes in housing prices, including households with negative housing equity.

[3] This chapter uses aggregates of asset types in three categories: financial wealth (bonds and other debt securities, deposits, mutual funds and other investment funds, net equity in own unincorporated enterprises, stocks, other financial non-pension assets, unlisted shares and other equity, and voluntary pensions and whole life insurance), real estate wealth (principal residence and other real estate), and other wealth (valuables, vehicles, and other non-financial assets).

[4] Some cross-country variation may be due to differences in data sources (e.g. administrative data or household surveys) and differences in oversampling of high-wealth households. Balestra and Tonkin (2018[2]) do not find a significant link between oversampling of wealthy households and differences

between the WDD and other wealth databases, suggesting that the degree of oversampling does not systematically bias cross-country differences in top wealth shares.

5 Austria, Belgium, Cyprus, Estonia, Finland, France, Germany, Greece, Ireland, Italy, Latvia, Luxembourg, Malta, Netherlands, Portugal, Slovakia, Slovenia, and Spain.

6 See Statistics Netherlands Statistical Trends, December 2020, Chapter 3, https://www.cbs.nl/nl-nl/longread/statistische-trends/2020/pensioenvermogen-en-vermogensongelijkheid/3-resultaten (Dutch).

7 The replacement rate assumes that a worker enters labour market at age 22, earns an average wage throughout their career, and retirees at the normal retirement age. Factors such as higher retirement ages, meaning longer contribution periods, raise the replacement rate. The high replacement rate modelled for Italy is driven by one of the highest minimum retirement ages (71 years with the current pre-COVID-19 demographic projections).

8 Wealth and Assets Survey (WAS) undertaken by the United Kingdom Office for National Statistics. Results are summarised by the Resolution Foundation: https://www.resolutionfoundation.org/app/uploads/2019/12/Who-owns-all-the-pie.pdf, accessed 14 January 2021.

9 An inheritance is a transfer of assets in connection with death of a decedent, while a gift is a transfer of assets made during the life of a donor, not connected to the death of that person.

2 Review of the arguments for and against inheritance taxation

Chapter 2 reviews the arguments for and against inheritance taxation, drawing on theoretical and empirical literature. Through the lens of equity, efficiency, and administration, the chapter assesses the pros and cons of taxing inheritances. The chapter also discusses gift taxes, as a necessary and common complement to inheritance taxation.

This chapter reviews the arguments for and against inheritance taxation. Largely based on existing theoretical and empirical literature, it assesses the pros and cons of taxing inheritances based on equity, efficiency, and administrative considerations. In this chapter, the term inheritance taxation is used to refer to all taxes levied on wealth transfers upon the death of donors, whether they are levied on donors' estates (i.e. estate taxes) or on the wealth received by heirs (i.e. inheritance taxes). As a necessary complement to inheritance taxation, the chapter also considers taxes on gifts made during the donor's lifetime. After briefly characterising inheritance taxation, the chapter starts by discussing the equity arguments in favour of inheritance taxation. The chapter then examines the efficiency effects of inheritance taxation on the behaviours of both donors and heirs. The last section of the chapter discusses the administrative implications of inheritance taxation. The chapter also compares the effects of inheritance taxes with the impact of other taxes that can be levied on wealthy households, including personal income taxes and net wealth taxes.

Overall, this chapter suggests that there is a good case for making greater use of inheritance taxation in OECD countries. There are strong equity arguments in favour of inheritance taxation, in particular of a recipient-based inheritance tax with an exemption for low-value inheritances. The case might be strongest where the effective taxation of personal capital income and wealth tends to be low. From an efficiency perspective, while the number of studies is limited, the empirical literature generally suggests that inheritance taxes tend to have more limited effects on savings than other taxes levied on wealthy taxpayers, and confirms their positive effects on heirs' labour supply and donors' charitable giving. In addition, while inheritance taxes might negatively affect family business successions (depending on tax design), they might at the same time reduce risks of misallocating capital. The chapter also shows that there is evidence of tax planning and migration among the very wealthy in response to inheritance taxation, but that these behaviours could largely be addressed through better tax design, as discussed in greater detail in Chapter 3. Finally, inheritance taxes have a number of administrative advantages compared to other forms of wealth taxation and recent progress on international tax transparency enhances the ability of countries to tax capital effectively.

2.1. Characteristics of inheritance taxation

Inheritance taxation is a specific form of wealth taxation. As opposed to net wealth taxes that are levied periodically (usually annually) on the ownership of wealth, wealth transfer taxes are levied when a transfer of wealth occurs and, in the case of inheritance and estate taxes, only upon the donor's death. Wealth transfer taxes can be further sub-divided into inheritance taxes, which are levied on the wealth received by heirs, and estate taxes, which apply to the total wealth transferred by donors. As with net wealth taxes, inheritance and estate taxes are typically levied on a broad range of assets, including immovable and movable property, as well as financial assets, and debts are deductible.

Some of the features of inheritance taxation make it different from other forms of property taxation. First, inheritance taxation inherently affects two related parties (Kopczuk, 2013[1]). Second, the fact that inheritance taxes are infrequent (at death in the case of inheritance taxation or on occasions during the donor's lifetime in the case of gift taxes) implies that they allow for a long period of planning. The potentially large amounts of money at stake may also make tax avoidance and planning worthwhile for some taxpayers (Kopczuk, 2013[1]). At the same time, the date of inheritances is uncertain, which may limit some behavioural responses, particularly among those who are less wealthy and cannot afford to give assets away prior to death or whose assets do not qualify for particular exemptions. Third, these taxes, even when they apply to a small group of taxpayers, can have significant distributional implications, in the short and the long term.

2.2. Equity considerations

This section examines the equity arguments in favour of inheritance taxation. It looks at equality of opportunity, horizontal and vertical equity, and the effects of inheritance taxes on the distribution of wealth. Using simple simulations, the last part of this section analyses how inheritance taxes, in combination with other taxes, can help prevent the build-up of dynastic wealth over generations.

2.2.1. Inheritance and gift taxation enhances equality of opportunity

A substantial share of wealth is inherited. Wealth inequality can result from inequality in self-made wealth – which is itself due to factors including differences in income from work or entrepreneurial activity, returns to savings and investments, and luck – and from inequality in inherited wealth. According to some estimates, the share of inheritances in overall wealth varies between 30% and 60% in Western countries (Wolff, 2015[2]; Piketty and Zucman, 2015[3]). In recent decades, evidence shows that the share of inherited wealth in total household wealth has increased in some countries, and the number and value of inheritances is expected to increase in the future (see Chapter 1).

From an equality of opportunity perspective, inheritances and gifts can create a divide between the opportunities that people face. Wealth transfers might give recipients a head start that is not linked to their personal efforts (Alstott, 2007[4]; Boadway, Chamberlain and Emmerson, 2010[5]) and reduce equality of opportunity, which can be understood as ensuring that people with similar abilities and levels of effort face similar prospects in life. This may be particularly true in the case of inter vivos gifts, which people receive earlier in life than inheritances.

Empirically, inheritances and gifts have been found to play a strong role in wealth persistence across generations, particularly between parents and their children. Intergenerational wealth mobility tends to be lower than intergenerational income mobility (Bastani and Waldenström, 2020[6]). Looking at the degree to which the wealth association between parents and children can be explained by inheritances in Sweden, Adermon, Lindahl and Waldenström (2018[7]) find that bequests and gifts account for at least half of the parent–child wealth correlation, while earnings and education can account for only a quarter. However, the authors also find that wealth tends to dissipate over time, with grandparent-grandchild wealth correlations being markedly lower than parent-child correlations. Boserup, Kopczuk and Kreiner (2018[8]) find that inter vivos transfers play a significant role, with wealth holdings in childhood, which are related to parental giving, being a strong predictor for wealth in adulthood.

Inheritance taxes can therefore be justified to enhance equality of opportunity. By breaking down the concentration of wealth and correcting for factors that are beyond recipients' control, inheritance and gift taxation can contribute to levelling the playing field across individuals, and thereby increase equality of opportunity and improve social mobility. Piketty, Saez and Zucman (2013[9]) have argued that, from a meritocratic perspective, inherited wealth should be taxed at higher rates than earned income and self-made wealth.

Results from theoretical optimal tax models on the design of inheritance taxes vary significantly. The optimal inheritance tax literature takes into account both equity and efficiency goals to draw insights about inheritance taxation. The optimal tax rate generally depends on a number of factors. These include the intent of the donor and the weights placed on the donor and recipients' utilities, the weights that the social planner assigns to efficiency and equity objectives, the type of social welfare function that the social planner is maximising, and the types of (linear or non-linear) tax instruments that the social planner can avail of to maximise social welfare. As discussed below, depending on their assumptions, some models find that bequests should not be taxed, some find that they should be subsidised, while others find that optimal tax rates are positive.

Based on highly restrictive assumptions, some optimal tax models have found that the optimal tax rate on bequests was zero or negative (i.e. that bequests should be subsidised). Farhi and Werning (2010[10]) analyse a two-generation model, assuming that all the capital comes from the work efforts of the first generation. Children are assumed not to work but to derive utility from the consumption they can finance with the bequest they receive from their parents. They show that if the social welfare function only considers the utility of parents, who are assumed to be altruistic (i.e. the children's consumption financed with the bequest provides utility to parents), but places no direct weight on the utility of children, the optimal tax on bequests is zero. When governments can levy a non-linear income tax, parents' intertemporal consumption choices should not be distorted, in line with the result in Atkinson and Stiglitz (1976[11]). When the utility of heirs is directly taken into account in social welfare, on the other hand, Farhi and Werning (2010[10]) find that bequests should be subsidised, but in a progressive way, i.e. with subsidies decreasing with the size of inheritances, to reduce consumption inequality amongst the generation of children.

When a society is assumed to have meritocratic and equality of opportunity preferences, however, optimal tax models find positive optimal inheritance taxes. In a model that builds upon their 2010 model, but assumes heterogeneity in the degree of parents' altruism towards their children, Farhi and Werning (2013[12]) find a range of possible optimal tax results, from subsidies to positive taxes, depending on redistributive objectives. They find that it can be optimal to tax inheritances if equality of opportunity weighs heavily in the objective function of the government. Piketty and Saez (2013[13]) develop a more realistic setup which considers that each generation both gives and receives inheritances. They find that the optimal tax rate is positive and high, up to 50%-60%, if the elasticity of bequests to tax is low, bequest concentration is high, and society cares primarily about those receiving small inheritances.

Equality of opportunity arguments have significant implications in terms of tax design. In particular, if promoting equality of opportunity is a major objective of inheritance taxation, then there is a strong case for a recipient-based inheritance tax rather than an estate tax levied on donors. Indeed, it is the amount of wealth received by each recipient that should matter rather than the overall amount bequeathed by the donor (Mirrlees et al., 2011[14]). Based on equality of opportunity arguments, it would also make sense to consider the overall amount of wealth received by individuals over their lifetime, regardless of who they received it from. These various design options are examined in Chapter 3.

2.2.2. Inheritance and gift taxation can strengthen horizontal and vertical equity

An inheritance tax can enhance horizontal equity. According to the horizontal equity principle, people receiving the same amount of income or assets should be taxed similarly. Thus, there should not be a difference in the tax burden of people in equal circumstances depending on whether they receive transfers from others in the form of earnings or in the form of gifts and inheritances. An inheritance tax can therefore be justified to level the playing field between inheritances and earnings from work or savings.

An inheritance tax, particularly a progressive one, would also enhance vertical equity. According to the vertical equity principle, taxpayers with a greater ability to pay tax should pay relatively more tax. By taxing wealth transfers, particularly at progressive rates, an inheritance tax ensures that those who receive more wealth pay more tax. In fact, inheritance taxes are often among the most progressive elements of countries' tax systems (Piketty and Saez, 2007[15]), although effective progressivity is often lowered by the way inheritance and gift taxes are designed (see Chapter 3).

Some have argued that wealth transfers should be taxed more heavily than earned income because wealth transfer recipients can be viewed as better off than income earners. Batchelder (2020[16]) recently proposed reforming the US estate tax by treating inheritances as taxable personal income in the hands of recipients, but she argues that large inheritances should be taxed at a higher rate than income from work. Indeed, recipients of inheritances are better off than people who accumulate the same amount of money by working as the former do not incur opportunity costs: they do not have to relinquish any leisure to receive the bequest. Besides, people who inherit a lot generally also benefit from other economic and social advantages, which may reinforce the case for taxing inheritances at higher rates than income from work (Batchelder, 2020[16]). In existing tax systems, however, inheritances are often taxed far more favourably than income from work and savings (see Chapter 3; and Batchelder, 2020[3], for the United States and the Resolution Foundation, 2018[10], for the United Kingdom).

2.2.3. Inheritance and gift taxes can reduce wealth inequality, particularly in the longer run and if revenues are redistributed

A number of studies simulating intergenerational wealth transfers have looked at the impact of inheritances on the distribution of wealth and shown mixed results. Results differ depending on the assumptions used. Some studies suggest that inheritances can be equalising, reflecting the role of imperfect correlation of spousal background in the sense that the partner in a couple from a financially less privileged background will benefit from the inheritance their partner receives (Laitner, 1979[17]) or the tendency to leave more to less well-off children (Tomes, 1981[18]). Others, however, suggest a disequalising effect of inheritances (Davies, 1982[19]; De Nardi, 2004[20]).

More recent studies based on individual level survey or administrative data have generally found that inheritances reduce relative wealth inequality but increase the absolute dispersion of wealth. Wolff and Gittleman (2014[21]), using data from the Survey of Consumer Finances in the United States, find that the rich inherit more than the less affluent, but that the rich inherit less relative to their existing wealth, causing inheritances to have an equalising effect on the distribution of wealth. Drawing on their methodology, Bönke, Werder and Westermeier (2017[22]) find the same results for eight European countries using data from the Household Finance and Consumption Survey. Other studies relying on administrative data reach similar conclusions. Using Swedish population register data on inheritances and wealth, Elinder, Erixson and Waldenström (2018[23]) find that inheritances reduce wealth inequality measured by the Gini coefficient or top wealth shares. However, they find that inheritances increase the absolute dispersion of wealth among heirs, measured as the difference in wealth between the heirs in the 25th and 75th percentiles of the distribution. In a similar study using Danish individual level tax register data on wealth, Boserup, Kopczuk and Kreiner (2016[24]) also find that inheritances cause an increase in the absolute dispersion of wealth and a decrease in relative wealth inequality.

In countries where inheritances are found to have an equalising effect, this effect tends to diminish over time, as inheritances received by the poor are much more likely to be consumed in the long run. Nekoei and Seim (2018[25]) show that the equalising effect of inheritances in Sweden is reverted in ten years. Heirs in the bottom 99% of the wealth distribution deplete almost all of their inherited wealth within a decade. In contrast, for the top 1%, the inherited wealth remains almost intact over time. Similarly, Elinder, Erixson and Waldenström (2018[23]) find that the equalising effect of inheritances is diluted over time, in line with findings that less wealthy heirs spend a larger share of their inherited wealth than wealthier heirs.

In addition, the overall impact of inheritance taxes – i.e. including income redistribution – is more likely to be equalising. In Sweden, Elinder, Erixson and Waldenström (2018[23]) find that inheritance taxes counteract the equalising effect of inheritances, but that this effect is reversed when tax revenues are redistributed to reduce inequality. The long-term impact of inheritance taxes might be even larger than the immediate redistributive effect. In their simulation model of intergenerational wealth transmissions, Cowell, Van De Gaer and He (2017[26]) find that the long-run effect of an inheritance tax in reducing wealth inequality (i.e. the "pre-distribution" effect) will be much larger than the immediate "redistribution" impact, as work, leisure, and saving rates all change in ways that reduce wealth inequality. Previous OECD research has also found that, overall, tax mixes that rely more on taxes on wealth transfers are associated with lower levels of income inequality (Akgun, Cournède and Fournier, 2017[27]). These findings reinforce the idea that the overall effect of inheritance taxation, including the redistribution of tax revenues, is equalising.

These findings provide valuable guidance for the design of inheritance taxes. Indeed, these findings suggest that a tax exemption threshold that allows small inheritances to be passed on free of tax, combined with a progressive inheritance tax rate schedule, may reduce absolute and relative wealth inequality. This would avoid taxing small inheritances that may have an equalising effect, at least in the short run, while taxing larger inheritances. Besides, since behavioural responses differ across the wealth distribution (i.e. the wealthiest heirs leave their inheritances intact, while the majority of heirs consume their inherited wealth) and wealthier heirs receive larger bequests, taxing large inheritances will have a long-run effect on the distribution of wealth (Nekoei and Seim, 2018[25]).

2.2.4. Inheritance taxes can help prevent the build-up of dynastic wealth

This section examines the impact of different taxes on wealth accumulation over several generations, based on a stylised lifecycle model. The purpose of the simulations presented in this section is to model the effects of different types of taxes on the pace of wealth accumulation over generations across different types of households and in different rate of return scenarios.

These simulations are meant as simple illustrations and rely on highly stylised assumptions. The first part of the simulation exercise models wealth accumulation over five generations across three types of households, assuming a 4% rate of return, when different types of taxes are levied. The only difference between household types is assumed to be their initial wealth levels. Apart from initial wealth endowments, the model assumptions remain unchanged across household types to ensure that the results are not driven by variations in labour and pension income, returns to savings or consumption behaviour. Across all household types and scenarios, wealth is also assumed to be equally split between two heirs at the end of each lifecycle. The second part of the simulation exercise looks at wealth accumulation dynamics for super-high wealth households earning a rate of return of 7%. The parameters of the model are specified in Box 2.1.

These simulations do not take into account potential economy-wide dynamic effects that may have a significant impact on wealth accumulation and inequality. In particular, it could be expected that if capital stocks continue to grow, the returns to capital could fall, depending on the elasticity of substitution between labour and capital, i.e. whether capital can easily be substituted to labour in the production process. If the elasticity of substitution is high (i.e. above one), the returns to capital are predicted to remain stable and higher than growth rates (Piketty, 2014[28]), but if the elasticity is lower, returns to capital could fall, and if they fall quickly enough when the capital stock grows, the capital share of income could fall rather than rise (Rognlie, 2014[29]). These dynamic effects are not taken into consideration in these simple simulations. The simulations also do not take into account the potential impact of the revenues raised through the different taxes that are modelled and how the increase in revenues and the size of the government may in turn affect private wealth accumulation.

These simulations also do not take account of observed changes in behaviours, including those of inheriting generations. The simple stylised scenarios assume that household behaviour does not change over time, and thereby assume that the steady accumulation of wealth between generations will continue uninterrupted over time. As discussed in sections 2.3.5 and 2.3.6, this assumption is in contrast to the empirical observation that inheriting generations tend to work less, consume more, and run companies less efficiently than their forebears.

Box 2.1. Model specifications

The model is estimated over five equally long generations. Each generation consists of a single taxpayer whose overall 60-year lifecycle is divided into a 40-year period of work and a 20-year period of retirement (this scenario corresponds to a taxpayer entering the labour market around the age of 20 and receiving an initial endowment in the same year from an inheritance).

At the beginning of the first generation, taxpayers are endowed with a certain amount of assets according to three different wealth categories: i) a medium-rich taxpayer with USD 40 000 of initial wealth, ii) a rich taxpayer with USD 500 000 and iii) a super-rich taxpayer with USD 10 000 000 of initial wealth. After death, the remaining assets are evenly split and passed on to two heirs with only one heir being followed up for further analysis. This heir is assumed to work also for 40 years, enjoy a 20-year retirement period and then pass on their accumulated wealth to two heirs, and this cycle repeats itself. The model disregards the fact that even if wealth is split between two heirs, it may continue to accumulate within the confines of the same family.

Apart from wealth endowments, taxpayers also earn a wage of USD 50 000 per year and a pension of USD 20 000 per year during retirement. Wage and pension income are kept constant for all wealth endowment levels and across generations. Every year, taxpayers consume a fraction of 30% out of their labour or pension income and consume a fraction of 1% out of their accrued wealth. The remainder is again invested into assets, which are assumed to yield a 4% rate of return. For simplicity, the model does not take inflation into account (although the accumulation of wealth in real terms will be affected by inflation).

A savings tax is levied on returns to savings accrued from wealth and labour income. The model imposes either an annual 20% flat tax or a progressive savings tax. In addition, an inheritance tax on wealth bequeathed above USD 300 000 is modelled; in one case a 10% flat rate applies and in another case progressive rates apply (see Table 2.1 for the respective income and bequest thresholds and tax rates). The impact of an annual 1% wealth tax levied on the wealth stock is also modelled.

Wages and pensions are subject to taxation. Wages are taxed at an average effective tax rate of 35%, and pensions at 20%. Consumption is subject to a 20% VAT.

To account for the fact that returns may vary with household wealth, a 7% return scenario for super-rich households is also modelled. Following for instance Lusardi, Michaud and Mitchell (2017[30]) and Fagereng et al. (2020[31]) who find that people systematically and persistently differ in their rates of return on capital depending on ability, risk-taking and wealth, the second part of the modelling exercise focuses on wealth accumulation for the super-rich, assuming a higher return on savings, in line with recent real-life returns.[1]

Table 2.1. Model parameters

	Medium wealth household	High wealth household	Super-high wealth household
Initial wealth endowment	USD 40 000	USD 500 000	USD 10 000 000
Labour income	USD 50 000	USD 50 000	USD 50 000
Pension income	USD 20 000	USD 20 000	USD 20 000
Consumption out of income	30%	30%	30%
Consumption out of wealth	1%	1%	1%
Consumption out of pension	30%	30%	30%
Consumption out of wealth during retirement	1%	1%	1%
Return on savings	4%	4%	4% / 7%
Savings tax progression	20% / 30% / 40% / 50%	20% / 30% / 40% / 50%	20% / 30% / 40% / 50%
Savings tax thresholds	USD 10 000 / 20 000 / 50 000 / 100 000	USD 10 000 / 20 000 / 50 000 / 100 000	USD 10 000 / 20 000 / 50 000 / 100 000
Inheritance tax progression	10% / 15% / 20% / 30%	10% / 15% / 20% / 30%	10% / 15% / 20% / 30%
Inheritance tax thresholds	USD 300 000 / 500 000 / 1 000 000 / 3 000 000	USD 300 000 / 500 000 / 1 000 000 / 3 000 000	USD 300 000 / 500 000 / 1 000 000 / 3 000 000
Wealth tax	1%	1%	1%
Labour income AETR	35%	35%	35%
Pension income AETR	20%	20%	20%
VAT rate	20%	20%	20%
Number of heirs in each generation	2	2	2

The simulation results show that, in the absence of taxes on savings and wealth, wealth accumulates unfettered for all three household types. Estimates in the top row of Figure 2.1 show that despite wealth stocks being split between two heirs at the end of each lifecycle, taxpayers still end up over time with a wealth level many times higher than the initial endowment. In this scenario, there are no taxes levied, and heirs are the only shock to wealth growth. There may be other factors that affect wealth accumulation (e.g. crises, low productivity growth), but these are not taken into consideration in the model. In this setting and in the absence of taxation, wealth accumulates fast and in a self-reinforcing way, and reaches extreme levels particularly for super-high wealth households (note the different scales used across household types).

The imposition of progressive savings taxes slows wealth accumulation significantly across all household types. Relative to a 20% flat tax on savings, which already slows wealth formation, the progressive savings tax that is modelled results in an even slower increase in wealth over time (Figure 2.1, second row). While wealth formation during the first generation almost matches the trajectory of wealth accumulation under a 20% flat tax for a medium-rich and a rich taxpayer, it slows in subsequent generations. Wealth levels for a super-rich taxpayer increase less in relative terms than for other households under a 20% flat tax (although they do increase more in absolute amounts) and actually decline under the progressive savings tax. This observation is explained by a combination of model parameters. Additional savings from non-consumed labour income, which form a relatively higher share of total wealth for medium-rich and rich taxpayers, are re-invested, making their wealth levels initially increase faster in relative terms. The progressive savings tax also affects lower wealth levels less, as they generate lower savings income. In contrast, re-invested savings from labour income form a smaller share of the super-rich taxpayers' existing wealth and progressive savings taxes have a higher impact given their higher income from savings. The impact of the progressive savings tax is also directly determined by the tax rates chosen in the model, and it should be noted that these rates are (significantly) higher than the tax rates that currently apply in most OECD countries. Under this progressive savings tax scenario, wealth levels across the different types of households would eventually converge, although this would take more generations than included in Figure 2.1.

Progressive inheritance taxes, in combination with a 20% flat savings tax, exert similar countervailing effects on wealth accumulation. While a 10% inheritance tax on wealth bequeathed in excess of USD 300 000 does not seem to alter the growth trajectory decisively for medium-rich and rich taxpayers, a progressive inheritance tax reduces wealth accumulation by half across generations compared to a scenario where only a 20% tax on savings is levied (Figure 2.1, third and fourth rows). For a super-rich taxpayer, the progressive inheritance tax results in a decrease in wealth over time. Depending on the tax rates, a progressive inheritance tax leads to similar, albeit slightly lower, effects on wealth accumulation dynamics over generations compared to the progressive savings tax and may thus act as an (imperfect) alternative to a progressive savings tax.

An annual 1% wealth tax, in combination with a 20% flat savings tax, exerts an overall lower impact on wealth formation than the progressive savings tax. Wealth growth trajectories across all three types of taxpayers flatten when a 1% annual wealth tax is combined with a 20% flat savings tax, with wealth growth turning negative for the super-rich taxpayer (Figure 2.1, bottom row). The reduction in wealth growth (or negative wealth growth for the super-rich) is slightly lower than under the progressive savings tax. In this context, it is important to recall the similarity of savings and wealth taxes absent capital market imperfections. If savings yield a return of 4%, a 1% tax on the wealth stock is equivalent to a 25% tax on the income from savings.

Figure 2.1. Simulations of wealth accumulation over five generations for different types of households under different tax scenarios

Estimated wealth accumulation in USD million for a medium-rich, rich and super-rich taxpayer at a 4% rate of return

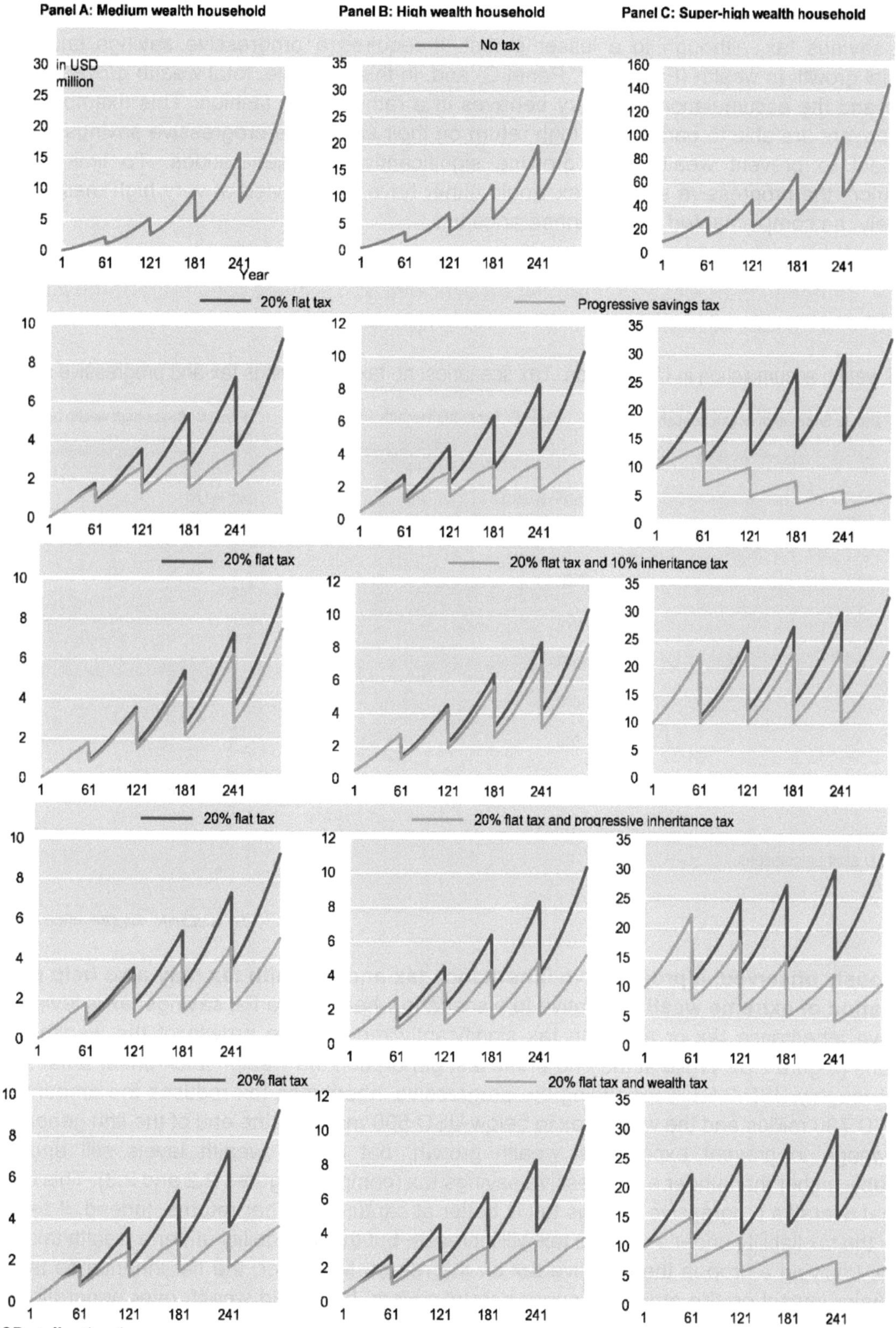

Source: OECD staff estimations.

StatLink https://stat.link/4t305f

To account for the fact that returns may vary with household wealth and significantly affect wealth accumulation dynamics, a 7% return scenario for super-rich households is also modelled. Under this scenario, Panel A in Figure 2.2 shows that wealth increases exponentially over time in the absence of any tax: it grows from an initial USD 10 million to over USD 50 billion over five generations (despite the fact that wealth is split into two at the end of each generation). A similar pattern can be observed under a 20% flat savings tax, although to a lesser extent. It requires a progressive savings tax to slow the exponential growth in wealth (Figure 2.2, Panel C) and, in this example, total wealth grows "only" six-fold over time and the accumulation trajectory behaves in a rather linear fashion. This example shows that when taxpayers are able to earn a very high return on their savings, a progressive savings tax might not be sufficient to prevent wealth from growing significantly over generations. To limit such wealth accumulation, the progressive savings tax would either have to be levied at very high marginal rates or, alternatively, be complemented with an inheritance tax.

Figure 2.2. Simulations of wealth accumulation over five generations for a super-high wealth household at a 7% rate of return

Estimated wealth accumulation in USD million. Tax scenarios: no tax, flat savings tax and progressive savings tax

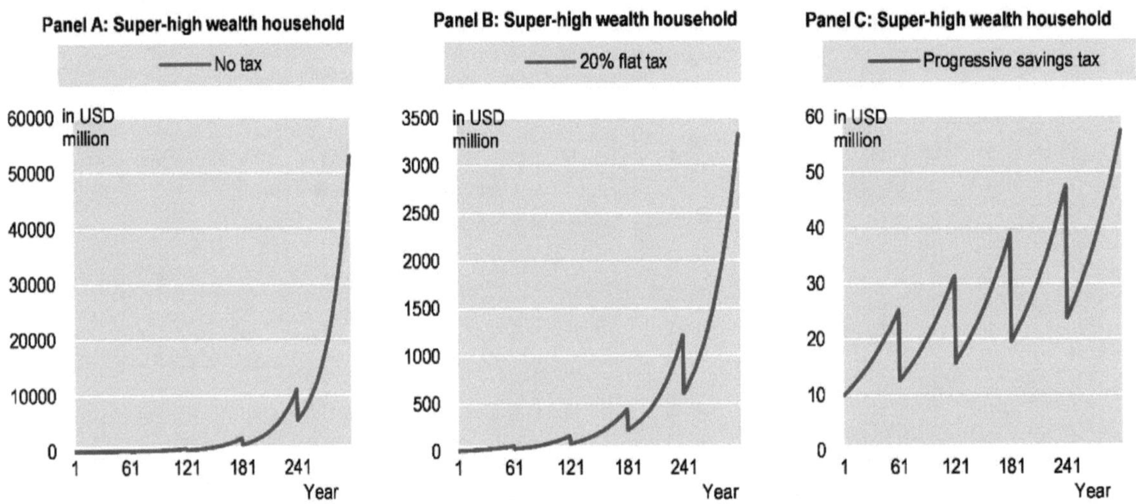

Source: OECD staff calculations.

StatLink https://stat.link/tcbhs0

As previously observed, a progressive inheritance tax and a wealth tax may also help prevent the accumulation of extreme wealth. Relative to a scenario where only a flat savings tax is levied, adding a progressive inheritance tax or a wealth tax significantly reduces the growth of the wealth stock over generations (Figure 2.3). While at the end of the last generation the wealth stock under a flat savings tax stands at roughly USD 3.5 billion, adding the progressive inheritance tax reduces the amount to slightly above USD 700 million and the wealth tax to below USD 500 million at the end of the fifth generation. Both taxes manage to prevent exponential wealth growth, but overall wealth levels still end up being considerably higher than under a progressive savings tax (compare Figures 2.2 and 2.3). This comparison shows that overall a progressive savings tax is better at capturing higher returns. Indeed, if asset returns increase, the tax liability under a savings tax will increase, but the tax liability under a wealth tax will remain the same, implying a drop in the effective tax on the return. Moreover, the flat inheritance tax does not exert a major impact on the growth of super-rich taxpayers' high-yield wealth over generations. Finally, Figure 2.4 shows wealth accumulation patterns when inheritance or wealth taxes are combined with a progressive savings tax. When a progressive savings tax is combined with a progressive inheritance tax or an annual wealth tax, wealth levels progressively decline over generations for super-rich households earning a 7% return on their assets.

Figure 2.3. Simulations of wealth accumulation over five generations for a super-high wealth household at a 7% rate of return

Estimated wealth accumulation in USD million. Tax scenarios: inheritance or wealth taxes, in combination with a flat savings tax

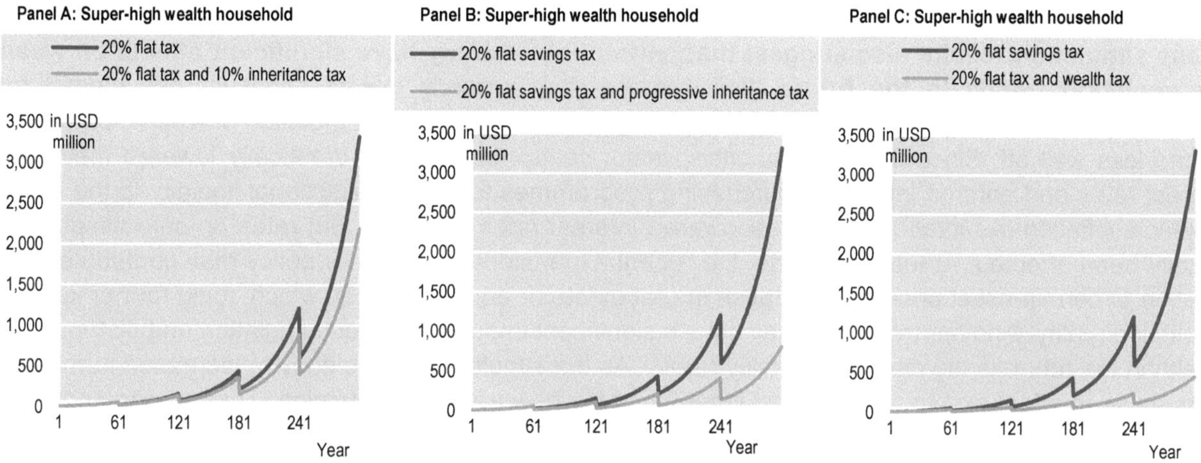

Source: OECD staff calculations.

StatLink https://stat.link/6o0fys

Figure 2.4. Simulations of wealth accumulation over five generations for a super-high wealth household at a 7% rate of return

Estimated wealth accumulation in USD million. Tax scenarios: inheritance or wealth taxes, in combination with a progressive savings tax

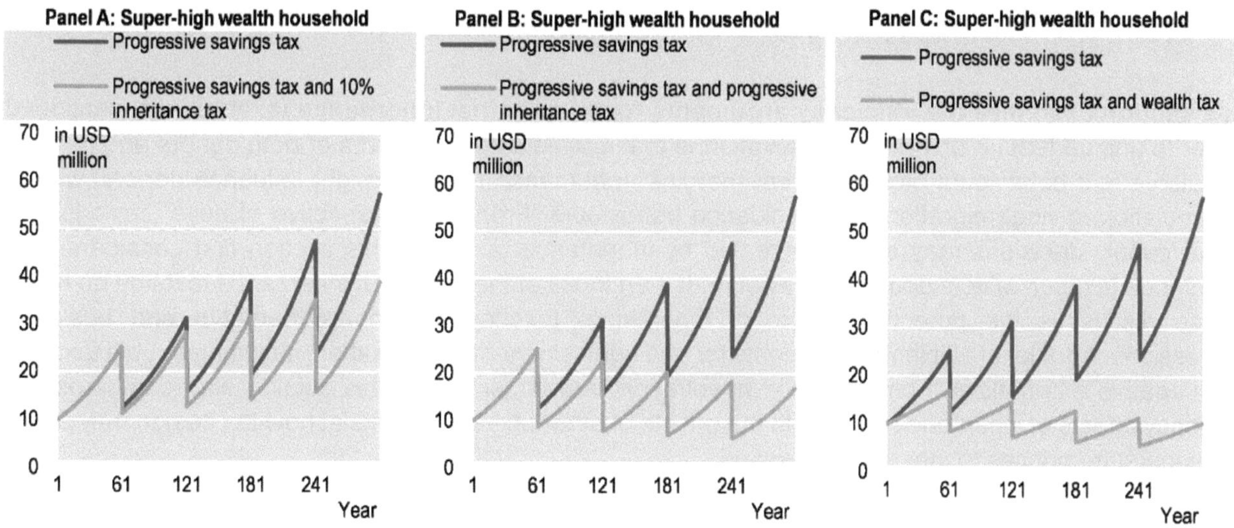

Source: OECD staff calculations.

StatLink https://stat.link/3ev8hf

Overall, the results suggest that a high progressive savings tax, or a lower savings tax combined with a progressive inheritance tax, may help prevent large wealth accumulation over generations. From an efficiency point of view, the combination of a more moderate progressive savings tax with a progressive inheritance tax may be preferable, given the overall limited negative efficiency effects of inheritance taxes (see Section 2.3). An annual wealth tax, in combination with a progressive savings tax, could also be a powerful tool to reduce wealth concentration over generations, but depending on its design, it could lead to very high marginal effective tax rates, particularly in low asset return scenarios. Besides, as discussed further in the chapter, a wealth tax is more administratively challenging than an inheritance tax.

These simulation results also suggest that certain factors may have significant effects on wealth accumulation trends in the future. For instance, the currently low to negative real interest rate environment poses a significant challenge to savings returns and the accumulation of wealth, particularly for the less well off. Since the financial crisis, major central banks have drastically lowered their policy interest rates and entered into asset purchasing programmes to provide additional liquidity to the market amid low inflation. As intended, this has lowered interest rates for credit, but rates on safe assets have equally been affected. At the same time, the recent expansionary monetary policy may contribute to the inflation of certain asset prices, for instance in real estate or equity markets, which could further increase wealth inequality. Another trend that may have a significant impact on the accumulation and distribution of wealth in the future is the decline in fertility rates.[2] As the simulations have shown, increased numbers of heirs have an effect akin to an additional inheritance tax on wealth accumulation. The growing shortfall of heirs as a "demographic shock to wealth accumulation" (Piketty, 2015[32]) might exacerbate intra- and inter-generational wealth inequality as wealth will be split between fewer heirs.

Finally, the build-up of significant wealth in one generation is not considered in the simulations but it has important implications for tax design. The simulations presented above consider the build-up of wealth over generations, through saving and investments, but the build-up of extreme wealth has often been the result of successful entrepreneurship in a single generation, supported by rapid technological change (e.g. industrialisation, financial innovation or digitalisation), as well as factors enabling economic rents, or supernormal returns, such as reduced market competition. This highlights that inheritance taxation is not a silver bullet and that other tax reforms, in particular in relation to personal capital income, as well as non-tax reforms are needed to address wealth inequality.

2.3. Efficiency considerations

This section examines the efficiency arguments for and against inheritance taxation. As mentioned earlier, a unique feature of inheritance taxation is that it affects the incentives of both donors and heirs. It can also affect behaviours along different margins. Inheritance taxation might influence donors' wealth accumulation, giving, migration, and avoidance behaviours. From the perspective of heirs, savings and labour supply decisions may also be affected by inheritance taxation. This section first considers how inheritance taxation affects donors' behaviours. It then looks at the impact of inheritance taxation on heirs. It also discusses the potential impact of inheritance taxation on entrepreneurship and business successions. Additional efficiency arguments for and against inheritance taxation, including double taxation and negative externalities from wealth concentration, are considered. This section also compares the efficiency effects of inheritance taxes with the effects of other taxes and looks at how tax design may affect behavioural responses to inheritance taxation.

2.3.1. Inheritance taxation may have a small negative impact on wealth accumulation by donors

An inheritance tax directly reduces wealth accumulation over generations (see Section 2.2.4). However, without taking into account potential effects on donors' behaviours, this effect only materialises when assets are transferred to the next generation by reducing the net amount of wealth that is transferred to heirs. As discussed below, inheritance taxes may also affect wealth accumulation prior to being levied by encouraging changes in donors' behaviours.

In theory, inheritance taxation may have varying effects on the behaviour of donors. Prospective donors might save less knowing that a part of their wealth will not be passed on to their heirs (substitution effect). On the other hand, if donors have their mind set on passing on a certain amount of wealth to the next generation, an inheritance tax could make them save more (income effect). Donors may also seek to transfer their assets earlier, in countries where inter vivos transfers result in lower taxation than if assets are transferred at death. Prospective donors might also prefer to invest more heavily in their children's education as opposed to accumulating wealth in a taxable form.

A vast theoretical literature has emphasised how donors' bequest motives influence their responses to inheritance and gift taxation. Potential donors accumulate wealth for different reasons (see Box 2.2) and the theoretical literature has found that bequest motives strongly influence donors' behavioural responses to changes in inheritance taxation. Potential donors might save to meet their needs in retirement (i.e. lifecycle saving). They might also save because they enjoy being wealthy and value the power and prestige that wealth confers while they are alive (egoistic saving). In these cases, donors might leave unintentional or "accidental" bequests if they die before using up all their wealth. Such unintentional bequests are expected to be unresponsive to inheritance taxation (Gale and Slemrod, 2001[33]). From a tax design perspective, this may justify having higher tax rates on transfers to distant relatives or non-related heirs, as the likelihood of accidental transfers may be greater than in the case of bequests to direct descendants (Cremer and Pestieau, 2009[34]). There are other cases, however, where bequests are not accidental but are at least partly planned by donors, and where inheritance taxes will affect donors' savings and consumption decisions to some extent. For altruistic parents who care about the welfare of their children, the effect of an inheritance tax is ambiguous, depending on income and substitution effects. On the one hand, they may have fewer incentives to save and work if part of their wealth cannot be passed on to their children. On the other hand, altruistic parents may save more if an inheritance tax is levied in order to compensate for the tax that heirs will face (Joulfaian, 2016[35]). If inter vivos transfers are tax-advantaged, altruistic parents may also be expected to increase the amount of inter vivos transfers to avoid a reduction in the post-tax amount of transfers that their children receive (Niimi, 2019[36]). Other models consider exchange-related motives, where parents transfer wealth in exchange for services from their descendants, such as taking care of them in old age. If inter vivos transfers are taxed preferentially compared to bequests, parents may avoid a tax increase by accelerating the timing of transfers, as altruistic parents would. However, parents with an exchange motive may also decide not to accelerate the timing of transfers and make wealth transfers conditional upon their children supporting them in old age (Niimi, 2019[36]).

Box 2.2. Bequest motives

The role of bequest motives in determining behavioural responses to inheritance taxation has been closely studied. A body of theoretical literature has suggested the following bequest motives (Cremer and Pestieau, 2009[34]):

(1) **accidental bequests**: Wealth transfers may be unintentional or "accidental" when people die before they were able to use up all their wealth (Abel, 1985[37]; Hurd, 1987[38]). Accidental bequests may occur when a part of donors' savings for consumption smoothing has not been consumed before death. Accidental or unplanned bequests may also occur when wealthy households accumulate wealth for the utility that wealth provides, rather than for dynastic or lifecycle purposes (Carroll, 2000[39]). The assumption is that donors do not obtain any utility from accidental bequests.

(2) **strategic motive**: Donors may transfer wealth to their heirs in exchange for a service, i.e. to induce their heirs to behave in certain ways, such as taking care of them in old age (Bernheim, Shleifer and Summers, 1985[40]).

(3) **altruistic bequests**: Donors may derive utility directly from the welfare of their heirs and seek to compensate for the lower earnings or earnings abilities of their children (Becker, 1974[41]; McGarry and Schoeni, 1995[42]).

(4) **"joy of giving" bequests** – also known as "warm glow": Donors may derive utility simply from the act of giving to their children (Andreoni, 1990[43]). Unlike altruistic bequests, "joy of giving" is a private benefit experienced only by the donor and benefits that heirs receive from bequests are not valued by the donor.

Estimations of bequest motives have differed. For example, Hurd (1987[38]) found that households with children do not save more and, based on this finding, concluded that bequests are largely accidental. On the other hand, Kopczuk and Lupton (2007[44]) found that approximately 75% of the elderly population have a bequest motive. Their results on whether bequests are altruistic or strategic are not statistically significant. Wealth is a major driver of having a bequest motive, as wealthy people "have more than enough assets to sustain their required consumption through retirement" (Burman, Mcclelland and Lu, 2018[45]; Kopczuk and Lupton, 2007[44]). As discussed in the main text, the impact of inheritance and gift taxes on donors' behaviours is expected to be different depending on the presence and type of bequest motive.

However, this highly theoretical literature on bequest motives has had limited influence in practice. Despite a large body of work on bequest motives, there is no consensus on what drives bequest behaviours. In fact, determining the intent of donors is extremely difficult and they usually have more than one motive. In addition, different individuals may have different motives (Kopczuk, 2013[1]). For instance, wealthier people are more likely to have a (non-accidental) bequest motive because they have more assets than they need to finance consumption in retirement (Burman, Mcclelland and Lu, 2018[45]; Kopczuk and Lupton, 2007[44]). Despite the strong emphasis on the role of bequest motives in theoretical work, most empirical studies assessing behavioural responses to inheritance taxation do so without establishing explicit links with donors' bequest motives (Niimi, 2019[36]). From a practical tax design perspective, findings on bequest motives have also been of limited use as tailoring tax rules to bequest motives would not be feasible.

The empirical literature on the impact of inheritance taxation on donors' wealth accumulation is very limited and generally shows negative, but small effects. There are very few empirical studies looking at the impact of inheritance taxation on wealth accumulation. Using different approaches, Holtz-Eakin and Marples (2001[46]), Slemrod and Kopczuk (2000[47]) and Joulfaian (2006[48]) estimate similar modest elasticities of taxable estates with respect to the estate tax rate of between 0.1 and 0.2, meaning that a one percent increase in the marginal tax rate reduces estates by between 0.1 and 0.2 percent (Kopczuk, 2009[49]). However, given that Slemrod and Kopczuk (2000[47]) and Joulfaian (2006[48]) rely on estate tax data, real wealth accumulation effects cannot be clearly distinguished from tax avoidance behaviours. On the other hand, Holtz-Eakin and Marples (2001[46]) use actual wealth data, but their estimates do not cover the richest households who are the most affected by estate taxes. More recently, Goupille-Lebret and Infante (2018[50]), using discontinuities in the French inheritance tax treatment of life insurance assets transferred at death depending on the age at which contributions were made and the date the account was opened, sought to disentangle real wealth accumulation effects from avoidance responses and found modest effects on capital accumulation.

Savings and wealth accumulation responses to inheritance taxation tend to be lower than responses to net wealth taxes. Recurrent net wealth taxes might be expected to have stronger disincentive effects on savings and wealth accumulation decisions than inheritance taxes given that they have to be paid by savers every year, while inheritance taxes are only levied once at the end of the donor's life and, in the case of recipient-based taxes, have to be paid by the recipients rather than by the savers themselves. In addition, inheritance taxes may be less distortive than net wealth taxes because a part of inheritances is likely to be unplanned and hence not affected by inheritance tax rules. Empirically, estimated taxable wealth elasticities are on balance larger in the case of net wealth taxes than with respect to one-off taxes on bequests (Advani and Tarrant, 2020[51]; OECD, 2018[52]).

2.3.2. There is evidence of significant inheritance and gift tax planning

Susceptibility to tax planning is one of the most common criticisms levelled against inheritance taxes. Some have argued that given the ease with which inheritance and estate taxes can be avoided, they have largely been "voluntary taxes" (Cooper, 1979[53]). As mentioned earlier, the fact that inheritance and estate taxes are levied at death leaves significant time for planning and the potentially large amounts of wealth at stake may make tax avoidance worthwhile for some taxpayers (Kopczuk, 2013[54]). In some countries, inheritance taxes only apply above high thresholds, affecting predominantly very wealthy and well-advised households. Schmalbeck (2001[55]) highlights the existence of many estate tax avoidance strategies, which can substantially reduce tax burdens on bequests in the United States. Such strategies include transferring wealth as gifts while alive, converting property into assets that benefit from exemptions or relief (e.g. business and farm assets), as well as using trusts, deductions for charitable bequests, and generous valuation discounts.

There is evidence of widespread inheritance tax planning, particularly through inter vivos gifts. A basic tax planning strategy consists of passing on wealth as inter vivos gifts, where these benefit from a more favourable tax treatment. In addition to exploiting the differential tax treatment between gifts and bequests, gifting allows future asset appreciation to escape inheritance and estate taxation. Studies generally find that the size and timing of gifts are responsive to inheritance and gift taxation (Bernheim, Lemke and Scholz, 2004[56]; Joulfaian, 2004[57]; Joulfaian, 2005[58]). Looking at the German inheritance tax, Sommer (2017[59]) finds that in the case of gifts between close relatives, gift amounts are particularly responsive to tax incentives. There is also heterogeneity in behaviour across taxpayers, with a higher responsiveness of gifts to tax among wealthier households. In the case of France, for instance, Arrondel and Laferrère (2001[60]) use inheritance data to show that the probability of gift giving depends on the amount of taxable wealth. Escobar, Ohlsson and Selin (2019[61]) find that the high elasticity of the Swedish inheritance tax base was due to tax-favoured inter vivos gifts and that there is a strong correlation between acquiring legal advice and making inter vivos gifts. At the same time, however, studies have found that gifts are not fully used as tax planning tools. For instance, McGarry (1999[62]) and Poterba (2001[63]) show that taxpayers do not take full advantage of the annual gift exemption in the United States.

Empirical findings on deathbed inheritance tax planning have varied across countries. Relying on estate tax returns filed in 1977 in the United States, Kopczuk (2007[64]) focuses on behaviours following the onset of terminal illnesses. He finds that there are significant adjustments to the size and structure of estates shortly before death, reflecting deathbed estate planning. This suggests that the wealthy care about what they leave as bequests but at the same time postpone important succession decisions until shortly before death. Erixson and Escobar (2020[65]), following the empirical approach used by Kopczuk (2007[64]), find no evidence of deathbed tax planning in Sweden. One of the explanations they offer is that Swedes have fewer interactions with professional tax advisers than US citizens and may have been less informed about tax planning strategies. Looking at Germany, Sommer (2017[59]) does not find evidence of deathbed inheritance tax planning either. The lack of evidence of deathbed tax planning in Sweden and Germany may also partly reflect more limited inheritance tax avoidance opportunities than in the United States.

The fact that tax-minimising strategies are not fully pursued may be explained by various factors. Many inheritance and gift tax avoidance techniques, including in-life giving, require people to give up control of their assets, which they may not be ready to do (Kopczuk, 2007[64]; Schmalbeck, 2001[55]). This could be for either wealth-loving or precautionary savings reasons, although precautionary savings is likely not to be the main factor at the top of the distribution. Maintaining control over one's assets may not be the only reason why tax planning is not more widely pursued. For instance, looking at French life insurance policies, which are commonly used as tax planning tools, Goupille-Lebret and Infante (2018[50]) find behavioural responses of a small magnitude, which cannot be explained by the desire to retain control over assets, as life insurance policies actually allow people to retain control over their assets until death. A lack of awareness of tax minimising strategies and myopic biases may be potential explanations, although this may be more likely for households with moderate wealth, compared to the very wealthy who are well-advised by professionals.

Possibilities for tax planning have reduced the effective progressivity of inheritance taxes. In addition to reducing horizontal equity, there is evidence that inheritance tax planning has reduced vertical equity because tax planning opportunities are mostly available to the wealthy. In Sweden, Henrekson and Waldenström (2016[66]) find that new laws combined with more efficient avoidance strategies during the 1990s enabled the wealthiest people to avoid paying the inheritance tax, while significant portions of the population experienced rapid increases in their inheritance tax liability. Various studies confirm that the provision of exemptions and reliefs have reduced the progressivity of inheritance taxes. A recent study in France shows that exempt assets under the inheritance tax generate a much greater reduction in the effective tax rate for very large wealth transfers than for small ones (Dherbécourt, 2017[67]). In the United States, Gravelle and Maguire (2006[68]) find that charitable deductions are the primary reason for the lower average effective tax rate on the highest estate bracket. In the United Kingdom, a recent study shows that relief for business and agricultural assets predominantly benefit the wealthiest households, significantly reducing the effective tax burden on some of the largest estates (Office of Tax Simplification, 2018[69]). These issues are discussed further in Chapter 3.

Opportunities for tax planning are far from unique to inheritance taxes, however, and highlight the need for reform rather than for their repeal. Opportunities for tax avoidance, and the lack of horizontal and vertical equity stemming from narrow tax bases, are not unique to inheritance taxation. In fact, it is a criticism that is very much applicable to net wealth taxes and personal capital income taxes as well (OECD, 2018[52]; OECD, 2018[70]). Moreover, the availability of tax planning opportunities is primarily a consequence of the way inheritance and gift taxes are designed, and could therefore be addressed in large part through reform. Well-designed reforms could address the concerns raised by tax avoidance by the wealthy, weakening the argument for repealing inheritance taxes altogether.

2.3.3. Migration responses to inheritance taxation appear generally limited

Taxpayers' location decisions may be affected by estate or inheritance taxes, but the few available empirical studies generally do not find high tax-induced mobility, except for the very wealthy. Bakija and Slemrod (2004[71]) find that state estate taxes in the United States have a statistically significant but modest negative effect on the number of federal estate tax returns filed in a state. Conway and Rork (2006[72]) find no statistical evidence that bequest taxes affect the inter-state migration patterns of elderly taxpayers in the United States. Looking at Switzerland, a much smaller country characterised by a great degree of heterogeneity in sub-national bequest taxation, Brülhart and Parchet (2014[73]) also find that cuts in bequest tax burdens across cantons had little noticeable impact on the migration patterns of elderly taxpayers. This suggests that there may be more important factors determining elderly taxpayers' location decisions, such as being close to family or trusted medical services. Moretti and Wilson (2020[74]), on the other hand, find significant mobility responses among billionaires to heterogeneity in estate taxation across US states, especially as they grow older. This suggests higher sensitivity at the very top of the distribution. Yet, despite the high elasticity of geographical location with respect to estate taxation, they find that for most states, the additional revenue from the estate tax exceeds the cost of foregone income tax revenue by a significant margin. This nevertheless suggests that the risk that very wealthy taxpayers may migrate to other countries should be carefully examined and prevented. Tax design may help limit such migration: for instance, in several jurisdictions, taxpayers continue to be liable for inheritance or estate taxes for a number of years after leaving the country. Exit taxes may also be considered (see Chapter 3).

Mobility responses to inheritance taxation may be lower than in the case of other taxes on wealthy households, such as taxes on net wealth or personal income. A recurrent tax on net wealth may provide stronger incentives to migrate than a one-off or infrequent tax on wealth transfers. There are very few studies on migration responses to wealth taxes, but these find substantial within-country migration responses to net wealth taxes. In the case of Switzerland, Brülhart et al. (2020[75]) find that 24% of the aggregate response to changes in net wealth taxes is due to taxpayer mobility. Looking at Spain, Agrawal, Foremny and Martínez-Toledano (2020[76]) find evidence of wealthy individuals flocking to Madrid following the reintroduction of the net wealth tax in 2011, with Madrid serving as an "internal tax haven" with a tax rate of 0%. They find that five years after the reform, the stock of wealthy individuals in the region of Madrid increased by 10% relative to other regions. Recent studies looking at personal income taxes have also found sizeable tax-induced migration among wealthy taxpayers, although behavioural responses are highly context- and population-specific (Kleven et al., 2020[77]) and the ultimate economic effects of such migration may be limited.

2.3.4. Inheritance taxation encourages charitable giving

In theory, levying an inheritance tax with an exemption for charitable giving could potentially have two opposing effects. An inheritance tax provides greater price incentives to give to charity rather than to other beneficiaries. At the same time, an inheritance tax has a wealth effect, as it reduces the wealth that is available to heirs, which could reduce overall charitable giving (Kopczuk, 2013[54]).

Empirical evidence shows that inheritance taxation encourages charitable giving. In general, the empirical literature has found strong price and wealth effects, with the first effect dominating, which implies that eliminating estate or inheritance taxes would likely result in a reduction in charitable giving (Kopczuk, 2013[1]). Using data for estates of US decedents in 1992, Joulfaian (2000[78]) finds taxes to be an important determinant of charitable transfers, suggesting that in the absence of the estate tax, charitable bequests may decline by around 12%. Bakija, Gale and Slemrod (2003[79]) find a much higher estimate of the drop in bequests that would result from repealing the estate tax, of up to 37%. McClelland (2004[80]) re-examines the results of Joulfaian (2000[78]) and Bakija, Gale and Slemrod (2003[79]) by applying their methods to 1999 and 2000 data and arrives at an estimate of around 20% (McClelland, 2004[80]).

However, exemptions for charitable giving tend to be regressive and may in some cases be used for tax planning purposes. Exemptions granted to charitable giving are primarily used by the wealthiest households, ultimately reducing the progressivity of inheritance or estate taxes (e.g. Gravelle and Maguire, 2006[55], for the United States). Exemptions for charitable giving may also provide greater benefit to high wealth households, whose inheritances would be taxed at higher marginal tax rates in countries that levy progressive inheritance tax rates. In addition, the preferential tax treatment for charitable giving may in some cases create tax avoidance opportunities. In the United States, for instance, there may be cases where special structures taking advantage of the preferential tax treatment for charitable giving are set up largely to transfer wealth to family members partially or entirely free of tax. The structures typically involve partial transfers to charities and allow assets to be transferred to ultimate beneficiaries at reduced values (see Chapter 3).

2.3.5. Inheritance taxation has been found to increase heirs' labour supply and savings

Inheritance taxation is also expected to affect the behaviour of heirs. A higher level of inheritance taxation leaves them with a lower net inheritance, which might give them an incentive to work and save more. At the same time, inheritance taxes may lower the probability that heirs start a business since bequests are often a source of seed capital for potential entrepreneurs (see the discussion in the next subsection).

Empirical evidence shows that inheritance receipts depress heirs' labour supply and that inheritance taxes could raise their incentives to work. In an early study, Holtz-Eakin, Joulfaian and Rosen (1993[81]) found results that were consistent with the "Carnegie conjecture" using tax-return data on the labour force behaviour of people before and after they receive inheritances. They found that those who received a large inheritance were more likely to exit the labour force and that for those remaining in the labour force, high-inheritance recipients tended to experience lower earnings growth than low-inheritance recipients, suggesting that inheritances reduce the heirs' hours of work. Relying on data from the US 1992–2002 Health and Retirement Study, Brown, Coile and Weisbenner (2010[82]) show that the receipt of an inheritance is associated with a significant increase in the probability of early retirement and that the effect increases with the size of the inheritance. They also find that unexpected inheritances have a larger effect than expected ones. Using Swedish tax register data, Elinder, Erixson and Ohlsson (2012[83]) find that the receipt of an inheritance depresses labour income, with stronger effects for older recipients than for younger heirs. They also find evidence of anticipation effects, with labour income declines prior to wealth transfers. Using a lifecycle model that they calibrate to the German economy, Kindermann, Mayr and Sachs (2020[84]) show that an inheritance tax has a positive fiscal externality. They find that for every euro of revenue raised directly from inheritance taxes, the government obtains an additional EUR 9 cents of labour income tax revenue (in net present value) as a result of higher labour supply.

In addition to labour supply effects, some studies suggest that an inheritance tax may generate an increase in potential heirs' savings. Different approaches have been used to study the impact of inheritances on heirs' saving behaviours. One approach considers changes in consumption after the receipt of an inheritance. For instance, Joulfaian and Wilhelm (1994[85]) find small consumption increases after the receipt of an inheritance using Panel Study of Income Dynamics data. Another approach consists in looking at changes in wealth after the receipt of an inheritance. Using estate tax records linked to the income tax records of beneficiaries, Joulfaian (2006[86]) shows that wealth increases by less than the full amount of the inheritance received. Elinder, Erixson and Ohlsson (2012[83]) find a temporary increase in capital income following the receipt of an inheritance, which they speculate may partly reflect the realisation of previously unrealised capital gains and may indicate increases in consumption. Overall, these studies may be interpreted as suggesting that savings tend to decrease following the receipt of an inheritance, although an increase in consumption cannot be directly equated with a decrease in savings as households may still be saving a significant part of their bequest. Overall, findings by Akgun, Cournède and Fournier (2017[27]) suggest that greater reliance on inheritance and gift taxes, as well as other one-off property taxes, tend to be output-enhancing in comparison with other revenue sources. Although such findings should be interpreted with caution, they may suggest that the negative efficiency effects of inheritance taxes (e.g. reduced incentives to save by donors) may be more than compensated by their positive efficiency effects (e.g. increased incentives to work and save among heirs).

2.3.6. Inheritance taxation may negatively affect entrepreneurship by heirs and family business successions, but reduce risks of misallocating capital

Inheritance taxes might lower entrepreneurship by heirs, as bequests can be sources of "seed capital" for entrepreneurial activity. Inheritance taxes may lower the probability that heirs start a business since bequests often constitute a source of seed capital (Burman, Mcclelland and Lu, 2018[45]). Thus, in theory, a reduction in bequests could lead to a reduction in new business creations. Empirically, Holtz-Eakin, Joulfaian and Rosen (1994[87]) find that the size of the inheritance has a significant impact on the probability of heirs becoming entrepreneurs by combining federal income tax returns for a group of people who received inheritances in 1982 and 1983 with information on the size of those inheritances from estate tax returns. Moreover, they find that conditional on becoming an entrepreneur, the size of the inheritance has a statistically significant and quantitatively large effect on the amount of capital employed in a new firm. This suggests that an inheritance tax may lower entrepreneurship among heirs. However, these results are old and the context is likely to have changed. For instance, it might be easier for entrepreneurs today to find capital and start a business than it used to be, by borrowing from a bank or through venture capital, which means that the link between receiving an inheritance and starting a business may have weakened.

Inheritance taxes may also jeopardise existing businesses when they are transferred if business owners do not have enough liquid assets to pay for the tax. Some studies shed light on the potential difficulties that inheritance taxes may generate for businesses, but do not directly assess whether they force business sales. For instance, based on two nationally representative samples of older individuals, Holtz-Eakin, Phillips and Rosen (2001[88]) find that, in anticipation of the estate tax, business owners purchase more life insurance than non-business owners, but that even with these purchases, business owners do not have enough money to cover estate taxes. Based on a survey of small business owners in upstate New York, Holtz-Eakin (1999[89]) also looked at the effect of the estate tax on employment growth and found a strong negative relationship between the expected estate tax liability and the number of jobs created. Other studies have explored more directly the link between estate or inheritance taxation and business sales. Using San Francisco probate records from 1980-1982, Brunetti (2006[90]) found a small positive relationship between the estate tax and business sales by heirs, but did not find statistically significant evidence that this was linked to the lack of liquidity. The study relied on a small sample, however (Kopczuk, 2013[1]; Houben and Maiterth, 2011[91]). Using a 2002 reform that substantially reduced the tax on family transfers of businesses in Greece, Tsoutsoura (2015[92]) found that, in addition to leading to a significant decline in investment, slower sales growth, and a depletion of cash reserves, inheritance taxes strongly affected the decision to sell or retain the firm within the family.

Liquidity constraints might be more acute for small businesses. First, SMEs might be more impacted by inheritance taxes as they are more likely to be run as family businesses, in comparison with larger firms that tend to have more atomised ownership structures (Redonda, 2017[93]). Moreover, SMEs often face more significant constraints in accessing credit markets, which may reinforce liquidity issues. In her analysis, Tsoutsoura (2015[92]) finds that the negative effects of inheritance taxes on investment hold for both large and small firms, but that they are stronger for family firms with low asset tangibility and businesses owned by people with low income from other sources.

Such liquidity pressures have often been used to justify generous business asset relief under inheritance and estate taxes. Indeed, most countries provide inheritance tax relief for business assets. However, these reliefs are not always well targeted, primarily benefit the wealthy and may sometimes be unnecessarily generous (see Chapter 3). For instance, Houben and Maiterth (2011[91]) examined the significant expansion of tax reliefs for family business successions introduced in Germany in 2009, but concluded that the reform was unnecessary to protect businesses against liquidity issues, as their analysis showed that the previous (less generous) system did not jeopardise transferred businesses. In the United States, Gravelle and Maguire (2010[94]) showed that, even when the federal estate tax exemption threshold was considerably lower than it is now, very few family businesses actually paid the estate tax, with less than 5% of businesses and farms affected. They also found that only a very small fraction of family-owned businesses (less than half of 1%) lacked the liquid resources to meet their estate tax liability, and highlighted that these businesses still had the option of paying the tax in instalments, borrowing, or selling a partial interest in the business (Gravelle and Maguire, 2010[94]).

More fundamentally, however, the goal itself of supporting family business succession has been questioned by some, in particular due to evidence of underperformance by businesses managed by heirs. While countries may wish to support family business successions because family businesses are often a significant economic sector and a large employer, evidence shows that heirs tend to not be as skilled as their parents in running family businesses. Using a dataset with more than 5 000 successions in limited liability firms in Denmark between 1994 and 2002, Bennedsen et al. (2007[95]) find that family succession has a large negative causal impact on firm performance: operating profitability on assets falls by at least four percentage points around CEO transitions. Bloom and Van Reenen (2007[96]) used data from 732 medium-size manufacturing firms in the United States, France, Germany and the United Kingdom, collected in a survey measuring management practices, and found that poor management practices are more prevalent when family-owned firms pass management control down to the eldest sons. Other studies looking at larger or publicly traded companies find similar results. Using data from 355 CEO successions in publicly traded US corporations, Pérez-González (2006[97]) finds lower firm performance in terms of profitability and market-to-book ratios when incoming CEOs are related to the departing CEO, a founder, or a large shareholder by either blood or marriage. Using proxy data on all Fortune 500 firms during the 1994-2000 period, Villalonga and Amit (2006[98]) find that family ownership creates value only when the founder serves as CEO or as Chairman with a hired CEO, but that when descendants serve as CEOs, firms underperform.

Thus, while inheritance taxes might negatively affect entrepreneurship by heirs and family business successions, they might reduce skills-capital mismatches and enhance efficiency. If heirs are not found to perform as well as their parents, or better than other individuals, reducing the amount of capital that they receive through an inheritance tax may reduce the risks of misallocating capital and possibly enhance productivity.

2.3.7. The double taxation argument appears to be weak

Double taxation is a popular objection to inheritance taxes, but it is far from unique to inheritance taxation. If the wealth transferred is accumulated from wage earnings, savings or personal business income, then these flows will have in many cases already been taxed. However, multiple levels of taxation are far from unique to taxes on wealth transfers. Consumption taxes, for instance, are paid out of post-tax income. In the area of wealth taxation, the double taxation argument is stronger in the case of net wealth taxes, levied on self-made wealth on a recurrent (usually annual) basis, than in the case of inheritance taxes which are levied once at the end of the donor's life (OECD, 2018[52]). Economically, it is important to point out that what really matters is overall effective tax rates, rather than the number of times assets or income are subject to taxation.

Opponents of inheritance taxation on the grounds that it generates double taxation tend to look at the issue from the perspective of donors. This view holds that donors who have built savings over the course of their lives and paid taxes during their lifetime should not be subject to another round of taxation upon their death. Evidence shows, however, that in some cases, an inheritance or an estate tax might be the first time that asset returns are taxed. This is particularly the case where some forms of personal capital income, including some capital gains, escape taxation (see below). The case for an inheritance tax might therefore be strongest for those countries where there are significant differentials in the way the accumulation of wealth may have been taxed and there are questions around the efficacy of the taxation of savings.

The double taxation argument is weaker when inheritance taxation is considered from the perspective of beneficiaries. The inherited wealth is only taxed once in the hands of the recipient and the wealth received provides them with what can be viewed as an unearned gain, which can, in some circumstances, exacerbate existing inequalities. More generally, opponents of inheritance taxation on the grounds that it generates double taxation tend to look at it from the donor's perspective, while those in favour of inheritance taxation tend to consider the issue from the recipient's perspective (Mirrlees et al., 2011[14]).

In some cases, inheritance taxes might be a way of taxing some income that would otherwise go untaxed. For instance, increases in the value of main residences are often exempt from capital gains tax. As a consequence, while the purchase price may well have been paid out of taxed earnings, any subsequent increases in value will not have been subject to tax and inheritance taxes may be the first time any taxation is levied on the capital gains (Boadway, Chamberlain and Emmerson, 2010[5]). Gale and Slemrod (2001[33]) highlight that in the United States, the estate tax also serves as a backstop to the income tax, taxing some forms of income, in particular unrealised capital gains, which would otherwise go untaxed. Capital gains taxes are only levied upon realisation, which means that capital gains are not taxed if the owner holds on to their assets until they die and if the country does not treat death as a realisation for the purpose of capital gains taxes. In most OECD countries, assets are bequeathed to recipients with a so-called step-up in basis, which implies that when heirs sell these assets, they only pay tax on the capital gains made from the day they inherited them (see Chapter 3). This creates strong incentives for individuals to hold onto appreciated assets until they die. In fact, Poterba and Weisbenner (2000[99]) found that unrealised capital gains constituted more than half of the value of US estates above USD 10 million. Auten and Joulfaian (2001[100]) find that the estate tax reduces these lock-in incentives, by encouraging earlier capital gains realisations, which can in turn improve capital allocation and economic efficiency. These figures also suggest that the case for imposing an inheritance tax might be stronger in the case of high-value wealth transfers, as the wealthiest households are more likely to have accumulated undertaxed forms of capital income, such as unrealised capital gains.

2.3.8. Negative externalities from wealth concentration may strengthen the case for inheritance taxation

The existence of negative externalities from wealth concentration imply that inheritance taxes could be justified on efficiency grounds. Negative externalities arise when the social costs of a behaviour outweigh its private costs. In such cases, a corrective tax can be used to ensure that agents internalise (part of) the negative social costs of their actions. If high wealth concentration was found to have a negative effect on the welfare of society at large, then targeting wealth concentration through an inheritance tax may be part of an optimal tax structure (Kopczuk, 2009[49]). However, justifying an inheritance tax on those grounds would require identifying externalities that directly stem from intergenerational wealth transfers or wealth concentration, rather than from the income or consumption resulting from wealth.

Inheritances and wealth concentration may indeed be associated with a number of undesirable effects. Regarding the negative externalities stemming directly from inheritances, the discussion above highlighted the increased opportunities for heirs and the misallocation of entrepreneurial and managerial talent as evidenced by the underperformance of businesses run by heirs. The perpetuation of wealth accumulation and family business successions over generations may also reduce competition, with potentially longer-term detrimental consequences on entrepreneurship and innovation. Additionally, increased wealth concentration over generations may have a detrimental impact on democratic political processes (Solt, 2008[101]) and be a source of social unrest.

2.4. Tax administration considerations

This section briefly discusses the administrative aspects of inheritance taxation. Interestingly, while administrative complexity is often put forward as an argument against inheritance taxes, it may be argued that some forms of wealth are easier to observe than income and that, historically, taxes on wealth – including on successions – have preceded the taxation of income (Kopczuk, 2013[1]) (see also Chapter 3, Table 3.1). This section highlights that inheritance taxes may also have advantages over other forms of wealth taxation and that the potential for tax evasion has significantly decreased thanks to recent progress on international tax transparency.

2.4.1. Inheritance taxation has administrative advantages over other forms of wealth taxation

The cost of administering and complying with inheritance taxes may seem high in comparison to the limited revenues they typically raise. Chapter 3 contains information on the revenues raised from inheritance and gift taxes, as well on the administrative and compliance procedures they involve. Inheritance taxes generally require a full statement of the donor's 'wealth' i.e. assets at death, detailed valuations where necessary and the computation and payment of the tax on a wide range of assets for which different reliefs apply. While these administrative and compliance costs may seem high, they include a number of unavoidable fixed costs that are linked to the legal recognition of transmissions and changes in property ownership. In addition, part of these administrative and compliance costs arise from the way inheritance and estate taxes have been designed, particularly from their narrow tax bases, and could therefore be reduced through tax reform.

Inheritance taxation has administrative advantages compared to net wealth taxation. One of the advantages of inheritance taxes is that they are levied only once (or infrequently in the case of gift taxes), as opposed to annually, and at a time when the tax administration can appropriately observe inherited assets and when assets often need to be valued anyway (Kopczuk, 2013[1]). Net wealth taxes require regularly updating asset values, while valuing assets under an estate or inheritance tax typically involves determining their market value (or their realistic selling price) only once, at the time of the transfer of assets between donors and recipients (OECD, 2018[52]). Thus, the tax administration and compliance costs, relative to the revenue raised, are likely to be lower for inheritance taxes than for net wealth taxes (OECD, 2018[52]). Nevertheless, there are still some important valuation and administrative issues involved in taxing wealth transfers, including for instance complexities in relation to jointly held assets or due to the presence of two parties (donors and recipients) with different jurisdictional affiliations (Iara, 2015[102]) (see also Chapter 3). It may be argued that net wealth taxes, which can be levied at low annual rates, are less salient and may therefore result in greater tax compliance than inheritance taxes, which are levied only once and apply at higher rates. Inheritance or estate taxes also give taxpayers ample time to engage in tax planning compared to annual net wealth taxes. Empirical evidence shows, however, that annual net wealth taxes can have a sizeable impact on wealth reporting and tax avoidance and evasion (Brülhart et al., 2020[75]; Durán-Cabré, Esteller-Moré and Mas-Montserrat, 2019[103]).

Uncovering wealth and identifying ownership is also likely to be easier under inheritance taxes than under net wealth taxes. Indeed, taxes on wealth transfers are assessed when property changes hands. As mentioned above, this happens infrequently and makes the administration of the tax easier than for recurrent taxes on wealth. Importantly as well, wealth transfer recipients have a clear interest in ensuring that all the legal requirements to attest the transfer of ownership are completed properly to secure their ownership rights (Rudnick and Gordon, 1996[104]). Rules may also be put in place to disallow the transfer of ownership if inheritance taxes have not been duly paid (Rudnick and Gordon, 1996[104]).

Liquidity issues, while they may arise, are also likely to be lower than under other property and net wealth taxes. Liquidity constraints may arise from the fact that taxpayers may not have sufficient liquid assets to pay their inheritance tax bill. However, unlike other property taxes, there may be less of a concern regarding liquidity as inherited immovable property may have multiple recipients and thus would be sold to divide the value amongst the recipients (Boadway, Chamberlain and Emmerson, 2010[5]). Regarding closely held businesses and farms, the lack of liquidity to pay the inheritance tax can be more problematic. However, there are a number of practical solutions that can be implemented to limit such issues (see Chapter 3). Liquidity issues are also likely to be less severe under inheritance taxes than under a net wealth tax levied every year (depending on the level of the wealth tax).

2.4.2. Capital tax evasion has become harder with recent progress on international tax transparency

Historically, rising international capital mobility has made capital taxes harder to enforce. The increasing mobility of financial assets as well as the use of low-tax jurisdictions, combined with the development of information and communication technology and the elimination of barriers to cross-border capital transfers have allowed taxpayers to hold their capital offshore without declaring it to their tax authorities and have made the enforcement of capital taxes much more difficult (Krenek and Schratzenstaller, 2018[105]). In fact, capital mobility has been a major factor behind the reduction of taxes on capital in the last few decades. In addition to generating revenue losses, the mobility of capital may have significant effects on the incidence of taxes on capital and wealth transfers, which may end up bearing primarily on taxpayers who do not engage in such tax planning or evasion and on immobile assets.

Empirical evidence of tax evasion directly linked to inheritance and estate taxes is scarce. Some US audit-based studies have estimated estate tax non-compliance to be between 8% and 13% of the overall tax liability (Kopczuk, 2013[54]), although they sometimes suggest that the true value is likely to be higher (Eller, Erard and Ho, 2000[106]). As audits of estate tax returns used to be fairly common, Kopczuk (2013[54]) argues that the scope for easily detectable and clearly illegal tax evasion tends to be limited and that non-compliance is likely to take the form of "plausibly legal but often legally uncertain strategies". Recent research in the United States has showed that the wealth reported by decedents from the Forbes 400 richest Americans on their estate tax returns is only half the wealth estimated by Forbes magazine (Raub, Johnson and Newcomb, 2010[107]). The authors find that the values reported for tax purposes and those estimated by Forbes are closest when valuations were relatively objective and amounts of debt were low, and much further apart when portfolios mainly consisted of assets for which valuation was difficult or involved some subjectivity, which tends to be the case for very wealthy individuals who typically own unique and hard-to-value assets, and when individuals held relatively more debt. While previous research suggested that differences between tax and Forbes estimates reflected evasion, the authors point out that the tax returns they looked at were those of very wealthy individuals, which tend to be carefully prepared by licensed professionals. They concluded that "while values reported for tax purposes may be conservative, they will fall within legally defensible parameters".

However, estimations point to significant wealth held offshore, and to the concentration of offshoring practices among the wealthiest households. Alstadsaeter, Johannesen and Zucman (2018[108]) estimate that globally the equivalent of about 10% of the world GDP is held offshore, but reveal significant heterogeneity across regions — from limited levels in Scandinavia, to about 15% in Continental Europe, and more than 50% in Russia, some Latin American countries, and Gulf countries. Offshore wealth is also highly concentrated. Using leaked data from offshore financial institutions and tax amnesty data, matched to population-wide administrative income and wealth records in Norway, Sweden, and Denmark, Alstadsæter, Johannesen and Zucman (2019[109]) find that the top 0.01% of the wealth distribution owns about 50% of the wealth in tax havens. They also find that the top 0.01% evades about 25% of their income and wealth tax liability by concealing assets and investment income abroad. These findings use data that predates the implementation of the Automatic Exchange of Information (see below), but the concentration of offshoring practices among the very wealthy may mean that this a potentially significant margin of response to wealth taxation (Advani and Tarrant, 2020[51]), and possibly to inheritance taxation as well.

The recent progress made on international tax transparency standards is greatly increasing countries' ability to tax capital effectively. Information exchange agreements as well as further international cooperation on the exchange of information on request (EOIR) and the automatic exchange of information (AEOI) reduce opportunities for tax evasion. These standards mean that information on foreign financial assets is now being shared between tax authorities globally, making it harder for taxpayers to evade taxation by concealing their assets overseas. Research has shown this has a deterrence effect, with the value of bank deposits held offshore decreasing with the densification of the information exchange network (O'Reilly, Parra Ramirez and Stemmer, 2019[110]). In the context of inheritance taxation, rules on the availability and accessibility of beneficial ownership information also help prevent donors and beneficiaries from concealing their ownership of assets through the use of opaque structures. Such progress is enhancing countries' ability to effectively tax inheritances, but progress needs to continue to ensure that jurisdictions effectively implement information exchange standards and to ensure that persons, assets, and institutions not covered under existing EOI standards do not offer opportunities for continued tax evasion (see Chapter 3).

References

Abel, A. (1985), "Precautionary Saving and Accidental Bequests", *The American Economic Review*, Vol. 75/4, pp. 777-791. [37]

Adermon, A., M. Lindahl and D. Waldenström (2018), "Intergenerational Wealth Mobility and the Role of Inheritance: Evidence from Multiple Generations", *The Economic Journal*, Vol. 128/612, pp. F482-F513, http://dx.doi.org/10.1111/ecoj.12535. [7]

Advani, A. and H. Tarrant (2020), *Behavioural responses to a wealth tax, Wealth Tax Commission, Evidence Paper 5*. [51]

Agrawal, D., D. Foremny and C. Martínez-Toledano (2020), "Paraísos Fiscales, Wealth Taxation, and Mobility", *SSRN Electronic Journal*, http://dx.doi.org/10.2139/ssrn.3676031. [76]

Akgun, O., B. Cournède and J. Fournier (2017), "The effects of the tax mix on inequality and growth", *OECD Economics Department Working Papers*, No. 1447, OECD Publishing, Paris, https://dx.doi.org/10.1787/c57eaa14-en. [27]

Alan J. Auerbach, R. (ed.) (2013), *Taxation of Intergenerational Transfers and Wealth*, http://dx.doi.org/10.3386/w18584. [1]

Alstadsæter, A., N. Johannesen and G. Zucman (2019), "Tax evasion and inequality", *American Economic Review*, Vol. 109/6, pp. 2073-2103, http://dx.doi.org/10.1257/aer.20172043. [109]

Alstadsaeter, A., N. Johannesen and G. Zucman (2018), "Who owns the wealth in tax havens? Macro evidence and implications for global inequality", *Journal of Public Economics*, Vol. 162, pp. 89-100, http://dx.doi.org/10.1016/j.jpubeco.2018.01.008. [108]

Alstott, A. (2007), "Equal Opportunity and Inheritance Taxation", *Yale Law School, Public Law Working Paper No. 117.* [4]

Andreoni, J. (1990), "Impure Altruism and Donations to Public Goods: A Theory of Warm-Glow Giving", Vol. 100/401, pp. 464-477. [43]

Arrondel, L. and A. Laferrere (2001), *Taxation and wealth transmission in France*, http://www.elsevier.nl/locate/econbase (accessed on 4 November 2020). [60]

Atkinson, A. and J. Stiglitz (1976), "The design of tax structure: Direct versus indirect taxation", *Journal of Public Economics*, Vol. 6/1-2, pp. 55-75, http://dx.doi.org/10.1016/0047-2727(76)90041-4. [11]

Auten, G. and D. Joulfaian (2001), "Bequest taxes and capital gains realizations", *Journal of Public Economics*, Vol. 81/2, pp. 213-229, http://dx.doi.org/10.1016/S0047-2727(00)00088-8. [100]

Bakija, J., W. Gale and J. Slemrod (2003), *Charitable bequests and taxes on inheritances and estates: Aggregate evidence from across states and time*, http://dx.doi.org/10.1257/000282803321947362. [79]

Bakija, J. and J. Slemrod (2004), "Do the Rich Flee from High State Taxes? Evidence from Federal Estate Tax Returns", *NBER Working Paper* No. 10645, http://dx.doi.org/10.3386/w10645. [71]

Bastani, S. and D. Waldenström (2020), "How should capital be taxed?", *Journal of Economic Surveys*, Vol. 34/4, http://dx.doi.org/10.1111/joes.12380. [6]

Batchelder, L. (2020), *Leveling the Playing Field between Inherited Income and Income from Work through an Inheritance Tax*. [16]

Becker, G. (1974), "A Theory of Social Interactions", *Journal of Political Economy*, Vol. 82/6, pp. 1063-1093, http://dx.doi.org/10.1086/260265. [41]

Bennedsen, M. et al. (2007), "Inside the family firm: The role of families in succession decisions and performance", *Quarterly Journal of Economics*, Vol. 122/2, pp. 647-691, http://dx.doi.org/10.1162/qjec.122.2.647. [95]

Bernheim, B., R. Lemke and J. Scholz (2004), "Do estate and gift taxes affect the timing of private transfers?", *Journal of Public Economics*, Vol. 88/12, pp. 2617-2634, http://dx.doi.org/10.1016/j.jpubeco.2003.11.004. [56]

Bernheim, B., A. Shleifer and L. Summers (1985), "The Strategic Bequest Motive," Journal of Political Economy, University of Chicago Press, vol. 93(6), pages 1045-1076, December. [40]

Bloom, N. and J. Van Reenen (2007), "Measuring and Explaining Management Practices Across Firms and Countries" The Quarterly Journal of Economics, Volume 122, Issue 4, November, Pages 1351–1408, https://doi.org/10.1162/qjec.2007.122.4.1351. [96]

Boadway, R., E. Chamberlain and C. Emmerson (2010), "Taxation of Wealth and Wealth Transfers", in *Dimensions of Tax Design; The Mirrlees Review*, Oxford University Press, Oxford. [5]

Bönke, T., M. Werder and C. Westermeier (2017), “How inheritances shape wealth distributions: An international comparison”, *Economics Letters*, Vol. 159, http://dx.doi.org/10.1016/j.econlet.2017.08.007. [22]

Boserup, S., W. Kopczuk and C. Kreiner (2018), “Born with a Silver Spoon? Danish Evidence on Wealth Inequality in Childhood”, *The Economic Journal*, Vol. 128/612, pp. F514-F544, http://dx.doi.org/10.1111/ecoj.12496. [8]

Boserup, S., W. Kopczuk and C. Kreiner (2016), “The Role of Bequests in Shaping Wealth Inequality: Evidence from Danish Wealth Records”, *American Economic Review*, Vol. 106/5, pp. 656–661, http://dx.doi.org/10.1257/aer.p20161036. [24]

Brown, J., C. Coile and S. Weisbenner (2010), “The effect of inheritance receipt on retirement”, *Review of Economics and Statistics*, Vol. 92/2, pp. 425-434, http://dx.doi.org/10.1162/rest.2010.11182. [82]

Brülhart, M. et al. (2020), *Behavioral Responses to Wealth Taxes: Evidence from Switzerland*, http://www.hec.unil.ch/mbrulhar/papers/wealthtax.pdf (accessed on 4 November 2020). [75]

Brülhart, M. and R. Parchet (2014), “Alleged tax competition: The mysterious death of bequest taxes in Switzerland”, *Journal of Public Economics*, Vol. 111, pp. 63-78, http://dx.doi.org/10.1016/j.jpubeco.2013.12.009. [73]

Brunetti, M. (2006), “The estate tax and the demise of the family business”, *Journal of Public Economics*, Vol. 90/10-11, pp. 1975-1993, http://dx.doi.org/10.1016/j.jpubeco.2006.05.012. [90]

Burman, L., R. Mcclelland and C. Lu (2018), *The Effects of Estate and Inheritance Taxes on Entrepreneurship*, Tax Policy Center. [45]

Conway, K. and J. Rork (2006), “State “Death” Taxes and Elderly Migration-The Chicken or the Egg?”, *National Tax Journal*, Vol. 59/1, pp. 97-128. [72]

Cooper, G. (1979), *A Voluntary Tax? New Perspectives on Sophisticated Estate Tax Avoidance*, Brookings Institution Press. [53]

Cowell, F., D. Van De Gaer and C. He (2017), *Inheritance Taxation: Redistribution and Predistribution*. [26]

Cremer, H. and P. Pestieau (2009), *Wealth and wealth transfer taxation: a survey. 1*. [34]

Davies, J. (1982), “The Relative Impact of Inheritance and other Factors on Economic Inequality”, *The Quarterly Journal of Economics*, Vol. 97/3, p. 471, http://dx.doi.org/10.2307/1885873. [19]

De Nardi, M. (2004), “Wealth inequality and intergenerational links”, *Review of Economic Studies*, Vol. 71/3, pp. 743-768, http://dx.doi.org/10.1111/j.1467-937X.2004.00302.x. [20]

Dherbécourt, C. (2017), “Peut-on éviter une société d’héritiers ? Estimation haute Estimation basse”*, La note d’analyse*, No. 51, France Stratégie, Paris. [67]

Durán-Cabré, J., A. Esteller-Moré and M. Mas-Montserrat (2019), “Behavioural responses to the (re)introduction of wealth taxes. Evidence from Spain”*, Working Papers 2019*, No. 04, Institut d’Economia de Barcelona (IEB). [103]

Elinder, M., O. Erixson and H. Ohlsson (2012), "The Impact of Inheritances on Heirs' Labor and Capital Income", *The B.E. Journal of Economic Analysis & Policy*, Vol. 12/1, pp. 1-37, https://EconPapers.repec.org/RePEc:bpj:bejeap:v:12:y:2012:i:1:p:1-37:n:61 (accessed on 4 November 2020). [83]

Elinder, M., O. Erixson and D. Waldenström (2018), "Inheritance and wealth inequality: Evidence from population registers", *Journal of Public Economics*, Vol. 165, pp. 17-30, http://dx.doi.org/10.1016/j.jpubeco.2018.06.012. [23]

Eller, M., B. Erard and C. Ho (2000), *The Magnitude and Determinants of Federal Estate Tax Noncompliance*. [106]

Erixson, O. and S. Escobar (2020), "Deathbed tax planning", *Journal of Public Economics*, Vol. 185, p. 104170, http://dx.doi.org/10.1016/j.jpubeco.2020.104170. [65]

Escobar, S., H. Ohlsson and H. Selin (2019), "Taxes, frictions and asset shifting: when Swedes disinherited themselves", *Working Paper Series*, https://ideas.repec.org/p/hhs/ifauwp/2019_006.html (accessed on 4 November 2020). [61]

Fagereng, A. et al. (2020), "Heterogeneity and Persistence in Returns to Wealth", *Econometrica*, Vol. 88/1, pp. 115-170, http://dx.doi.org/10.3982/ecta14835. [31]

Farhi, E. and I. Werning (2013), "Estate Taxation with Altruism Heterogeneity", *NBER Working Paper No. 18792*, http://dx.doi.org/10.3386/w18792. [12]

Farhi, E. and I. Werning (2010), "Progressive Estate Taxation [*]", *Quarterly Journal of Economics*, Vol. 125/2, pp. 635-673, http://dx.doi.org/10.1162/qjec.2010.125.2.635. [10]

Gale, W. and J. Slemrod (2001), "Rethinking Estate and Gift Taxation", *NBER Working Paper* No. 8205, p. 532, http://dx.doi.org/10.3386/w8205. [33]

Goupille-Lebret, J. and J. Infante (2018), "Behavioral responses to inheritance tax: Evidence from notches in France", *Journal of Public Economics*, Vol. 168, pp. 21-34, http://dx.doi.org/10.1016/j.jpubeco.2018.09.016. [50]

Gravelle, J. and S. Maguire (2010), *Estate Taxes and Family Businesses: Economic Issues Estate Taxes and Family Businesses*, Economic Issues Congressional Research Service, http://www.crs.govRL33070.c11173008 (accessed on 4 November 2020). [94]

Gravelle, J. and S. Maguire (2006), *CRS Report for Congress: Estate Taxes and Family Businesses: Economic Issues*. [68]

Henrekson, M. and D. Waldenström (2016), "Inheritance taxation in Sweden, 1885–2004: the role of ideology, family firms, and tax avoidance", *Economic History Review*, Vol. 69/4, pp. 1228–1254, http://dx.doi.org/doi.org/10.1111/ehr.12280. [66]

Holtz-Eakin, D. (1999), *The Death Tax: Impact on Investment, Employment, and Entrepreneurs*. [89]

Holtz-Eakin, D., D. Joulfaian and H. Rosen (1994), *Entrepreneurial Decisions and Liquidity Constraints*. [87]

Holtz-Eakin, D., D. Joulfaian and H. Rosen (1993), *The Carnegie Conjecture: Some Empirical Evidence*. [81]

Holtz-Eakin, D. and D. Marples (2001), "Distortion Costs of Taxing Wealth Accumulation: Income Versus Estate Taxes", *NBER Working Papers*. [46]

Holtz-Eakin, D., J. Phillips and H. Rosen (2001), "Estate taxes, life insurance, and small business", *Review of Economics and Statistics*, Vol. 83/1, pp. 52-63, http://dx.doi.org/10.1162/003465301750160036. [88]

Houben, H. and R. Maiterth (2011), "Endangering of Businesses by the German Inheritance Tax? — An Empirical Analysis", *Business Research*, Vol. 4/1, pp. 32-46, http://dx.doi.org/10.1007/BF03342725. [91]

Hurd, M. (1987), "Savings of the Elderly and Desired Bequests", *The American Economic Review*, Vol. 77/3, pp. 298-312. [38]

Iara, A. (2015), "Wealth distribution and taxation in EU Members", *Taxation Papers*. [102]

Jordà, Ò. et al. (2019), "The Rate of Return on Everything, 1870–2015*", *The Quarterly Journal of Economics*, Vol. 134/3, pp. 1225-1298, http://dx.doi.org/10.1093/qje/qjz012. [111]

Joulfaian, D. (2016), "What Do We Know About the Behavioral Effects of the Estate Tax?", *Boston College Law Review*, Vol. 57/3, https://lawdigitalcommons.bc.edu/bclr/vol57/iss3/5 (accessed on 4 November 2020). [35]

Joulfaian, D. (2006), *Inheritance and Saving*, National Bureau of Economic Research, Cambridge, MA, http://dx.doi.org/10.3386/w12569. [86]

Joulfaian, D. (2006), "The Behavioral Response of Wealth Accumulation to Estate Taxation: Time Series Evidence", *National Tax Journal*, Vol. 59/2, pp. 253-268. [48]

Joulfaian, D. (2005), "Choosing between gifts and bequests: How taxes affect the timing of wealth transfers", *Journal of Public Economics*, Vol. 89/11-12, pp. 2069-2091, http://dx.doi.org/10.1016/j.jpubeco.2004.11.005. [58]

Joulfaian, D. (2004), "Gift taxes and lifetime transfers: Time series evidence", *Journal of Public Economics*, Vol. 88/9-10, pp. 1917-1929, http://dx.doi.org/10.1016/j.jpubeco.2003.06.002. [57]

Joulfaian, D. (2000), "Estate Taxes and Charitable Bequests by the Wealthy", *NBER Working Papers, No 7663*. [78]

Joulfaian, D. and M. Wilhelm (1994), "Inheritance and labor supply", *Journal of Human Resources*, Vol. 29/4, pp. 1205-1234, http://dx.doi.org/10.2307/146138. [85]

Kindermann, F., L. Mayr and D. Sachs (2020), "Inheritance taxation and wealth effects on the labor supply of heirs", *Journal of Public Economics*, p. 104127, http://dx.doi.org/10.1016/j.jpubeco.2019.104127. [84]

Kleven, H. et al. (2020), "Taxation and migration: Evidence and policy implications", *Journal of Economic Perspectives*, Vol. 34/2, pp. 119-142, http://dx.doi.org/10.1257/JEP.34.2.119. [77]

Kopczuk, W. (2013), "Taxation of intergenerational transfers and wealth", in *Handbook of Public Economics*, Elsevier B.V., http://dx.doi.org/10.1016/B978-0-444-53759-1.00006-6. [54]

Kopczuk, W. (2009), *Economics of estate taxation: Review of theory and evidence*. [49]

Kopczuk, W. (2007), “Bequest and Tax Planning: Evidence from Estate Tax Returns”, *The Quarterly Journal of Economics*, Vol. 122/4, pp. 1801-1854, https://doi.org/10.1162/qjec.2007.122.4.1801 (accessed on 27 April 2020). [64]

Kopczuk, W. and J. Lupton (2007), “To Leave or Not to Leave: The Distribution of Bequest Motives”, *Review of Economic Studies*, Vol. 74/1, pp. 207-235. [44]

Krenek, A. and M. Schratzenstaller (2018), “A European Net Wealth Tax”, *WIFO Working Papers*. [105]

Laitner, J. (1979), “Household Bequests, Perfect Expectations, and the National Distribution of Wealth”, *Econometrica*, Vol. 47/5, p. 1175, http://dx.doi.org/10.2307/1911957. [17]

Lusardi, A., P. Michaud and O. Mitchell (2017), “Optimal financial knowledge and wealth inequality”, *Journal of Political Economy*, Vol. 125/2, pp. 431-477, http://dx.doi.org/10.1086/690950. [30]

McClelland, R. (2004), “Charitable Bequests and the Repeal of the Estate Tax”, *Congressional Budget Office Technical Paper Series*, Vol. 2004/8. [80]

McGarry, K. (1999), “Inter vivos transfers and intended bequests”, *Journal of Public Economics*, Vol. 73/3, pp. 321-351, http://dx.doi.org/10.1016/S0047-2727(99)00017-1. [62]

McGarry, K. and R. Schoeni (1995), “Transfer Behavior in the Health and Retirement Study: Measurement and the Redistribution of Resources within the Family”, *The Journal of Human Resources*, Vol. 30/special, pp. S184-226. [42]

Mirrlees, J. et al. (2011), *Chapter 15: Taxes on Wealth Transfers*, Oxford University Press. [14]

Moretti, E. and D. Wilson (2020), *Taxing Billionaires: Estate Taxes and the Geographical Location of the Ultra-Wealthy*, National Bureau of Economic Research, Cambridge, MA, http://dx.doi.org/10.3386/w26387. [74]

Nekoei, A. and D. Seim (2018), “How do Inheritances Shape Wealth Inequality? Theory and Evidence from Sweden”, *CEPR Discussion Papers*. [25]

Niimi, Y. (2019), “The Effect of the Recent Inheritance Tax Reform on Bequest Behaviour in Japan”, *Fiscal Studies*, Vol. 40/1, pp. 45-70, http://dx.doi.org/10.1111/1475-5890.12181. [36]

O’Reilly, P., K. Parra Ramirez and M. Stemmer (2019), “Exchange of information and bank deposits in international financial centres”, *OECD Taxation Working Papers*, No. 46, OECD Publishing, Paris, https://dx.doi.org/10.1787/025bfebe-en. [110]

OECD (2018), *Taxation of Household Savings*, OECD Tax Policy Studies, No. 25, OECD Publishing, Paris, https://dx.doi.org/10.1787/9789264289536-en. [70]

OECD (2018), *The Role and Design of Net Wealth Taxes in the OECD*, OECD Tax Policy Studies, No. 26, OECD Publishing, Paris, https://dx.doi.org/10.1787/9789264290303-en. [52]

Office of Tax Simplification (2018), *Inheritance Tax Review - first report: Overview of the tax and dealing with administration*, Office of Tax Simplification, London. [69]

Pérez-González, F. (2006), “Inherited control and firm performance”, *American Economic Review*, Vol. 96/5, pp. 1559-1588, http://dx.doi.org/10.1257/aer.96.5.1559. [97]

Piketty, T. (2015), “Capital and Wealth Taxation in the 21st Century”, *National Tax Journal*, Vol. 68/2, pp. 449-458. [32]

Piketty, T. (2014), *Capital in the Twenty-First Century*, Harvard University Press. [28]

Piketty, T. and E. Saez (2013), “A Theory of Optimal Inheritance Taxation”, *Econometrica*, Vol. 81/5, pp. 1851-1886, http://dx.doi.org/10.3982/ECTA10712. [13]

Piketty, T. and E. Saez (2007), *How Progressive is the U.S. federal tax system? A historical and international perspective*, http://dx.doi.org/10.1257/jep.21.1.3. [15]

Piketty, T., E. Saez and G. Zucman (2013), *Rethinking capital and wealth taxation*. [9]

Piketty, T. and G. Zucman (2015), *Wealth and Inheritance in the Long Run*, Elsevier. [3]

Poterba, J. (2001), “Estate and gift taxes and incentives for inter vivos giving in the US”, *Journal of Public Economics*, Vol. 79/1, pp. 237-264, http://dx.doi.org/10.1016/S0047-2727(00)00102-X. [63]

Poterba, J. and S. Weisbenner (2000), “The Distributional Burden of Taxing Estates and Unrealized Capital Gains at the Time of Death”, *NBER Working Papers*. [99]

Raub, B., B. Johnson and J. Newcomb (2010), *A Comparison of Wealth Estimates for America’s Wealthiest Decedents Using Tax Data and Data from the Forbes 400.* [107]

Redonda, A. (2017), “Inheritance Taxation, Corporate Succession and Sustainability”, *Discussion Notes*. [93]

Rognlie, M. (2014), *A note on Piketty and diminishing returns to capital*, http://mattrognlie.com/piketty_diminishing_returns.pdf (accessed on 23 November 2021). [29]

Rudnick, R. and R. Gordon (1996), *Taxation of Wealth*, IMF. [104]

Schmalbeck, R. (2001), “Avoiding Federal Wealth Transfer Taxes”, in Gale, W., J. Hines Jr. and J. Slemrod (eds.), *Rethinking Estate and Gift Taxation*, Brookings Institution Press, Washington, D. C. [55]

Slemrod, J. (ed.) (2000), *Why do the Rich Save so Much?*, Harvard University Press. [39]

Slemrod, J. and W. Kopczuk (2000), “The Impact of the Estate Tax on the Wealth Accumulation and Avoidance Behavior of Donors”, *NBER Working Papers*. [47]

Solt, F. (2008), “Economic inequality and democratic political engagement”, *American Journal of Political Science*, Vol. 52/1, pp. 48-60, http://dx.doi.org/10.1111/j.1540-5907.2007.00298.x. [101]

Sommer, E. (2017), *Wealth Transfers and Tax Planning: Evidence for the German Bequest Tax*, http://www.iza.org (accessed on 4 November 2020). [59]

Tomes, N. (1981), “The Family, Inheritance, and the Intergenerational Transmission of Inequality”, *Journal of Political Economy*, Vol. 89/5, pp. 928-958. [18]

Tsoutsoura, M. (2015), “The Effect of Succession Taxes on Family Firm Investment: Evidence from a Natural Experiment”, *Journal of Finance*, Vol. 70/2, pp. 649-688, http://dx.doi.org/10.1111/jofi.12224. [92]

Villalonga, B. and R. Amit (2006), "How do family ownership, control and management affect firm value?", *Journal of Financial Economics*, Vol. 80/2, pp. 385-417, http://dx.doi.org/10.1016/j.jfineco.2004.12.005. [98]

Wolff, E. (2015), *Inheriting Wealth in America. Future Boom or Bust?*, Oxford University Press. [2]

Wolff, E. and M. Gittleman (2014), "Inheritances and the distribution of wealth or whatever happened to the great inheritance boom?", *Journal of Economic Inequality*, Vol. 12/4, pp. 439-468, http://dx.doi.org/10.1007/s10888-013-9261-8. [21]

Notes

[1] These assumptions are close to real life returns. For instance, the average annual return on a relatively risk-free 30-year US Treasury bill in the last 10 years was 3.28% (Federal Reserve Bank of St. Louis, 2020). Jordà et al. (2019[111]) provide evidence that across residential real estate and equities asset classes the mean return was about 7% on a global level over the period 1870-2015. Both asset classes have been shown, for instance in Norway, to play a dominant role in the investment portfolios of the top 5% in the net worth distribution (Fagereng et al., 2020[31]).

[2] https://www.oecd.org/els/family/SF_2_1_Fertility_rates.pdf.

3 Inheritance, estate, and gift tax design in OECD countries

Chapter 3 describes and assesses the design of inheritance, estate, and gift taxes across OECD countries. Beginning with a discussion of tax revenues, the chapter provides a comparative examination of the main design features of OECD countries' inheritance, estate, and gift taxes.

This chapter describes and assesses the design and implementation of inheritance, estate, and gift taxes across OECD countries.[1] After a brief discussion of tax revenues across countries and over time, the chapter provides a comparative overview of the main design features of OECD countries' inheritance, estate, and gift taxes[2] including rules regarding taxable events, tax exemption thresholds, tax rate schedules, the treatment of various tax-preferred assets, tax filing and payment procedures, valuation rules, gift tax design and the interaction between the tax treatment of unrealised capital gains at death and inheritance and estate taxes. The final section of the chapter discusses tax planning and avoidance opportunities as well as tax evasion risks. The discussion in this chapter primarily draws upon responses to an OECD questionnaire on inheritance, estate, and gift taxes provided by country delegates to Working Party No. 2 on Tax Policy Analysis and Tax Statistics of the OECD's Committee on Fiscal Affairs.

There are many common design features of inheritance, estate, and gift taxes across OECD countries. The majority of countries levy recipient-based inheritance and gift taxes, but a minority levy donor-based estate taxes. Most countries favour spouses and direct descendants through higher tax exemption thresholds and lower tax rates. Countries also typically exempt charitable giving and apply preferential tax treatment to certain assets, which contributes to a narrowing of the tax base. The most commonly tax-favoured assets include the main residence, business assets, pension assets, and life insurance policies. In a number of countries, the tax treatment of inter vivos (between living people) gifts as well as other tax design features have created opportunities for tax planning and avoidance. Overall, this chapter emphasises the importance of tax design to ensure that inheritance, estate, and gift taxes achieve their objectives.

3.1. Use of inheritance, estate, and gift taxes across OECD countries

3.1.1. The majority of OECD countries tax inheritances

24 of 36 OECD countries levy wealth transfer taxes. Of these, 20 levy inheritance taxes on the beneficiaries of wealth transfers. Only four countries (Denmark, Korea, the United Kingdom, and the United States) levy estate taxes on deceased donors. Most countries that levy inheritance or estate taxes also levy a gift tax on inter vivos transfers, typically on the beneficiary. One country – Ireland – levies a combined inheritance and gift tax (a tax on lifetime wealth transfers), which considers all wealth transfers received by beneficiaries over their lifetime. Latvia and Lithuania tax inter vivos gifts through the personal income tax (PIT), but Latvia does not tax inheritances while Lithuania levies a separate inheritance tax.

A minority of OECD countries tax inheritances or estates at the sub-central level. Central governments may retain partial authority over the design of inheritance taxes, but in some countries sub-central governments have substantial autonomy. The regions in Belgium and the cantons in Switzerland have full autonomy over the imposition and design of inheritance, estate, and gift taxes. The local municipalities in Lithuania and the regions in Spain instead levy inheritance taxes in concert with the central government, which sets the main design features from which sub-central governments can deviate. The United States levies an estate tax at the federal level and some states additionally levy inheritance taxes. The report examines the taxes levied by the central/federal government in Lithuania, Spain, and the United States, and examines the taxes levied at the local/regional level in Belgium (Brussels-Capital Region) and Switzerland (Canton of Zurich).

Ten OECD countries have abolished their estate or inheritance taxes and two countries have never taxed wealth transfers (Table 3.1). Austria, Czech Republic, Norway, Slovak Republic, and Sweden have abolished their inheritance or estate taxes since 2000. Israel and New Zealand abolished these taxes between 1980 and 2000, Australia, Canada, and Mexico abolished these taxes before 1980, and Estonia and Latvia have never levied inheritance or estate taxes. In response to the OECD questionnaire, countries reported their motives for repealing or not imposing inheritance, estate, and gift taxes. Lack of political support for inheritance and estate taxes was a key driver of the repeal or non-imposition of inheritance and estate taxes. This is consistent with evidence that inheritance and estate taxes tend to be unpopular (Section 3.14). Unpopularity may have also stemmed in some cases from tax design. For instance, before repealing its inheritance tax, Sweden had very low tax exemption thresholds (around USD 31 000 for spouses and USD 8 000 for children). Tax minimisation opportunities that primarily benefited wealthier taxpayers also eroded the legitimacy of inheritance, estate, and gift taxes, generating support for their removal (Henrekson and Waldenström, 2016[1]). Some countries reported high administrative burdens compared to relatively meagre revenues, in part due to the preferential treatment granted for certain assets.

Table 3.1. Current and historical inheritance and estate taxes in OECD countries

Country	Tax name (national language)	Tax name (English)	Tax first introduced	Current tax introduced	Year of repeal	Government level[1]
Current inheritance and estate taxes						
Belgium	Droit de succession	Inheritance Duty	1795	1936	..	Regional / State[2]
Chile	Impuesto a las Herencias y Donaciones	Inheritance and Gift Taxes	1915	1915	..	National
Denmark	Boafgiftsloven	Inheritance Estate and Gift Taxes	1792	1995	..	National
Finland	Perintövero	Inheritance Tax	1940	1940	..	National
France	Droits de mutations titre gratuit	Tax on Free Transfers	1791	1791	..	National
Germany	Erbschaftsteuer und Schenkungsteuer	Inheritance Tax and Gift Tax	1906	1974	..	National
Greece	Φόρος Κληρονομιάς	Inheritance Tax	1836	2001	..	National
Hungary	öröklési illeték	Inheritance Duty	1918	1918	..	National
Iceland	Erfðafjárskattur	Inheritance Tax	1792	2004	..	National
Ireland	Capital Acquisitions Tax	Capital Acquisitions Tax	1894	1976	..	National
Italy	Imposta sulle successioni e donazioni	Inheritance and Gift Tax	1862	2006	..	National
Japan	相続税	Inheritance Tax	1950	1950	..	National
Korea	상속세및증여세법	The Inheritance Tax and Gift Tax	1950	1950	..	National
Lithuania	Paveldimo turto mokesčio įstatymas	Law on Inheritance Tax	1990[3]	2003	..	National / Local
Luxembourg	Droits de succession	Inheritance Tax	1817	1817	..	National
Netherlands	Erfbelasting en schenkbelasting	Inheritance and Gift Tax	1859	1956	..	National
Poland	Podatek od spadków i darowizn	Tax on Inheritance and Donation	1920	1983	..	National
Portugal	Imposto do selo sobre transmissões gratuitas	Stamp Duty on Inheritance and Gifts	1959	2004	..	National
Slovenia	Davek na dediščine in darila	Inheritance and Gift Tax	1988	2006	..	National
Spain	Impuesto sobre Sucesiones y Donaciones	Inheritance and Gift Tax	1798	1988	..	National / Regional[4]
Switzerland	Erbschafts- und Schenkungssteuer	Inheritance and Gift tax	1870	1986	..	Regional / State[5]
Turkey	Veraset ve İntikal Vergisi	Inheritance and Gift Tax	1959	1959	..	National
United Kingdom	Inheritance Tax	Inheritance Tax	1894	1986	..	National
United States	Estate and Gift Tax	Estate and Gift Tax	1916	1916	..	National[6]
Past inheritance and estate taxes						
Australia	Estate Tax	Estate Tax	1851	1914	1979	National / State
Austria	Erbschaftssteuer	Inheritance Tax	1759	1955	2008	National
Canada	Estate Tax	Estate Tax	1941	1958	1972	National
Czech Republic	Zákon o dani dědické, darovací a dani z převodu nemovitostí	Act on Inheritance Tax, Gift Tax and Real Estate Transfer Tax	1993	1993	2014	National
Estonia	..	..	..	..	..	..
Israel	חוק מס עזבון	Inheritance Tax Law	1949	1949	1980	National
Latvia	..	..	..	..	..	..
Mexico	Impuesto sobre Herencias y Legados	Inheritance and Bequest Tax	1926[7]	1926	1961	National / State
New Zealand	Estate duty	Estate Duty	1866	1866	1992	National

Norway	Avgift på arv og gave	Inheritance and Gift Tax	1792	1792	2014	National
Slovak Republic	Daň z dedičstva	Inheritance tax	1993	1993	2004	National
Sweden	Arvskatt	Inheritance Tax	1884	1884	2004	National

1. This refers to the government level that has primary responsibility for legislating the tax, including the right to introduce or to abolish a tax, set tax rates, define the tax base, or grant tax allowances or reliefs. In some countries, one level of government has legislative authority but revenues accrue to another level of government. A cell with ".." indicates that the country has not abolished their inheritance, estate, and gifts taxes or that they have never levied inheritance, estate, and gift taxes. Belgium: refers to the Brussels-Capital Region. Switzerland: refers to the canton of Zurich.
2. Information on Belgium refers to the Brussels-Capital Region.
3. Due to tax relief inheritances were effectively untaxed between 1990 and 1998.
4. The central government administers the Inheritance and Gift Tax, however, regional governments may regulate tax base allowances, tax rates, tax deductions, and certain administrative procedures.
5. Information on Switzerland refers to the Canton of Zurich.
6. State-level inheritance taxes are not presented in this report, though some states levy an inheritance tax in addition to the federal Estate Tax.
7. This refers to taxes at the federal level. Prior to 1926, some local municipalities levied taxes on inheritances and gifts.

Source: OECD Questionnaire on Inheritance, Estate, and Gift Taxes (2020).

3.2. Tax revenues and shares of taxable estates

3.2.1. Revenues from inheritance and estate taxes are typically low, as a majority of estates go untaxed in a number of countries

Revenues from inheritance, estate, and gift taxes form a very small portion of total tax revenues across OECD countries (Figure 3.1). On average (unweighted) across the OECD, 0.36% of total tax revenues are sourced from these taxes and, among countries that levy these taxes, 0.51% of total tax revenues on average are sourced from these taxes. Revenues from inheritance, estate, and gift taxes exceed 1% of total taxation in only four OECD countries (Belgium, France, Japan, and Korea). As discussed further, this largely reflects broader tax bases and higher tax rates, particularly for heirs that are not close family, in these countries. The inheritance tax in Korea is examined in greater detail in Box 3.1. Twenty countries raise less than a quarter of a percent in total taxation from inheritance, estate, and gift taxes, and revenue is zero in eight countries (Australia, Estonia, Israel, Mexico, New Zealand, Portugal, Slovak Republic, and Sweden). Of these countries, all except Portugal[3] do not levy taxes on inheritances, estates, and gifts.

Figure 3.1. Inheritance, estate, and gift tax revenues, 2019, all OECD countries

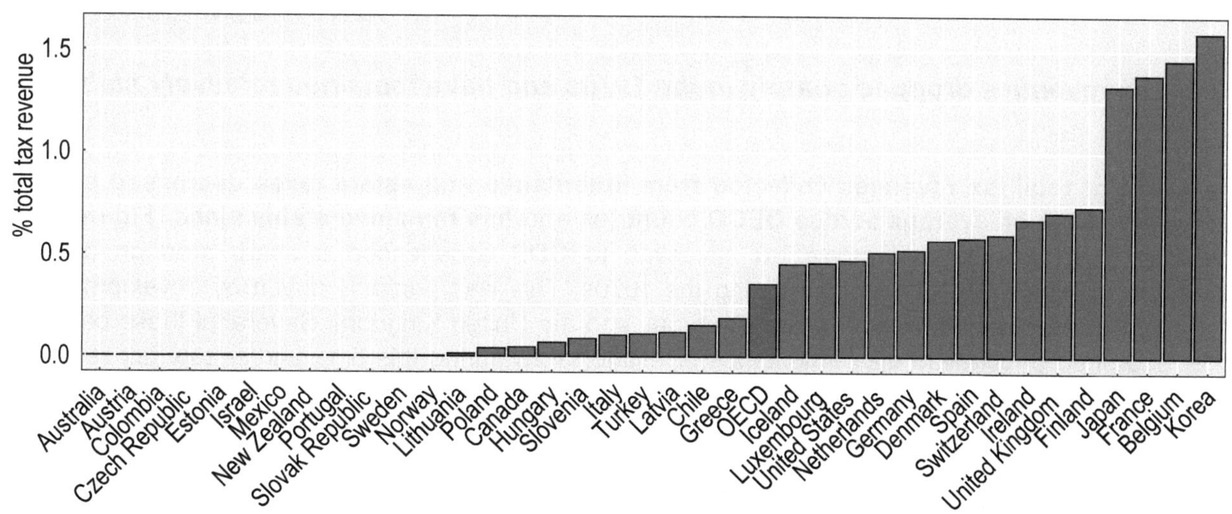

Note: Data are for 2018 for Australia, Greece, Japan, Mexico, and the OECD average.
Source: OECD Revenue Statistics.

StatLink https://stat.link/qtpwu6

Low inheritance and estate tax revenues are in part due to the low shares of taxable estates amongst total estates and transfers. Figure 3.2 shows the share of estates that were subject to inheritance or estate taxes in eight countries for which data were available. Most estates are not subject to inheritance or estate taxes and, in seven countries, less than 13% of estates were taxed. The shares of estates that were subject to inheritance or estate taxes ranges from 0.2% (United States) to 48% (Belgium, Brussels).

Figure 3.2. Share of estates subject to inheritance or estate taxes, select countries

2019 or latest available year

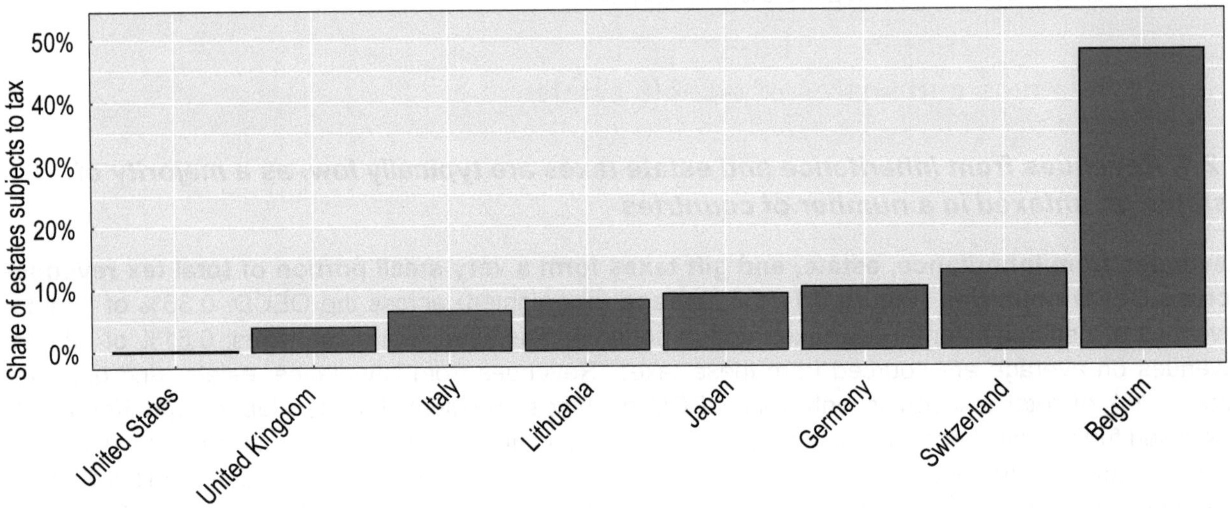

Note: Results presented for countries for which data were available. Belgium: refers to the Brussels-Capital Region. Switzerland: refers to the canton of Zurich.
Source: OECD Questionnaire on Inheritance, Estate, and Gift Taxes (2020).

StatLink https://stat.link/zx51p9

3.2.2. Tax revenues dropped sharply in the 1970s and have remained relatively stable since

The share of total tax revenues collected from inheritance and estate taxes decreased sharply during the 1970s on average across OECD countries and has remained stable since (Figure 3.3).[4] The ratio of inheritance and estate tax revenues to GDP experienced a sharp drop on average (unweighted) across OECD countries during the 1970s. This was primarily driven by developments in Australia, Canada, Ireland, New Zealand, Portugal, and the United Kingdom. Several of these countries either abolished or curtailed their inheritance or estate taxes during this time and/or saw tax revenues eroded by increasingly sophisticated tax planning. Inheritance and estate tax revenues were relatively stable between the mid-1980s and 2018. In contrast, revenues from gift taxes have been stable across the whole period in Figure 3.3, though they are substantially lower than revenues from inheritance and estate taxes.

Figure 3.3. Inheritance, estate, and gift tax revenues, 1965-2019, OECD average

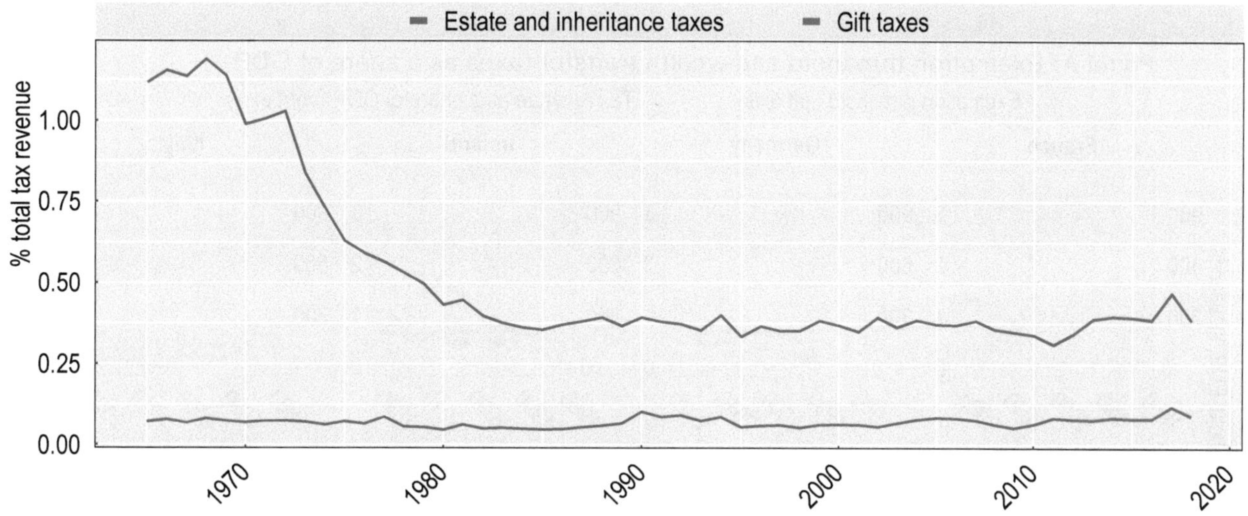

Note: Figure shows unweighted average across all OECD countries.
Source: OECD Revenue Statistics.

StatLink https://stat.link/2itdka

Inheritance and estate tax exemption thresholds have increased since the 1980s in several countries. Panel A of Figure 3.4 compares the exemption threshold for the donor's children (left axis) and inheritance and estate tax revenues as a share of GDP (right axis), between 1980 and 2020 (tax exemption data drawn from (Nolan et al., 2020[2]). Tax exemption thresholds for children have increased in all countries, either through periodic changes (e.g. Germany, Italy) or through yearly adjustments (e.g. United Kingdom). All else being equal, higher exemption thresholds would be expected to lead to lower revenue, but there is little evidence of this in Figure 3.4. Despite higher exemption thresholds, revenues from inheritance taxes have risen in France and Germany and remained largely stable in the United Kingdom. However, a decline in revenue was discernible in Italy and the United States at the time of substantial increases to tax exemption thresholds.

In parallel to narrower tax bases, there was a trend towards lowering top tax rates in most countries. Panel B of Figure 3.4 compares the top marginal estate or inheritance tax rate for the donor's children (left axis) and inheritance and estate tax revenue as a share of GDP (right axis), between 1980 and 2020 (tax rates data drawn from (Nolan et al., 2020[2]) A steady decrease in top marginal tax rates in the United States was accompanied by steadily declining tax revenues, while revenues in Italy decreased slightly around the time of a major drop in the top tax rate. The significant drop in top marginal tax rates in the United Kingdom, from 75% to 40% between 1980 and 1988, had no discernible impact on revenues, which remained largely stable throughout the period. Significant variation in top marginal rates in Ireland, dropping from 55% in 1984 to 20% in 2000 before rising to 33% in 2013, do not appear to affect tax revenue trends, which have shown a steady increase throughout the period. In contrast to other countries in Figure 3.4, France raised its top marginal tax rate between 1980 and 2020, and saw an increase in inheritance tax revenues over the period.

Figure 3.4. Inheritance and estate tax exemption thresholds and top marginal tax rates compared to inheritance, estate, and gift tax revenues as a share of GDP, 1980-2020, select countries

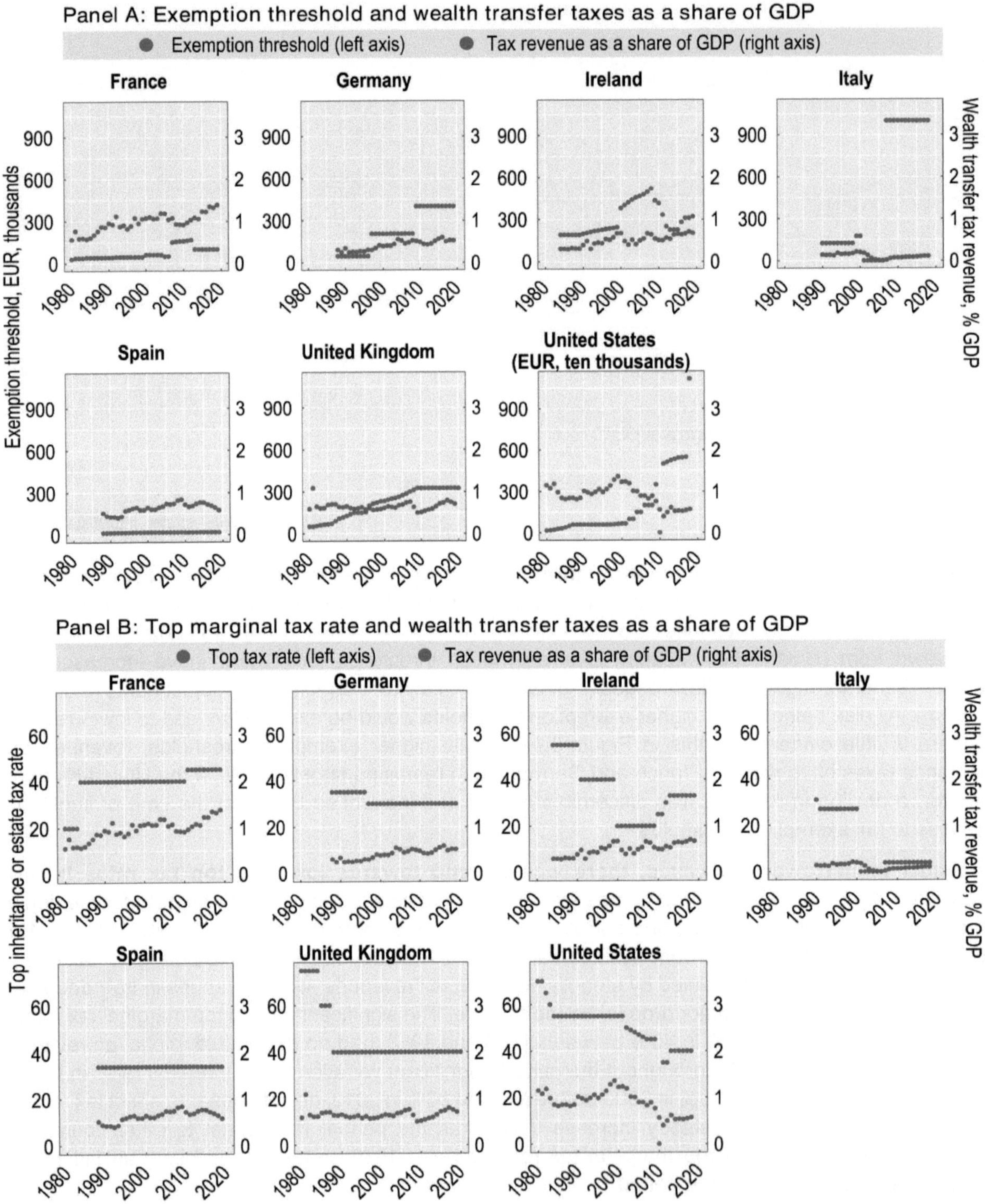

Note: Tax exemption thresholds and top marginal tax rates are shown for the donor's children. United States: The left axis of Panel A represents ten thousands, not thousands as for other countries, as the exemption threshold for children was around USD 11.6 million in 2020.

Source: OECD Revenue Statistics (2020) and Nolan, B., J. Palomino, P. Van Kerm and S. Morelli (2020), 'The Wealth of Families: The Intergenerational Transmission of Wealth in Britain in Comparative Perspective', Nuffield Foundation, Oxford.

StatLink https://stat.link/r4uw27

The stability or slight increase in inheritance, estate, and gift tax revenues in most countries in Figure 3.4, despite increases in tax exemption thresholds and decreases in top marginal rates, may reflect different factors. The fact that tax revenues have held up is likely due in part to the rise in the importance of inherited wealth (Figure 1.15). In some countries, it may also reflect tax reforms involving an increase in effective tax burdens, such as compensating base broadening measures. Countries may have also offset the lower tax burden on the donor's children, observed in some countries in Figure 3.4, with lower tax exemptions and higher tax rates for other heirs. Revenue trends may also possibly reflect greater tax compliance and more effective tax administration.

While inheritance, estate, and gift taxes are generally a minor source of revenue, they can support important objectives beyond raising revenue. In response to the OECD questionnaire, the most common rationale cited by countries for levying an inheritance or estate tax was to redistribute wealth, increase equality of opportunity or tax unearned windfalls. Chapter 2 outlines and assesses the various equity arguments in favour of inheritance taxation, underlining that it can enhance equality of opportunity as well as horizontal and vertical equity, and reduce wealth inequality over time.

Box 3.1. The distribution of wealth transfers and inheritance taxation in Korea

Drawing on data provided by the Korea Institute for Public Finance (KIPF), which provided financial support for this project, this box examines Korea's estate tax. Korea's estate tax, in place since 1950, shares many features of inheritance and estate taxes in other OECD countries. It applies to resident donors' worldwide assets and to non-resident donors' local assets (Table 3.2), spouses benefit from the most generous tax treatment (Figure 3.8), and estates are taxed at progressive rates (Figure 3.11). Korea, like nearly all countries that levy an inheritance or estate tax, also levies a gift tax on inter vivos transfers (Table 3.9). Unlike most OECD countries, only different-sex married couples benefit from spousal treatment (Table 3.5) and only one set of rates applies across different groups of heirs (Figure 3.12).

Korea's estate tax is levied mostly on wealthier taxpayers. While only 2.2% of successions give rise to estate taxes (Figure 3.2), taxable wealth transfers amount to 39.3% of total transferred wealth. Donors whose wealth transfers are subject to the estate tax made taxable transfers of KRW 18 278 billion (USD 15.5 billion) in 2018, compared to KRW 28 344 billion (USD 24.0 billion) by the remaining 97.8% of donors whose wealth transfers were not subject to estate taxes (Figure 3.5). This is partly due to the standard deduction of KRW 500 million (around USD 420 000), plus the spousal deduction of KRW 3 billion (USD 2.5 million).

Figure 3.5. Total wealth transferred by size of the donor's estate, 2018

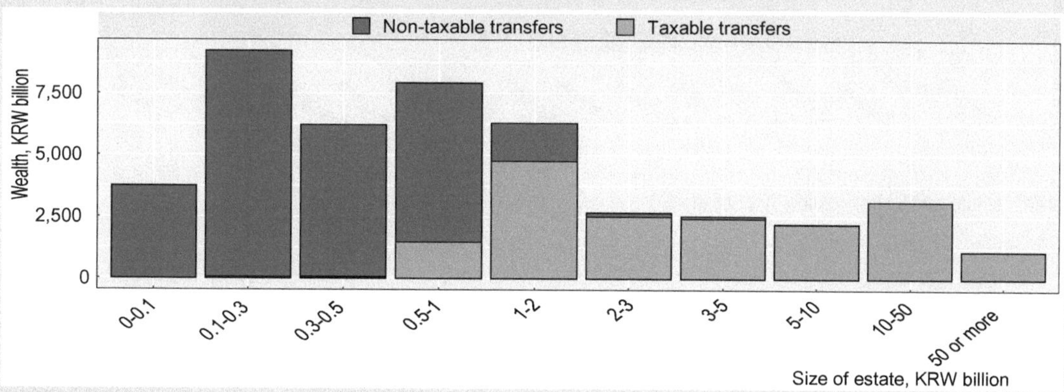

Source: Korea Institute for Public Finance, unpublished.

StatLink https://stat.link/0sd9ez

Figure 3.6 illustrates the asset composition of taxable estates by the size of the donor's estate. The main component of taxable estates up to KRW 2 billion (USD 1.7 million) is buildings, while the main component of taxable estates between KRW 2 and 50 billion (USD 1.7 million to 42.4 million) is land. Securities comprise 54% of the estates over KRW 50 billion (USD 42.4 million), compared to 26% and 12% of donors' assets for estates worth KRW 10 to 50 billion (USD 8.5 million to 42.4 million) and estates worth KRW 5 to 10 billion (USD 4.2 million to USD 8.5 million), respectively.

Figure 3.6. Asset composition of taxable estates by size of the donor's estate, 2018

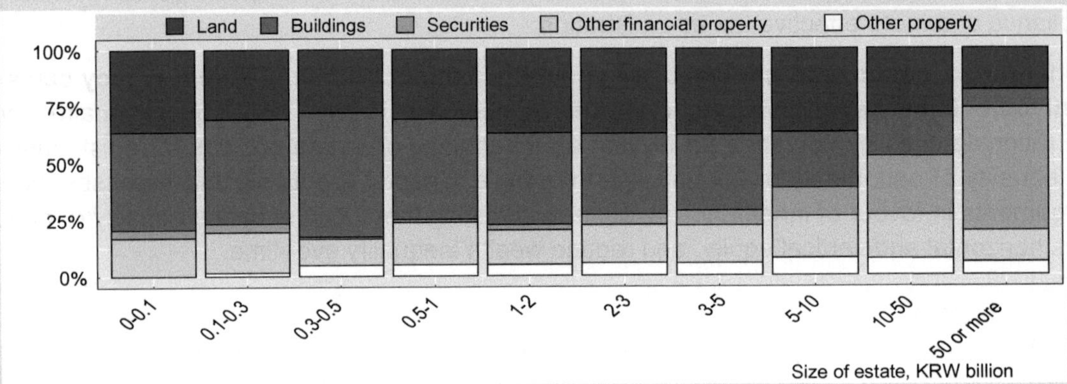

Source: Korea Institute for Public Finance, unpublished.

StatLink https://stat.link/qh7lvz

Wealth transfers are highly concentrated among donors in the capital, Seoul, and the region surrounding the capital, Gyeonggi Province (Figure 3.7). Taxable transfers in Seoul amount to KRW 8 833 billion (USD 7.5 billion), followed by KRW 3 782 billion in Gyeonggi (USD 3.2 billion), with the smallest taxable transfers taking place in Sejong (KRW 25.5 billion or USD 22 million). In total, 72% of taxable transfers and 46% of non-taxable transfers are made by donors in the Seoul Capital Area (Seoul, Gyeonggi, and Incheon).

Figure 3.7. Total wealth transferred by tax administration area, 2018

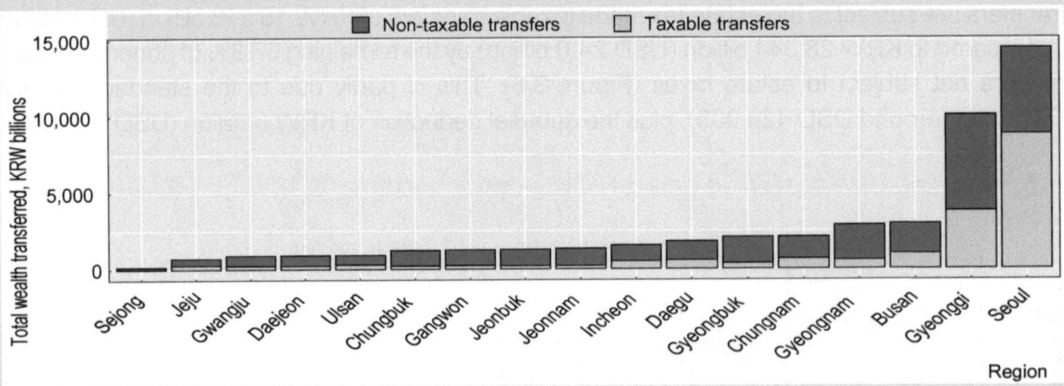

Source: Korea Institute for Public Finance, unpublished.

StatLink https://stat.link/isfxhe

Estate taxes have received much attention in recent years, particularly as ownership of several chaebol – large industrial groups run by founders and their families – will shift to the next generation in the coming years. As in other countries, business assets are subject to the estate tax and benefit from some preferential treatment (see section 3.8.3), but the question of business succession has generated substantial commentary.

3.3. The different types of wealth transfer taxes

3.3.1. Most OECD countries levy inheritance taxes on the recipients of wealth transfers

Wealth transfer taxes can take different forms. For end-of-life bequests, countries may impose donor-based estate taxes, levied on the deceased donor's total net wealth, or recipient-based inheritance taxes, levied on the value of the assets that beneficiaries receive from the deceased donor. For inter vivos transfers made during the donor's life, countries can apply gift taxes, which are levied on the beneficiary in most countries.

The most common approach across OECD countries is to tax wealth transfers received by beneficiaries through an inheritance tax. Out of the 24 countries that tax bequests, 20 OECD countries apply recipient-based inheritance taxes. These countries typically apply different treatment – including different tax exemption thresholds and tax rates – to different heirs depending on their relationship with the donor. Four countries levy an estate tax (Denmark, Korea, the United Kingdom, and the United States), but some additional criteria such as the beneficiaries' relationship to the donor may be taken into consideration to determine the tax liability. All these countries levy accompanying gift taxes (except Lithuania, which taxes gifts through the PIT).

Most countries treat each inheritance as a separate event. This approach implies that, for example, in a country applying a EUR 300 000 tax exemption threshold, a beneficiary receiving two inheritances of EUR 200 000 each would not be liable for inheritance taxes, whereas a beneficiary receiving one inheritance of EUR 400 000 would be liable. An alternative approach would consider all wealth received by beneficiaries over their lifetime through a tax on lifetime wealth transfers, which is the case in Ireland. In the above scenario, the two beneficiaries would face the same tax liability as they have received the same amount of wealth.

Inheritance or estate taxes are typically levied on net asset values, but some countries apply conditions on debt deductibility. In 12 countries, all the donor's debts are deductible for tax purposes (Belgium, Denmark, Finland, Hungary, Ireland, Korea, Luxembourg, Netherlands, Poland, Slovenia, Switzerland, and the United States). In some countries, debts that were contracted to purchase exempt assets are not deductible (Chile, France, Germany, Italy, Japan, and the United Kingdom) and in others, loans from heirs or close family to the donor are not deductible (Spain). A minority of countries allow debts to be deducted on the condition that they were contracted in normal circumstances or that they were not contracted with the intention to reduce the taxable base (France, Greece, and Japan). Debts are not deductible in Lithuania.

3.3.2. The type of tax chosen involves trade-offs

Inheritance taxes have a number of advantages compared to estate taxes. As discussed in Chapter 2, if promoting equality of opportunity is a major objective of inheritance taxation, there is a strong case for a recipient-based inheritance tax rather than an estate tax levied on donors. It is the amount of wealth received by each recipient that should matter for equality of opportunity rather than the overall amount bequeathed by the donor. In addition, because the tax liability will depend on the wealth received by each individual, donors that spread a bequest among more recipients may reduce the total tax liability. This may incentivise the division of estates and reduce concentrations of wealth. Inheritance taxes also allow countries to focus more on beneficiaries' personal situations, such as age, disability, and previous wealth received. The double taxation argument against wealth transfer taxes is also weaker in the case of inheritance taxes that are levied on recipients as there is no double taxation of the donor themselves and the inherited wealth is also only taxed once in the hands of the recipient. On the other hand, estate taxes may be easier to collect than inheritance taxes, as they are levied on the overall estate.

A tax on lifetime wealth transfers has a number of advantages over inheritance and estate taxes, but may be more difficult to administer. A tax on lifetime wealth transfers is levied on the gifts and bequests that beneficiaries receive over their lifetime. For each new wealth transfer, the tax liability is determined by taking into account the amount of wealth previously received by the beneficiary. Such a tax may be levied above a lifetime tax exemption threshold, i.e. above an amount of wealth that beneficiaries are entitled to receive tax-free during the course of their life. Such a tax improves horizontal equity, by ensuring that individuals who receive the same amount of wealth pay the same amount of tax, regardless of whether they receive one large transfer or several smaller transfers. A tax on lifetime wealth transfers also improves vertical equity, particularly if tax rates are progressive, ensuring those who receive more wealth over their lifetime pay more tax than individuals who only receive a small amount. A tax on lifetime wealth transfers may also incentivise donors to spread their wealth among several beneficiaries, including those that have received less wealth over their life. In its purest form, a lifetime wealth transfers tax would not consider who the beneficiary received the wealth from, however, in the case of the Capital Acquisitions Tax in Ireland – the only lifetime wealth transfers tax in an OECD country – different tax exemptions apply to three groups of donors (parents, other close family, other donors). Taxing lifetime wealth transfers also limits the importance of timing for gifts and inheritances, reducing avoidance opportunities. A tax levied on lifetime transfers increases the administrative complexity of the tax, but countries may choose between tracking taxpayers' history of wealth transfers and relying on self-reporting (as is the case in Ireland). Some tax administrations may need to invest in establishing or updating comprehensive records, which may be easier thanks to increasing digitalisation.

Gift taxes can be integrated with inheritance and estate taxes to ensure neutrality between inter vivos and end-of-life transfers and act as a backstop to prevent avoidance of inheritance and estate taxes. A gift tax levied on inter vivos transfers is an important complement to inheritance and estate taxes. Aligning the design of gift taxes and inheritance and estate taxes improves neutrality between transferring wealth during life or at death and ensures that the timing of the wealth transfer will be less central to the tax treatment.

A question that may arise is whether wealth transfers should be taxed through the personal income tax when they are received by beneficiaries. For instance, Latvia and Lithuania tax gifts through the personal income tax (PIT). Batchelder (2020[3]) recently proposed such an integrated approach for the United States, where inheritances would be taxed under income and payroll taxes above a large lifetime exemption. Such an approach would level the playing field between earned labour and/ or capital income and inheritances, but could create some difficulties. In particular, it would be necessary to apply income averaging to address the lumpiness of inheritances. Depending on tax design, taxing inheritances under the PIT could also lead to very high marginal effective tax rates for recipients who earn labour income and receive inheritances, which could have strong disincentive effects on labour supply. If inheritances were taxed jointly with capital income under a dual income tax, they would not introduce such labour supply distortions, but would still require income averaging for individuals who receive large amounts of capital income. In contrast, taxpayers who have greater control over the timing of their income may be able to minimise personal income in the year they receive an inheritance. If inheritances were redefined as personal income, there would also be important implications regarding the allocation of taxing rights between countries in the case of cross-border inheritances. Such effects can be avoided by having a separate tax on bequests. More generally, as discussed in Chapter 2, the distributional and behavioural effects of income and inheritance, estate, and gift taxes are likely to be different and may also justify a separate tax treatment.

3.4. Rules determining tax liability

3.4.1. Rules governing liability for inheritance and estate taxes vary substantially across countries

Liability for inheritance or estate taxes most commonly depends on the nationality or tax residence of the donor or the physical location of assets (Table 3.2). The most common approach across OECD countries is to levy inheritance or estate taxes on total worldwide assets of tax-resident donors and on total or immovable assets located within the jurisdiction for non-resident taxpayers. Three countries tax citizen donors, regardless of whether they are tax residents. One country – the United Kingdom – levies estate taxes on domiciled taxpayers, whose strongest ties are in the country, but not on tax residents, who may be domiciled abroad.[5] A minority of countries do not tax nationals' or residents' foreign immovable property; only moveable property located abroad and assets located within the jurisdiction. Some countries apply different taxes or thresholds to non-residents. For example, Belgium and Luxembourg apply a special transfer tax to non-residents, rather than the usual inheritance tax that would apply to residents, and the United States applies a significantly lower tax-free threshold to non-residents. The regional or local tax residency of the donor or the location of the assets are determining factors for the countries that levy inheritance taxes at the regional or local level.

Table 3.2. Taxable persons and assets

Taxable persons	Taxable assets	Countries
Donor is a tax resident or tax domicile	Worldwide assets	Belgium, Denmark, Finland, France, Germany[1], Ireland, Italy, Japan, Korea, Netherlands[2], Slovenia, Switzerland, United Kingdom[3], United States
	All assets within the jurisdiction and moveable property outside the jurisdiction	Greece[4], Hungary[5], Luxembourg
Donor is a national	Worldwide assets	Chile, United States
	All assets within the jurisdiction and moveable property outside the jurisdiction	Hungary
Beneficiary is a tax resident or tax domicile	Worldwide assets	Finland, France, Germany, Ireland, Japan[6], Lithuania, Poland, Spain
Beneficiary is a national	Worldwide assets	Hungary, Poland
Taxable person is not a tax resident, tax domicile or national	Immovable and moveable property within jurisdiction	Chile[7], France, Germany, Greece, Hungary, Ireland, Italy, Japan, Korea, Lithuania, Portugal[8], Spain, United Kingdom, United States
	Immoveable property within jurisdiction	Belgium[9], Denmark, Finland[10], Luxembourg[11], Poland, Slovenia, Switzerland

1. A German national is considered a taxable person if the donor has been non-resident for tax purposes for less than five years.
2. A Dutch national is considered a taxable person if the donor has been non-resident for tax purposes for less than ten years.
3. This includes taxpayers who were actually tax-domiciled in the United Kingdom in the preceding three years, even if were tax residents abroad, and taxpayers who were tax resident in the United Kingdom for 15 of the past 20 years, even if they were domiciled abroad. Some assets are exempt from inheritance taxation; non-domiciled taxpayers are exempt on certain types of collective investment funds (open-ended investment company and authorised unit trust) and non-resident taxpayers are exempt on government bonds.
4. A Greek national is considered a taxable person if the donor has been non-resident for tax purposes for less than ten years preceding the inheritance.
5. This applies if the donor is not a Hungarian citizen and no inheritance tax has been imposed on assets outside Hungary.
6. A Japanese national is considered a taxable person if both the beneficiary and the donor left have been non-resident for tax purposes for less than ten years. Non-citizen, tax resident beneficiaries are taxed on assets situated within Japan.
7. It includes property located outside the jurisdiction that was acquired using Chilean resources.
8. If the inheritance consists of listed shares, the beneficiary must be a tax resident.
9. Immovable property is subject to a transfer tax, if the donor is not a tax resident.
10. Includes shares or other rights in a corporate body where more than 50% of total gross assets consist of real property situated in Finland.
11. Immovable property is subject to a transfer tax, if the donor is not a tax resident.
Note: Belgium: refers to the Brussels-Capital Region. Switzerland: refers to the canton of Zurich.
Source: OECD Questionnaire on Inheritance, Estate, and Gift Taxes (2020)

Nine countries levy inheritance or estate taxes depending on the situation of the beneficiary (Table 3.2). Beneficiaries are typically liable if they were tax residents at the time that they received the inheritance. Hungary and Poland, on the other hand, tax citizen beneficiaries. Lithuania, Poland, and Spain are the only countries to exclusively consider beneficiaries; the remaining countries consider the residency or nationality of both beneficiaries and donors.

There are various administrative reasons why the donor's tax residence or citizenship is the most common connecting factor to determine where transferred assets are taxable. From an administrative perspective, it may be easier to identify the taxable event, as the distribution of a person's wealth following their death is tied to additional procedures like probate and there will likely already be people administering the donor's affairs. It is unclear whether the incentive for avoidance-related migration is stronger for beneficiaries or donors, however, as the donor is already linked to their wealth, and beneficiaries are only linked to wealth after they receive it, it may be easier to apply tail provisions, discussed in the following sub-section, to donors than to beneficiaries.

3.4.2. The risks of tax-related emigration, double non-taxation and double taxation can be minimised through tax design

Several jurisdictions apply "tail provisions", where taxpayers continue to be liable for inheritance or estate taxes for a number of years after leaving the country. In some countries, citizens and/or former tax residents are treated as tax residents for inheritance tax purposes if the donor passes away soon after the donor or beneficiary has left their home country.[6] Such tail provisions limit the risk of inheritance or estate tax avoidance by emigrating shortly before the donor's death. These provisions may also mitigate the need for provisions such as exit taxes, where citizens and former tax residents renounce their status. To distinguish avoidance-related emigration from genuine emigration, tail provisions may expire after a set number of years, so genuine emigrants cease to be liable for inheritance or estate taxes in their home country.

Provisions to relieve double taxation vary across countries. Given the differences across countries in rules determining liability for inheritance or estate taxation, double (or multiple) taxation may arise in cross-border wealth transfers. Double taxation relief is available under double tax treaties in some cases, although treaty networks to prevent inheritance or estate double taxation are very limited. A majority of countries levying inheritance or estate taxes provide unilateral relief. Under domestic legislation, relief is typically provided for inheritance and gift tax paid abroad in respect of assets located abroad (e.g. a tax credit or an exemption). In some cases, however, unilateral relief may be incomplete. For instance, relief may only be granted for taxes paid on certain types of foreign property. There may also be mismatches between inheritance tax rules regarding what is considered a local compared to a foreign asset and between valuation methods for the same property (European Commission, 2011[4]). In some countries, there is no relief provided for gifts, either through unilateral or double tax treaty relief.

Reforms could be considered to avoid risks of double taxation and double non-taxation by better aligning taxing rights across countries. Given the limited number of double tax treaties, there might be merit in focusing first on improving and harmonising domestic rules for inheritance or estate tax relief (European Commission, 2011[4]). As part of these efforts, the order of priority of taxing rights could also be clarified. Countries may coordinate on certain rules; for example, assigning the primary right to apply inheritance or estate taxes to the country where the taxpayer has the closest link; providing tax relief in the country where the beneficiary has personal links for the tax paid on the inheritance in the country where the donor had personal links; and establishing mutual agreement procedures for situations where a beneficiary or a donor had personal links to more than one country (e.g. resident in one country and domiciled in or a national of another). Consistent application of such rules across countries could reduce risks of double taxation and double non-taxation in cross-border inheritances.

3.5. Tax exemption thresholds

3.5.1. Close family members often benefit from more generous tax exemption thresholds

Inheritance and estate tax exemption thresholds typically depend on the relationship between the donor and the heir, with more favourable exemption thresholds applying to closer family members. Figure 3.8 shows family members arranged according to proximity to the donor, with darker shading indicating more favourable inheritance or estate tax treatment and lighter shading indicating less favourable tax treatment. Across countries, the donor's spouse and children are either exempt or benefit from the highest exemption thresholds. It is worth mentioning that these heirs are typically entitled to a share of the donor's estate under forced heirship rules (see Box 3.2). Some countries apply the same tax treatment to the immediate family and beyond (e.g. Poland), but in others, the most favourable treatment is restricted to the closest family members (e.g. Ireland). The tax treatment of parents and grandparents is generally among the more generous, while cousins receive the same tax treatment as aunts and uncles in most countries. Where more distant relatives receive the same treatment, it is usually because countries group together relatives that are not close family. As shown in Tables 3.3, some countries in practice have only two or three groups of beneficiaries, while countries such as France and Switzerland have as many as seven groups.

Table 3.3. Number of beneficiary groups, according to applicable tax rates and exemption thresholds, per country

Number of beneficiary groups	Countries
2	Hungary, Japan, Korea, Lithuania, Portugal
3	Chile, Denmark, Greece, Finland, Spain, United Kingdom, United States
4	Belgium, Ireland, Italy, Poland, Slovenia
6	Germany, Luxembourg, Netherlands
7	France, Switzerland

Note: This table considers the tax rate schedule and the tax exemption threshold that apply to heirs. Countries may have fewer beneficiary groups when considering only one of these dimensions or under relevant legislation. Belgium: refers to the Brussels-Capital Region. Korea: assumes that the standard deduction applies. Poland: the Tax on Inheritance and Donation Act specifies three beneficiary groups, but was amended in 2006 to exempt a subset of Group I beneficiaries. Switzerland: refers to the Canton of Zurich.
Source: OECD Questionnaire on Inheritance, Estate, and Gift Taxes 2020.

Figure 3.8. Tax exemption thresholds according to relationship with the donor, most to least favourable

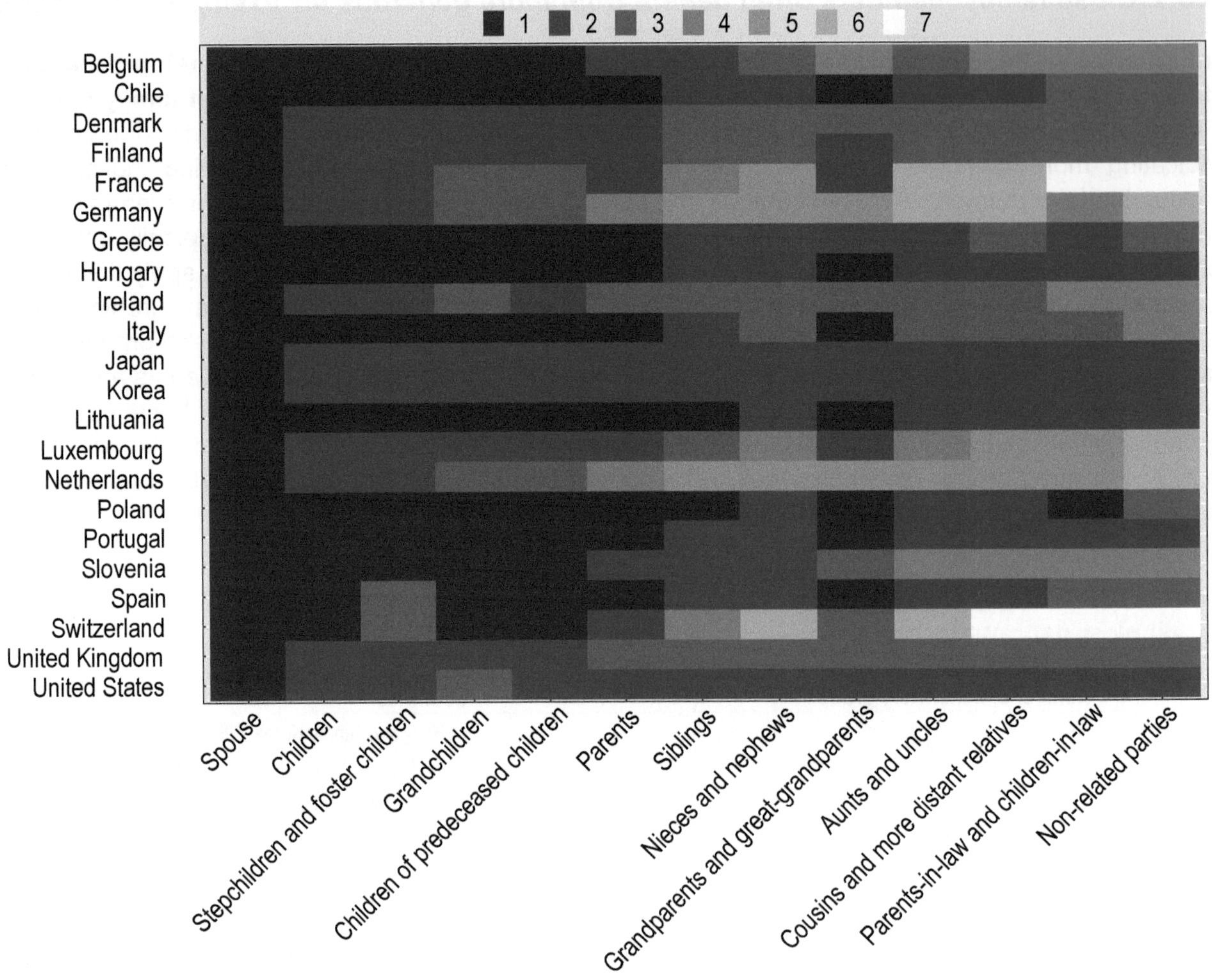

Note: The category "siblings" includes step-siblings. Beneficiaries are ordered first with respect to the applicable rates schedule and then to the tax-free threshold. This figure assumes that beneficiaries are adults and do not have a disability. Belgium: refers to the Brussels-Capital Region. Korea: assumes that the standard deduction applies. Lithuania: Step-siblings are not exempt. Netherlands: foster children are treated as children if they have been supported by the deceased for at least 5 years before their 21st birthday; otherwise they are treated as other family. Poland: Siblings receive the most favourable treatment and step-siblings receive the 4th most favourable treatment. Spain: children and grandchildren aged under 21 receive the most favourable tax treatment. Switzerland: refers to the Canton of Zurich, foster children receive the 6th most favourable tax exemption. United States: The Generation Skipping Tax (GST) applies to asset transfers to recipients, usually grandchildren, who are two or more generations younger than the donor. As the GST applies at the same rate and above the same exemption threshold as estate taxes, the effective taxation of wealth transfers is the same whether donors transfer directly to their grandchildren, or whether they transfer to their children, who then transfer the wealth to their children (the original donor's grandchildren).

Source: OECD Questionnaire on Inheritance, Estate, and Gift Taxes 2020

StatLink https://stat.link/kvlfyb

Box 3.2. Forced heirship rules

Forced heirship rules limit the freedom of donors to decide how their assets are distributed upon death. Countries may consider that spouses and parents have a responsibility to provide for their close family and so regulate the transfer of assets to them. Such rules may also limit unfair behaviour, preventing donors from favouring one child above another or from causing financial hardship to their spouse, while retaining some flexibility for donors to bequest a portion of their assets as they wish.

Most countries have some form of forced heirship (Table 3.4). Of the 24 OECD countries that levy inheritance or estate taxes, only three countries allow full testamentary freedom, where donors can dispose of their assets as they wish. Nineteen countries allow partial testamentary freedom but require donors to leave a fixed share of their wealth to specified persons. In the majority of countries that apply these rules, spouses and children are entitled to a share of the estate. Where spouses are the only forced heirs, children are entitled to some form of financial support. In other countries, a broader (parents, spouses, and children) or narrower (only children) category of beneficiaries are considered forced heirs. More distant relatives, such as grandchildren, can be considered forced heirs in 12 countries when the donor does not have closer relatives (Belgium, Chile, Germany, Italy, Japan, Korea, Lithuania, Netherlands, Portugal, Slovenia, Spain, and Switzerland).

Table 3.4. Forced heirship rules

Designated heirs	Countries
Parents, spouses, and children	Hungary, Poland, Switzerland
Spouses and children	Belgium, Chile, Denmark, Germany, Greece, Italy, Japan, Korea, Lithuania, Portugal, Slovenia, Spain
Spouses (some provision for children)	Ireland[1]
Children	Finland, France, Luxembourg, Netherlands
No forced heirs	Latvia, United Kingdom, United States

1. Children can apply for a provision of maintenance if the donor failed for provide for them in the will.
Note: The information in this table considers that donors have a spouse, children, and parents. Different rules may apply where this is not the case; in some countries, more distant family members are forced heirs where the donor does not have closer relatives. Belgium: refers to the Brussels-Capital Region. Switzerland: refers to the Canton of Zurich.
Source: OECD Questionnaire on Inheritance, Estate, and Gift Taxes (2020).

While forced heirship rules may help protect heirs, they may also prevent donors from sharing their wealth more widely or donating it to charitable causes. Forced heirship rules may also counter efforts to reduce wealth inequality by mandating that a minimum share of the donor's wealth pass to their closest heirs. Inheritance and estate tax revenue may also be limited if countries mandate that donors pass a significant share of their wealth to heirs that benefit from higher tax exemptions and lower tax rates.

3.5.2. Spouses are exempt or benefit from the highest tax exemption threshold

In all countries that levy inheritance and estate taxes, spouses benefit from the most generous tax exemption thresholds (Figure 3.8, Table 3.5). The surviving spouse is fully exempt from inheritance or estate taxes in most countries (Denmark, France, Hungary, Ireland, Japan, Lithuania, Luxembourg, Poland, Portugal, Slovenia, Switzerland, the United Kingdom,[7] and the United States). In other countries, spouses benefit from the highest tax-free threshold, applying only to spouses (Finland, Germany, Korea, and the Netherlands) or the highest tax-free threshold that also applies to other close family members

(Belgium, Chile, Greece, and Italy). In the United Kingdom, the unused fraction of the donor's tax-free threshold can pass to the surviving spouse. If, for example, the donor uses half of their exemption threshold bequeathing wealth to a taxable heir (i.e. any heir but their spouse), the surviving spouse would combine their own tax-free threshold with the remaining unused half of their deceased spouse's tax exemption threshold, allowing spouses to use the full value of their tax exemptions between them.

Table 3.5. Tax treatment for the donor's spouse and children

Country	Spousal treatment for married (MA), civil union (CU), and cohabiting couples (CH)	Tax exemption threshold spouse	Tax exemption threshold children
Belgium	MA, CU	USD 17 133	USD 17 133
Chile	MA, CU	USD 36 952	USD 36 952
Denmark	MA, CU	Exempt	USD 46 147
Finland	MA, CU	USD 102 798	USD 22 844
France	MA, CU[1]	Exempt	USD 114 220
Germany	MA, CU	USD 571 098[2]	USD 456 879
Greece	MA, CU	USD 171 329	USD 171 329
Hungary		Exempt	Exempt
Ireland	MA, CU	Exempt	USD 382 636
Italy	MA, CU	USD 1 142 197	USD 1 142 197
Japan	MA	Exempt	USD 337 159[3]
Korea	MA	USD 2 541 778	USD 423 630[4]
Lithuania	MA	Exempt	Exempt
Luxembourg	MA, CU	Exempt	Depends on value of estate[5]
Netherlands	MA, CU, CH[6]	USD 755 367[7]	USD 23 924
Poland	MA	Exempt	Exempt
Portugal	MA, CU	Exempt	Exempt
Slovenia	MA, CU, CH	Exempt	Exempt
Spain	MA, CU	USD 18 226	USD 18 226[8]
Switzerland	MA[9]	Exempt	Exempt
United Kingdom	MA, CU	Exempt	USD 641 026
United States	MA	Exempt	USD 11 580 000

1. Civil partners must have a valid will naming their partner as one of the beneficiaries. In case of intestate succession, the partner does not benefit from spousal treatment.
2. In case of acquisitions *mortis causa*, the threshold may increase by up to EUR 256 000 for spouses and by up to EUR 52 000 for children (depending on age). However, this additional exemption is reduced by the net present value of survivor pensions.
3. It assumes that the child is the only heir. The tax-free threshold is equal to 30 million yen + (6 million yen * number of statutory heirs).
4. It assumes that the child is the only heir and receives the full standard deduction of KRW 500 million. The alternate itemised deduction consists of a basic allowance of KRW 200 million and additional allowances for direct descendants, elderly and minor heirs and heirs with a disability, and a housing allowance.
5. Children are exempt on the inheritance that they would be attributed under intestate laws, defined as a share of the estate, and are taxed above this amount.
6. Co-habiting partners must have lived together for at least five years (six months if they have signed a notarial cohabitation agreement) and must have a valid will naming their partner as one of the beneficiaries. In case of intestate succession, the partner does not benefit from spousal treatment.
7. Inherited pension wealth counts towards the spouse's tax exemption threshold.
8. As many regions apply additional tax-exemption thresholds to donor's children, the tax exemption provided by the central government should be viewed as a lower bound.
9. Civil partners benefit from a small additional tax-free threshold, but this is less favourable than the full exemption available to married couples.

Note: Exemption thresholds are reported in USD 2020. This table assumes that beneficiaries are adult6s and do not have a disability. Data on tax treatment for civil union and cohabitating couples was not available for Hungary. Belgium: refers to the Brussels-Capital Region. Switzerland: refers to the canton of Zurich.

Source: OECD Questionnaire on Inheritance, Estate, and Gift Taxes

The tax treatment of spouses and partners may depend on the type of union (Table 3.5). In most OECD countries, couples are able to choose between marriage, a civil union, and cohabitation, which can determine the applicable inheritance or estate tax treatment. Two countries apply the same tax treatment to all married, civil union, and co-habiting partners, while 13 apply the same tax treatment to married partners and civil partners. Additional criteria may apply to non-married partners; for example, the Netherlands requires co-habiting partners to have lived together for at least five years[8] and France requires civil partners to have a valid will. Six countries only grant special treatment to married couples. Couples under the same type of union benefit from the same tax treatment regardless of sexual orientation, but some countries restrict certain unions to different- or same-sex couples.[9]

The tax exemption thresholds for children are typically among the highest, but the level varies across countries

The tax treatment of direct descendants is among the most favourable; the same as or second only to the spouse in nearly all countries (Figure 3.8, Table 3.5). The donors' children are fully exempt from inheritance taxes in Hungary, Lithuania, Poland, Portugal, Slovenia, and Switzerland (Canton of Zurich) and benefit from the highest tax-free threshold in Belgium, Chile, Greece, Italy, and Spain. In these 11 countries, children receive the same treatment as the donor's spouse. Children benefit from the second highest tax-free thresholds (after the spouse) in Finland, France, Germany, Ireland, Japan, Luxembourg,[10] and the United Kingdom.[11] In Luxembourg the tax-free threshold for children is a share of the donor's estate, so the threshold rises with the donor's wealth. There is an additional threshold for children in Korea[12] and an additional threshold for lineal descendants in the United Kingdom when donors bequeath their residence. The donor's children receive the same exemption as all heirs other than the spouse in Denmark (although children are taxed at lower rates than other heirs) and Japan. Stepchildren are nearly always treated as children for tax purposes. Figure 3.8 shows that, with the exception of Spain and Switzerland, stepchildren receive the same tax treatment as the donor's children in all countries.

Tax exemption thresholds for transfers to children vary widely (Figure 3.9, Figure 3.10). Several countries provide relatively low tax-exemption thresholds for the donor's children, including four countries with thresholds under USD 25 000 (Belgium, Finland, Netherlands, and Spain). At the upper end, however, there are large differences between countries, as tax-free thresholds range from around USD 640 000 (the United Kingdom) to around USD 1.1 million (Italy) and around USD 11.6 million (the United States). Figure 3.10 compares applicable inheritance or estate tax exemption thresholds for children in different countries with the average value of inheritances received across the wealth distribution. The tax-free thresholds in Germany, Greece, Ireland, and Italy are above the average value of inheritances received by heirs across the wealth distribution, while the threshold is above all but the highest quintile of inheritances in France. The relatively low tax-free thresholds in Belgium and Spain are still above the value of the average inheritance for the lowest quintile. These comparisons should be interpreted with caution, however, as the value of inheritances varies within quintiles and factors such as the asset type affect the tax liability. In addition, survey data may underestimate wealth at the top of the wealth distribution (see Chapter 1).

Figure 3.9. Tax exemption thresholds for donor's children, USD

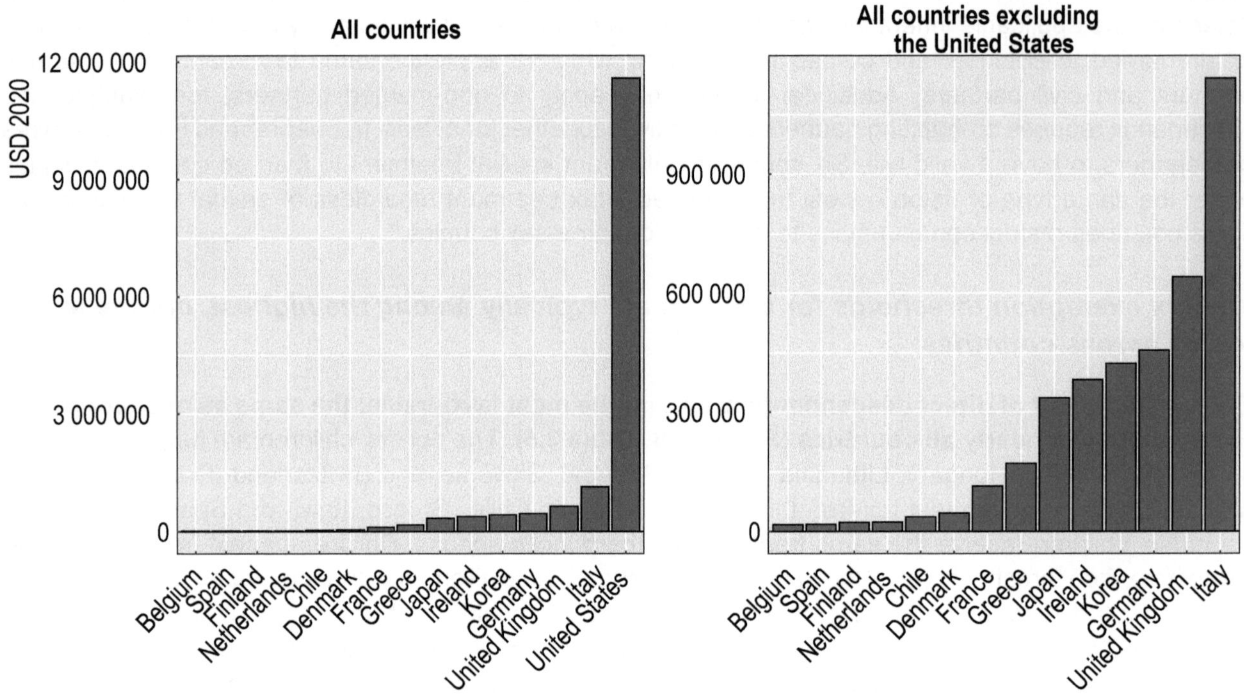

Note: Tax exemption thresholds are reported in USD 2020. Children of the donor are exempt in Hungary, Lithuania, Poland, Portugal, Slovenia, and Switzerland. This figure assumes that beneficiaries are adults and do not have a disability. Belgium: refers to the Brussels-Capital Region. Luxembourg: exemption thresholds depend on the value of the estate; children are exempt on the inheritance that they would be attributed under intestate laws, defined as a share of the estate, and are taxed above this amount. Switzerland: refers to the Canton of Zurich. United Kingdom: assumes that the donor uses the residence nil-rate band, but not the transferable nil-rate band (which applies if the donor's spouse had already passed away and did not made full use of the tax-exemption threshold).
Source: OECD Questionnaire on Inheritance, Estate, and Gift Taxes

StatLink https://stat.link/5nvbq6

Figure 3.10. Tax exemption threshold for donors' children compared to the average value of inheritances received by all heirs in each quintile, select countries

2015 or latest available year

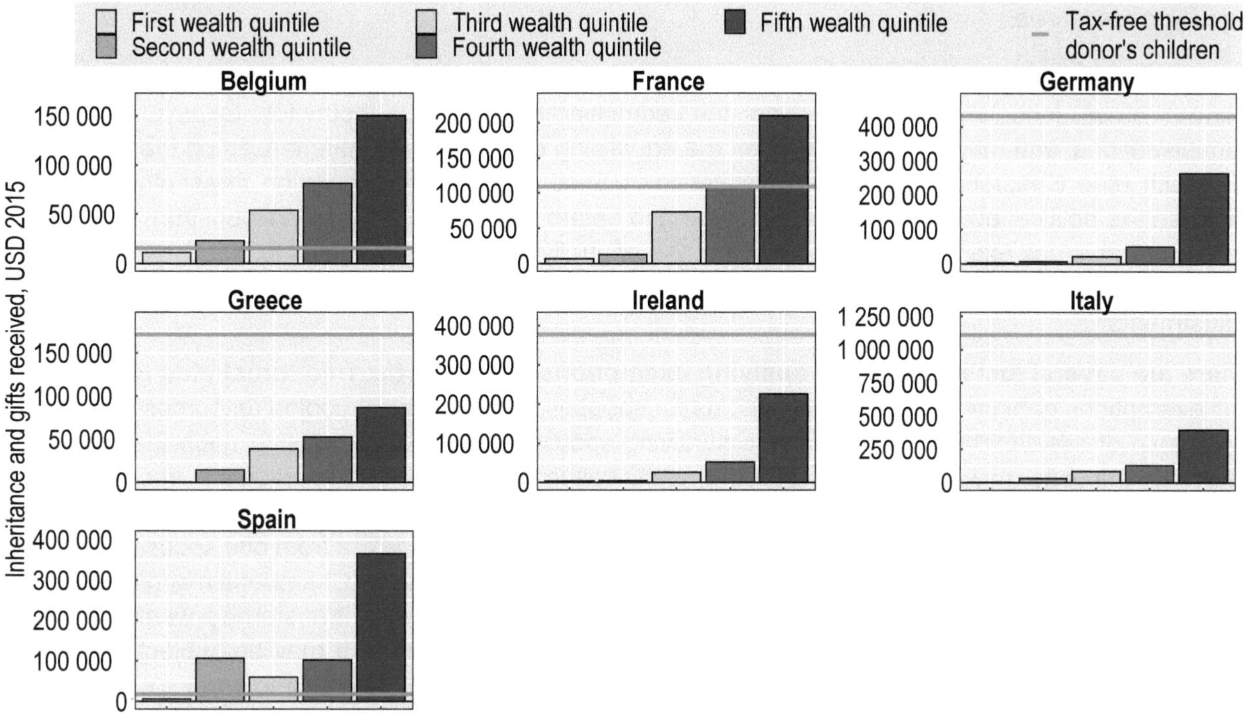

Note: Tax exemption thresholds and inheritances are reported in USD 2015. Children of the donor are exempt in Hungary, Lithuania, Poland, Portugal, Slovenia and Switzerland. Data from the Wealth Distribution Database were not available for Finland and the Netherlands and the remaining countries that levy inheritance or estate taxes were not included in the Wealth Distribution Database. This figure assumes beneficiaries are adults (over 21 years old) and do not have a disability. Belgium: refers to the Brussels-Capital Region. Switzerland: refers to the Canton of Zurich.
Source: OECD Wealth Distribution Database, oe.cd/wealth.

StatLink https://stat.link/p0gstl

3.5.3. Special tax exemption thresholds apply to minor heirs and heirs with a disability in a few countries

Few countries provide special treatment for minor heirs. In Ireland, where a donor's child passes away before the donor but has children themselves, the grandchildren under 21 years of age will receive the same treatment as the donor's children; otherwise, they are treated as grandchildren. In Korea, minors receive an additional deduction per year until they reach 20 years of age, but estates must choose itemised deductions, rather than the standard deduction, to obtain this relief. In Spain, children and grandchildren receive a more favourable tax treatment if they are under 21 years of age. Property left in trust for orphaned minor children in the United Kingdom can qualify for treatment that is slightly more favourable than the standard tax treatment for trusts.

Some countries apply special treatment to heirs who have a disability. In Ireland, gifts and inheritances received by heirs who have a disability are exempt if used for qualifying expenses, which include costs for medical treatment and associated maintenance. In five countries, heirs who have a disability benefit from an additional tax-free threshold (Italy, Korea, Netherlands, Switzerland, and Spain) or a reduction of the tax liability (Greece). The additional allowance in Korea is only available where estates opt for itemised deductions. Above the additional tax-free allowance, beneficiaries with a disability are taxed at usual rates in all countries. One country (Spain) conditions the additional thresholds on the degree of disability.

3.5.4. Tax exemption thresholds should balance the notion of care, with efficiency and equity objectives

Overall, there is a strong case for exempting small inheritances. Tax-free thresholds that effectively exempt small inheritances can reduce the administrative burden, both for taxpayers and tax administrations, and may be equitable given the equalising effect of small inheritances on the distribution of wealth (see Chapters 1 and 2). As discussed in Section 3.14, tax exemption thresholds may also increase the political acceptability of inheritance and estate taxes (Bastani and Waldenström, 2021[5]). In some countries, tax exemption thresholds increase annually. Indexing thresholds to inflation ensures that tax exemption thresholds retain their real value and may lessen political pressure to make large periodic adjustments.

There are several justifications for applying exemptions or higher tax-free thresholds to spouses. Full exemptions or higher exemption thresholds for spouses reflect couples' pooled resources and shared ownership of assets. This may prevent the surviving spouse experiencing hardship upon their spouse's death. Exemptions may also address gender imbalances in asset ownership, particularly in cases where one partner performs non-market work to support their partner's ability to engage in paid work and accumulate wealth and pension rights. Finally, taxing wealth when it transfers from one spouse to another and then to the couple's children may amount to double-taxation (Boadway, Chamberlain and Emmerson, 2010[6]). The risk of inheritance tax avoidance is generally limited when transferring wealth between spouses, as the wealth will eventually pass to the next generation, where it may be subject to taxation (Boadway, Chamberlain and Emmerson, 2010[6]).[13] Couples have a tax incentive to enter a civil union or to marry when more favourable tax treatment applies to these unions than to cohabitation or civil union, respectively. In cases where countries restrict access to civil unions and marriage based on the partners' sexual orientation, this may have significant implications for inheritance and estate tax treatment.

Higher tax-free thresholds for donors' children may be justified, but depending on their level, they might significantly reduce the tax base. A common justification for providing a more generous tax treatment of gifts and bequests to donors' children is based on the notion care, which may be particularly important when children are young, as the inheritance may contribute to living and education expenses. It also makes the tax more acceptable given that taxpayers place great value on passing on wealth to their children. Economically, it may be argued that wealth transfers to children may be less elastic than transfers to more distantly related heirs and could therefore be taxed at higher effective tax rates. However, it is likely that the negative behavioural response of donors in the form of reduced incentives to work and accumulate wealth might be more significant in response to high tax levels on transfers to children than in response to high tax levels on transfers to more distantly related heirs (see Chapter 2). In addition, parents may respond by changing the form of their transfers, for example by increasing in-kind giving. Thus, there might be some justification for higher tax exemption thresholds for transfers to direct descendants. However, if tax exemption thresholds for wealth transfers to children are very high, they may significantly reduce the revenue raising capacity of inheritance and estate taxes and may mean that a significant share of wealth transfers fully escape inheritance or estate taxation (Figure 3.2).

Narrowing tax exemption differentials between close and distant heirs where these differentials are significant may raise efficiency and reduce avoidance. In some cases, lower tax exemption thresholds (often combined with higher tax rates) on transfers to more distant relatives and non-family members may be questionable. These differentials raise a horizontal equity issue, where two individuals receive the same wealth but benefit from vastly different tax exemption thresholds depending on who they receive the wealth from. Applying higher tax rates to more distant family members also distorts donors' choices about how to distribute their wealth, incentivising them to concentrate their wealth transfers among closer family members. Reducing the difference in the tax treatment between closely related and distantly related heirs may encourage donors to spread their wealth among more heirs and thereby reduce concentrations of wealth, as well as improve horizontal equity.

3.6. Statutory tax rates

3.6.1. Tax rates typically depend on the amount of the wealth transfer and the relationship between the donor and the beneficiary

Inheritance and estate tax rates vary substantially across countries, as do the wealth levels to which they apply. Seven countries apply flat inheritance or estate tax rates, while 15 apply progressive rates. Of these 15 countries, all but one apply multiple progressive rate schedules, where, first, the marginal rate rises with the value of the inheritance and second, separate and typically higher tax rate schedules apply to more distant family and non-relatives (Belgium, Chile, Finland, France, Germany, Greece, Japan, Lithuania, Luxembourg, Netherlands, Poland, Slovenia, Spain, and Switzerland). Korea applies one progressive rate schedule to all heirs.

Flat inheritance or estate tax rates range from 4% to 40% (Figure 3.11). The same flat rates apply to all heirs in Ireland (tax rate of 33%), Hungary (18%), Portugal (10%), the United Kingdom (40%), and the United States (40%). Italy and Denmark apply a flat tax rate that depends on the relationship between the donor and the beneficiary: ranging from 4% for the closest family members to 8% for other beneficiaries in Italy, and from 15% to 36.25% in Denmark.

Progressive rates range from 1% (Chile) to 80% (Belgium) (Figure 3.11, Figure 3.12). Nearly all countries with progressive tax rates apply several schedules, depending on the proximity between the donor and the beneficiary. Progressive rates for spouses and children are typically lower and vary less widely across countries than the rates that apply to other family and non-related persons. For example, the minimum rate that applies to children ranges from 1% (Chile and Greece) to 10% (Japan, Korea, and the Netherlands) but the minimum rate that applies to siblings ranges from 1.2% (Chile)[14] to 35% (France). Top marginal rates applying to children range from 10% (Greece) to 55% (Japan), while top marginal rates applying to wealth transfers to siblings range from 14% (Slovenia) to 65% (Belgium).

Within some countries, tax rate schedules vary widely depending on the relationship between donors and beneficiaries. Among countries that apply multiple tax schedules that depend on proximity between the donor and the beneficiary, some exhibit only small differences between the tax rate schedules that apply to groups of beneficiaries (e.g. Chile, Poland, and Slovenia). However, in other countries, tax rates are much higher for wealth transfers beyond close family. In Belgium and Germany, for example, the donor's children benefit from rates as low as 3% (Belgium) and 7% (Germany), but the lowest rate for aunts and uncles is 30% (Germany) and 35% (Belgium).

Top marginal tax rates kick in at relatively low levels of transferred wealth in several countries with progressive tax rates. For instance, Belgium applies six marginal rates to the donor's children, with rates increasing for inheritances up to roughly USD 570 000. Beyond that threshold, inheritances are taxed at the top marginal rate. In contrast, the top marginal rate in Germany applies at around USD 33.3 million for the donor's children. Panel B of Figure 3.11, which shows tax thresholds as a multiple of countries' annual average wage, shows that for children, the threshold for the top marginal rate was lowest in the Netherlands (2.8 times annual average wage), Belgium (10.1), and Finland (22.1). For non-related heirs, the threshold for the top marginal rate was lowest in France (0.04 times annual average wage), Hungary (0.07), and Poland (0.3).

Figure 3.11. Statutory inheritance and estate tax rate schedules for spouse, children, and non-related parties

Panel A: value of inheritances in USD

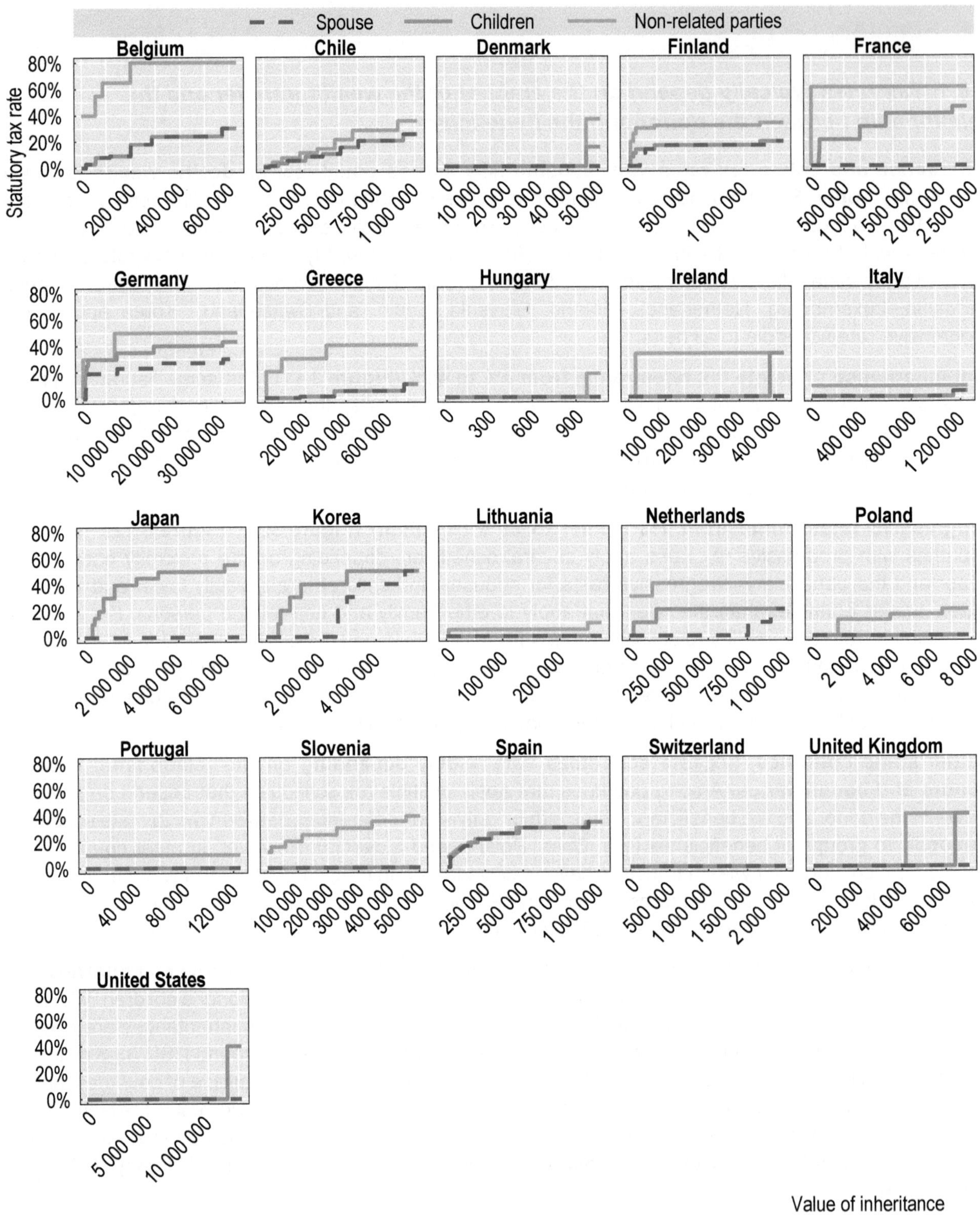

Panel B: value of inheritances as a multiple of the average annual wage

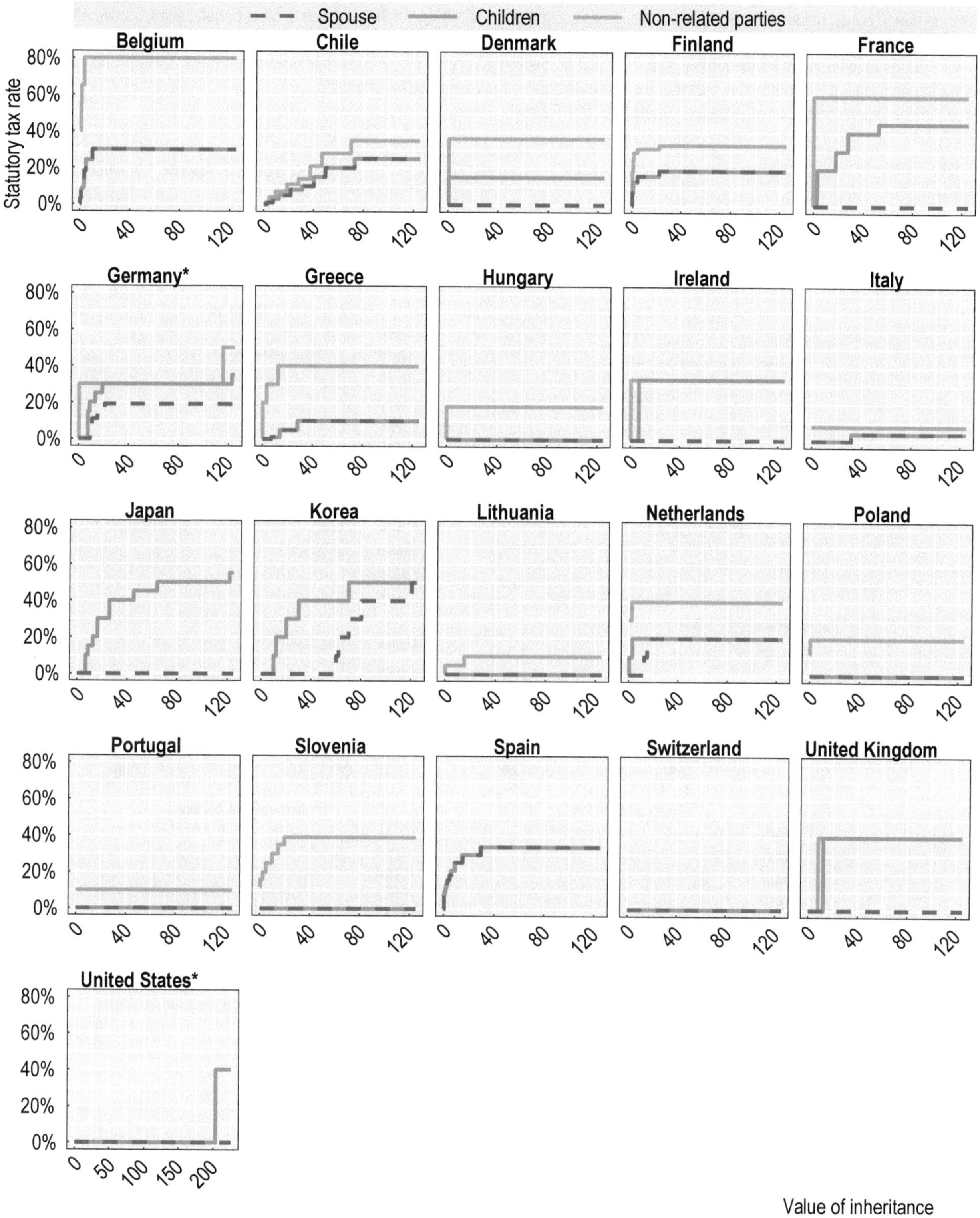

Note: *Germany applies additional rates that are not included in this graph. Spouse: 23% from 129-264 times average wage, 27% from 264-513 times average wage, and 30% above 513 times average wage. Children: 40% from 257-506 times average wage and 43% above 506 times average wage).

* United States: x-axis shows 0-200 times average wage; all other charts show 0-125 times average wage on x-axis.

Tax exemption thresholds are reported in USD 2020. This figure assumes that beneficiaries are adults (over 21 years old) and do not have a disability. Belgium: refers to the Brussels-Capital Region. Chile: a surcharge of 20% on the tax liability applies to 2nd rank relatives (siblings, nieces, nephews, aunts, uncles, cousins, great-aunts, great-uncles) and a surcharge of 40% applies to other beneficiaries. Japan: Assumes that there is only one heir, so the tax-free threshold is USD 337 159 [36 million yen = 30 million yen + (6 million yen * number of statutory heirs)]. Poland: Siblings receive the most favourable treatment and step-siblings receive the 4th most favourable treatment. Switzerland: refers to the canton of Zurich. United Kingdom: Assumes that the taxpayer applies the residence nil-rate band.
Source: OECD Questionnaire on Inheritance, Estate, and Gift Taxes

StatLink https://stat.link/ukzjam

Figure 3.12. Minimum and maximum statutory inheritance and estate tax rates, four groups of beneficiaries

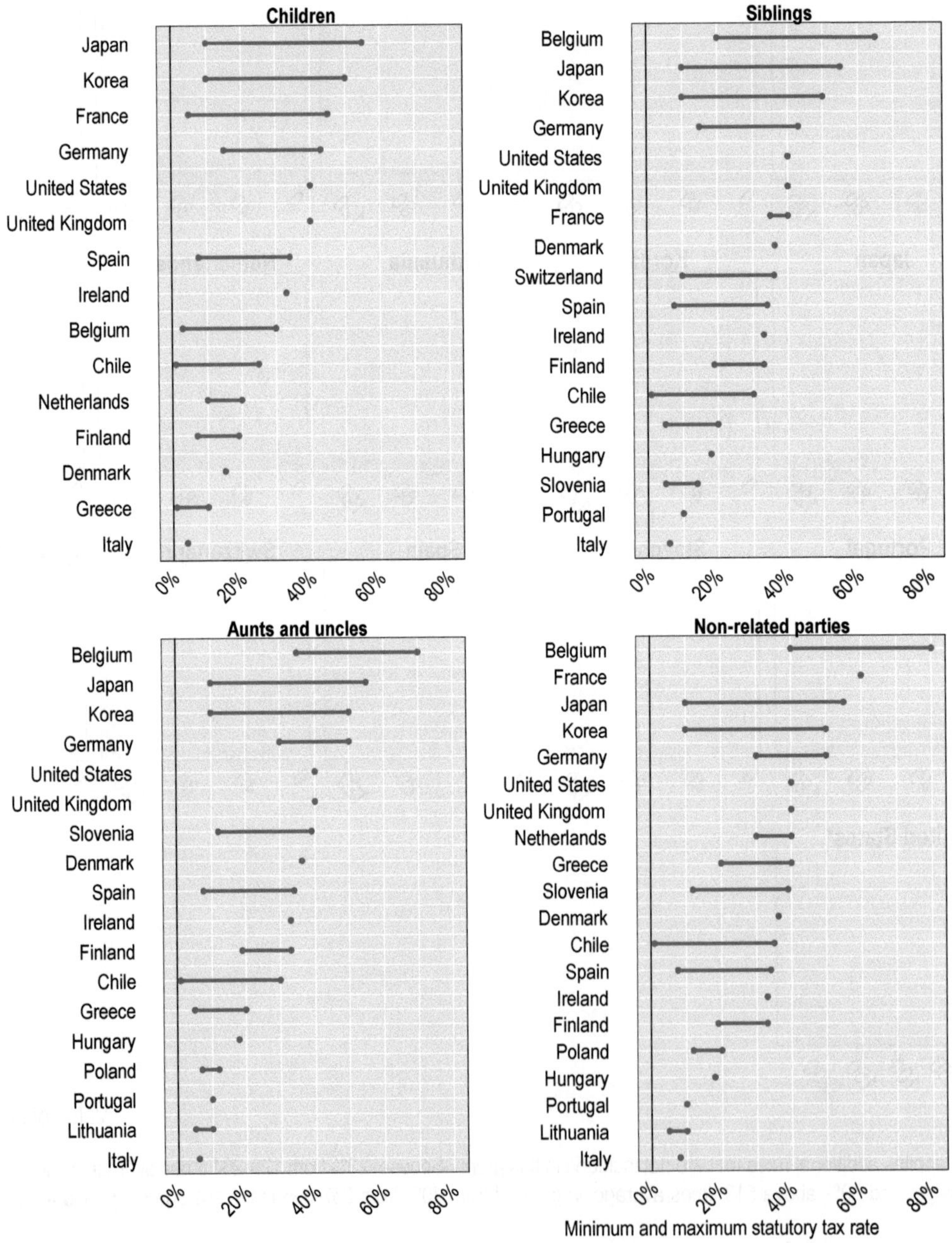

Note: Children are exempt in Hungary, Lithuania, Poland, Portugal, Slovenia, and Switzerland. Siblings are exempt in Lithuania, Poland. Belgium: refers to the Brussels-Capital Region. Lithuania: step-siblings are not exempt from inheritance taxes. Poland: Siblings receive the most favourable treatment and step-siblings receive the 4th most favourable treatment. Switzerland: refers to the Canton of Zurich.
Source: OECD Questionnaire on Inheritance, Estate, and Gift Taxes

StatLink https://stat.link/b3wyqs

Figure 3.13 shows countries with higher top marginal tax rates levy those on higher-value inheritances, while countries with lower top marginal tax rates apply these at lower thresholds. In addition to the tax rate schedules, the thresholds at which tax rates apply is a key determinant of heirs' tax liability and the overall progressivity of the inheritance or estate tax. Figure 3.13 shows that countries with relatively high top marginal tax rates apply these at relatively high levels, while the reverse tends to be true for countries with low top marginal tax rates. For example, for the donor's children, Korea applies a top marginal tax rate of 50% once the inheritance exceeds around USD 3 million, while the Netherlands applies a top marginal tax rate of 20% once the inheritance exceeds around USD 170 000. The relationship between top marginal tax rates and applicable thresholds is particularly strong for the donor's children, but is also visible for the donor's siblings. Among countries that levy flat rates, there is no clear connection between the level of the rate and the level of the threshold; relatively similar tax rates apply in Denmark (36.25%) and the United States (40%), but at very different thresholds (around USD 11.6 million in the United States, compared to around USD 46 000 in Denmark).

Figure 3.13. Maximum statutory inheritance and estate tax rates and applicable threshold (USD), donor's children and siblings

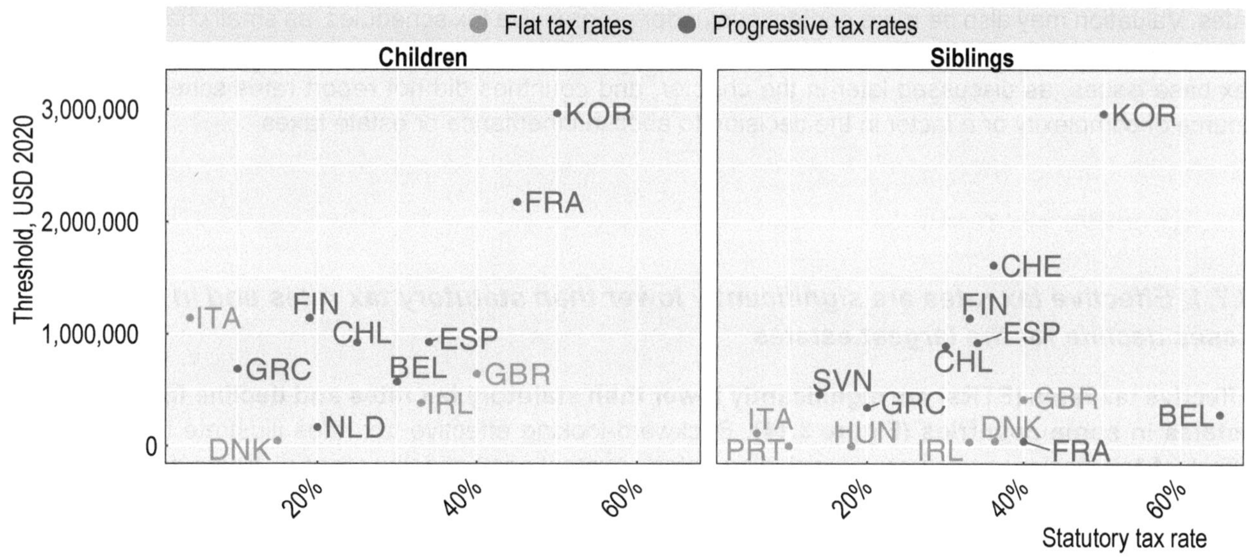

Note: Tax exemption thresholds are reported in USD 2020. The category "siblings" includes step-siblings. Three points have been removed for readability: Germany (43% applying at USD 30 153 991 [children] or USD 29 719 956 [siblings]), Japan (55% applying at USD 5 956 474 [children and siblings]), and the United States (40% applying at USD 11 580 000 [children and siblings]). Children are exempt in Hungary, Lithuania, Poland, Portugal, Slovenia, and Switzerland. Siblings are exempt in Lithuania, Poland. Belgium: refers to the Brussels-Capital Region. Lithuania: step-siblings are not exempt from inheritance taxes. Poland: Siblings receive the most favourable treatment and step-siblings receive the 4th most favourable treatment. Switzerland: refers to the canton of Zurich.
Source: OECD Questionnaire on Inheritance, Estate, and Gift Taxes

StatLink https://stat.link/3dl9bf

3.6.2. Progressive tax rates have several advantages compared to flat tax rates

Progressive inheritance or estate tax rates enhance vertical equity effects. Progressive rates increase vertical equity by ensuring that those who receive more wealth pay more tax. Illustrative simulations in Chapter 2 showed that where countries have a preference to prevent the build-up of excessive wealth over generations, progressive inheritance taxes and taxes on personal capital income can be powerful tools. Moreover, unlike flat rates, progressive rates can encourage donors to distribute their wealth among more heirs in order to avoid top marginal rates. As discussed, top marginal tax rates kick in at relatively low levels of transferred wealth in several countries with progressive rates. Where this is the case, applying higher tax rates to very high-value inheritances could improve the progressivity of inheritance and estate taxes. This requires finding a balance so that tax rate levels are not excessively high, as high tax rates strengthen the case for tax reliefs and may induce greater avoidance and evasion behaviours.

Progressive tax rate schedules may help avoid significant increases in marginal effective tax rates. If tax rates increase gradually with the value of the inheritance received, progressive rate schedules may avoid large increases in marginal tax rates. As flat inheritance and estate tax rates are typically high in OECD countries, they often result in high marginal tax rates above tax-free thresholds (Figure 3.11). For example, while Italy levies flat rates that vary between 4% and 8% (depending on the beneficiary), Denmark (depending on the beneficiary), Ireland, the United Kingdom and the United States all levy flat rates above 30%.

It is unclear whether progressive tax rates are more complex to administer. Progressive tax rates may be more complex to administer than flat rates, as taxpayers need to be attentive to multiple rates and thresholds. In addition, taxpayers may engage in greater avoidance behaviour to avoid higher marginal rates. Valuation may also be more contentious under progressive tax schedules, as small changes in value could push taxpayers into a higher marginal tax bracket. However, complexity generally stems more from tax base issues, as discussed later in the chapter, and countries did not report rates schedules to be a source of complexity or a factor in the decision to abolish inheritance or estate taxes.

3.7. Effective tax rates

3.7.1. Effective tax rates are significantly lower than statutory tax rates and in some cases decline for the largest estates

Effective tax rates (ETRs) are significantly lower than statutory tax rates and decline for the largest estates in some countries (Figure 3.14). Backward-looking effective tax rates illustrate the combined effect of tax design measures – including rates, exemptions, and the special treatment for certain assets – on taxpayers' effective tax burdens.[15] Figure 3.14 shows ETRs for five countries for which data were available. Care should be taken when comparing between countries, as these indicators were provided by participating countries and partly reflect differences in methodology. Several broad insights arise from these indicators. The tax burden tends to be lower at the bottom end of the wealth distribution and higher at the upper end of the distribution. However, in some countries, for donors in the lowest wealth grouping, the ETR is higher than the ETR for donors in the lower middle or middle of the wealth distribution. This may in part reflect the fact that poorer households tend to hold assets that do not benefit from special treatment. The figures also show that the tax rates faced by the wealthiest donors exhibit different patterns across countries. In Chile, the ETR at the top of the wealth distribution is far above even the ETR of the ninth wealth decile. In contrast, the ETRs of the wealthiest donors in the United Kingdom and the United States are below those of other wealthy donors. For example, the ETR on an estate owning GBP 8-9 million was twice as high as the ETR for estates owning GBP 10 million or more (19.5% versus 10.0%).

This is in part due to a greater share of their estate being covered by a tax relief such as agricultural or business property relief (Office of Tax Simplification, 2018[7]).

Figure 3.14. Effective tax rates across wealth groups or estate values, select countries

2019 or most recent year

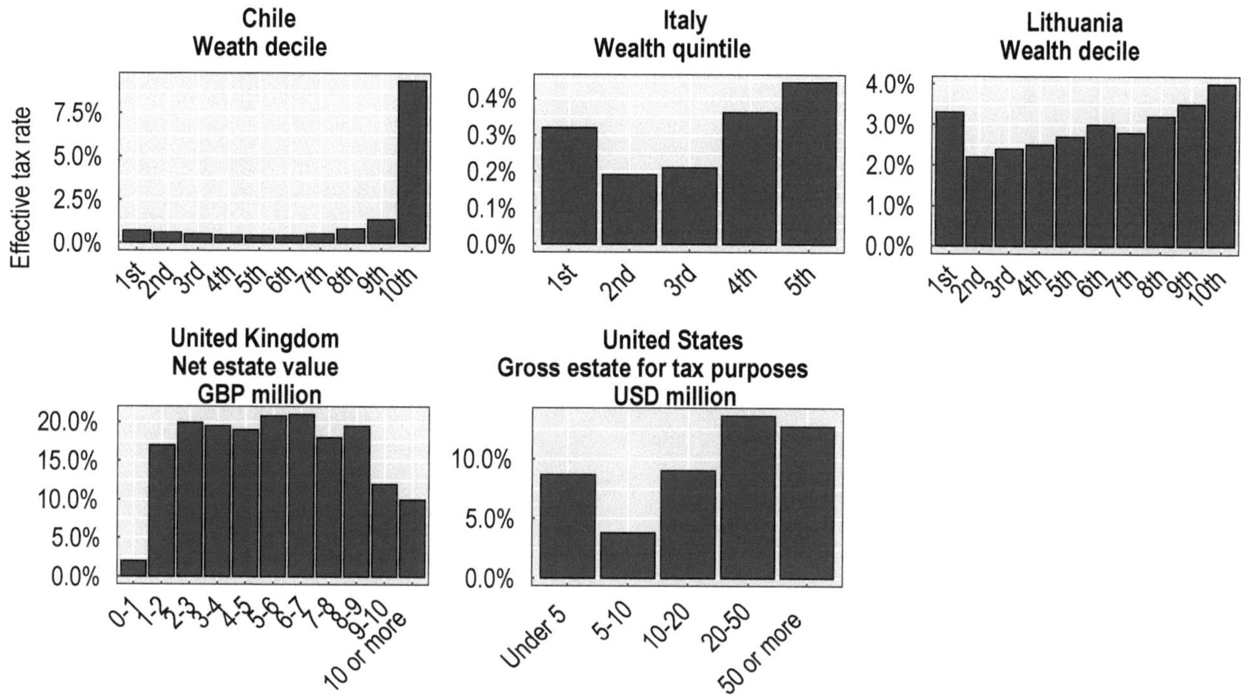

Note: United States: data are based on 2018 federal estate tax returns, which in most cases were filed for deaths occurring in 2017, as tax returned are submitted the year after the donor's death. In 2017, the filing threshold was USD 5.49 million of gross estate and from 2018, the filing threshold was USD 11.18 million.

Source: OECD Questionnaire on Inheritance, Estate, and Gift Taxes. Data for Italy are published in (Acciari and Morelli, 2020[8]).

StatLink https://stat.link/jnx1fm

Reforms to inheritance and estate taxes in recent decades suggest that ETRs may have declined over time, but further research is needed to explore long-term trends. Figure 3.15 shows the exemption threshold and the top marginal tax rate for children in six countries in two periods: 1980 and 2020 (or closest available year) (data drawn from (Nolan et al., 2020[2]) Four of the six countries shown in Figure 3.15 lowered their top marginal tax rates and increased their tax exemption thresholds over the last 30-40 years (Germany, Ireland, Italy, and the United Kingdom). Unlike other countries, France increased both the exemption threshold and the top marginal tax rate, while there was little change in Spain over the period. However, there have been many changes at the regional level in Spain, as regional governments have substantial autonomy over inheritance tax design. Information provided by countries in response to the questionnaire also confirms the trend in recent years to raise tax exemption thresholds. For example, in 2007, Poland introduced full exemptions for immediate family members and in 2018, the United States doubled the estate tax exemption threshold. These trends are suggestive of a decline in ETRs on wealth transfers over time. This may explain in part why inheritance, estate, and gift tax revenues have largely remained stable despite increases in the volume of wealth transfers in some countries (see Section 1.5). However, ETRs may not have declined if other measures were taken to compensate for the changes, including base broadening measures. Further research would be needed to understand how ETRs have evolved over time.

Figure 3.15. Changes in top marginal tax rates and tax exemption thresholds, donor's children, 1980-2020, select countries

Earliest year to latest year of data availability

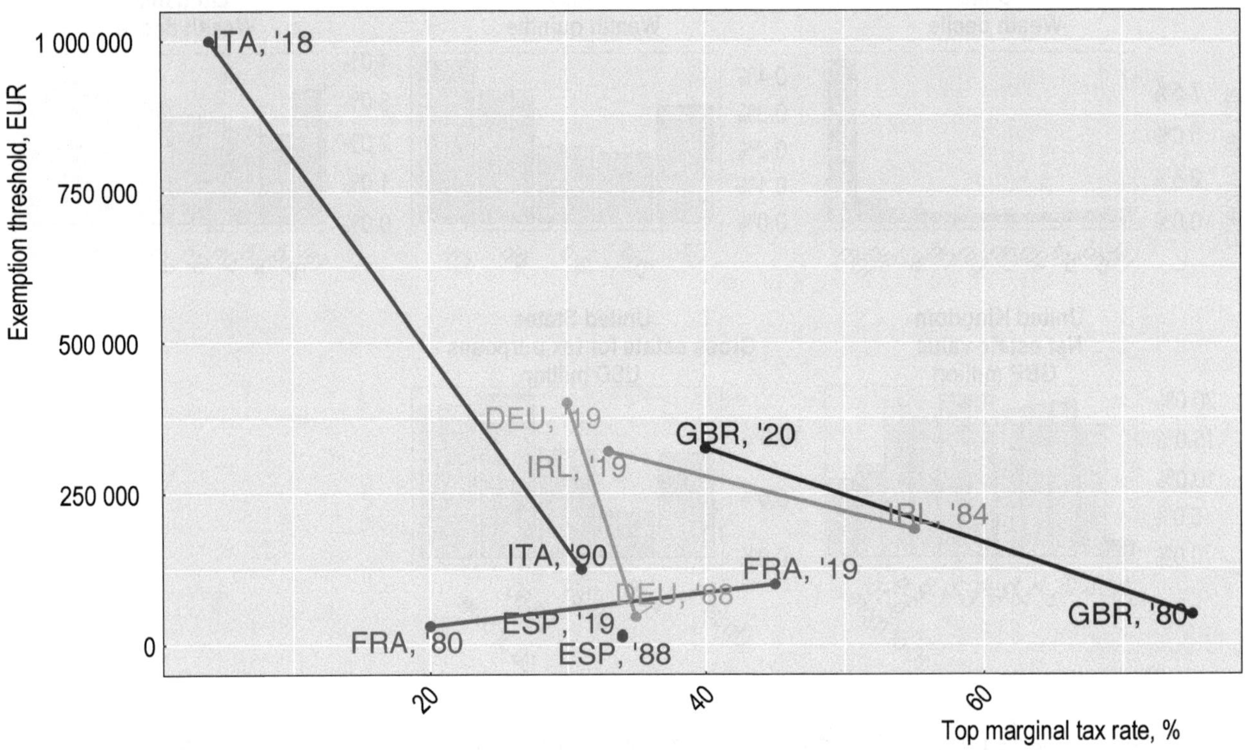

Source: OECD Revenue Statistics (2020), Nolan, B., J. Palomino, P. Van Kerm and S. Morelli (2020), 'The Wealth of Families: The Intergenerational Transmission of Wealth in Britain in Comparative Perspective', Nuffield Foundation, Oxford.

StatLink https://stat.link/aynvdm

3.8. Tax treatment of specific assets

3.8.1. A number of assets benefit from preferential tax treatment

Some asset classes benefit from exemptions or tax treatment that is more preferential than standard treatment under inheritance or estate taxes. Figure 3.16 sets out whether countries include asset classes in the tax base and whether preferential taxation is conditionally available for some heirs. In all countries, financial assets such as bank deposits, equities, and bonds are included in the inheritance or estate tax base and are subject to standard tax treatment. Standard tax treatment also applies in most countries to vehicles (all countries except Italy), jewellery (all countries except Portugal), and some types of residential property (all countries except Switzerland). Some assets benefit from preferential treatment in several countries, including family-owned businesses (16 countries) and main residences (12 countries). Full exemptions apply most commonly to private pensions (eight countries) and life or accidental death insurance (six countries). Land or immovable property used for agriculture or forestry is exempt or taxed preferentially in ten countries. Of the 14 asset classes in Figure 3.16, tax-exempt assets are most numerous in Portugal (four asset classes) and in Germany, Poland, and the United Kingdom (three asset classes each). Preferentially taxed assets are most numerous in Japan, Poland, and Switzerland (six asset classes each). In contrast, the broadest tax bases are found in Lithuania (13 asset classes are taxed) and in Belgium, Chile, Denmark, Greece, Luxembourg, the Netherlands, and the United States (12 asset classes).

Figure 3.16. Tax base for estate and inheritance taxes

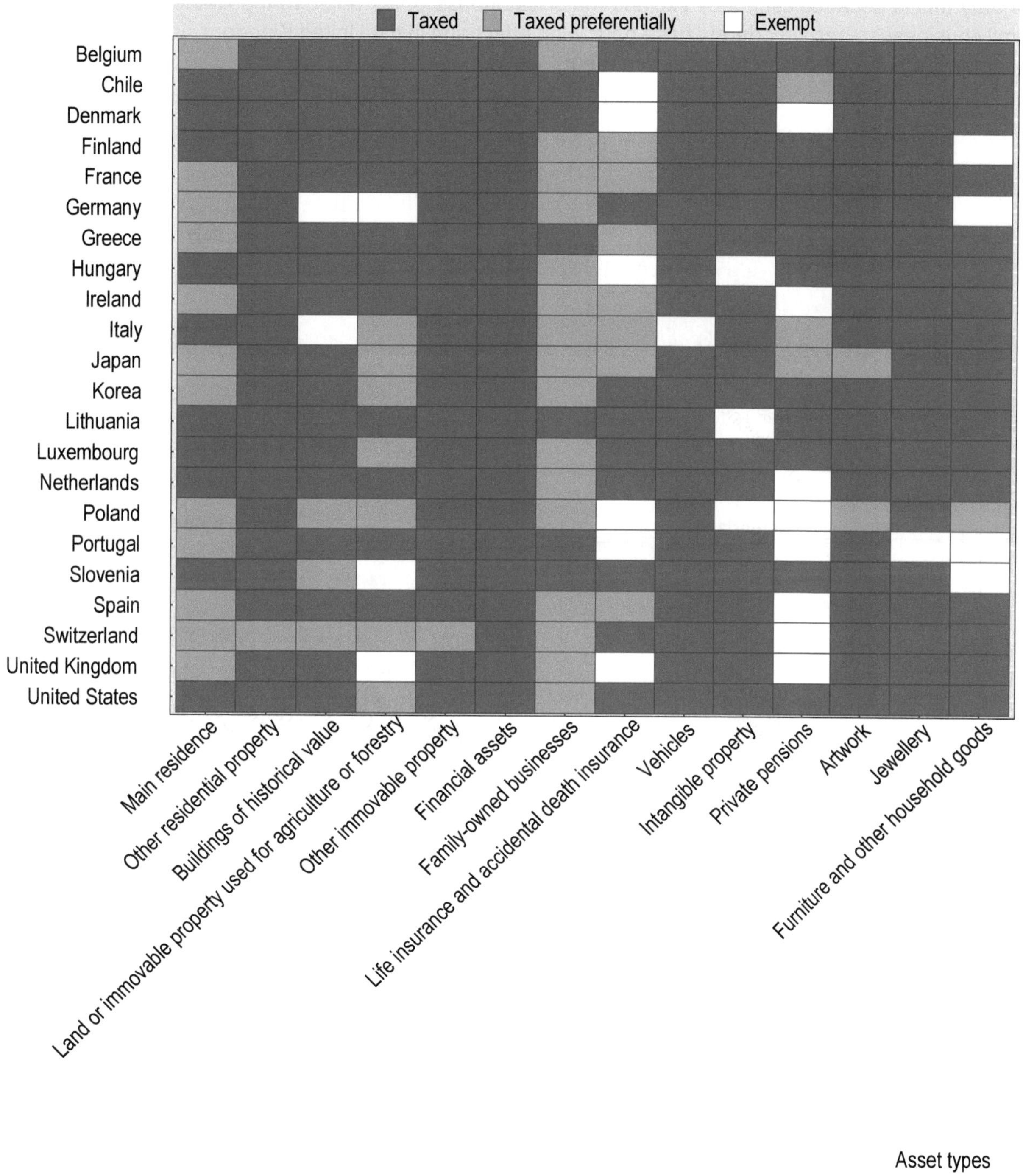

Note: 'Taxed' means assets are included in the tax base; 'Taxed Preferentially' means special treatment is available for some heirs under specified conditions and includes conditional exemptions, and 'Exempt' means assets are not included in the tax base.
Source: OECD Wealth Distribution Database, oe.cd/wealth.

StatLink https://stat.link/ybrqnu

While preferential tax treatment for some asset classes may be justified for equity or efficiency reasons, as discussed below, they substantially narrow the tax base and reduce potential revenues. Figure 3.17 illustrates the fiscal cost of certain tax reliefs in select countries, according to data availability. Care should be taken when comparing between countries, as these indicators were provided by participating countries and partially reflect differences in methodology and benchmark for what constitutes a tax expenditure. Tax reliefs do not substantially erode revenues in Belgium and Italy, though for Italy this is because estimates exclude major categories of tax relief. In the Netherlands, tax relief for family businesses has a moderate base narrowing effect and in the United Kingdom close to half of taxable inheritances benefit from preferential treatment.

Figure 3.17. Tax revenue foregone as a share of total inheritance transfers, select countries

2019 or latest available year

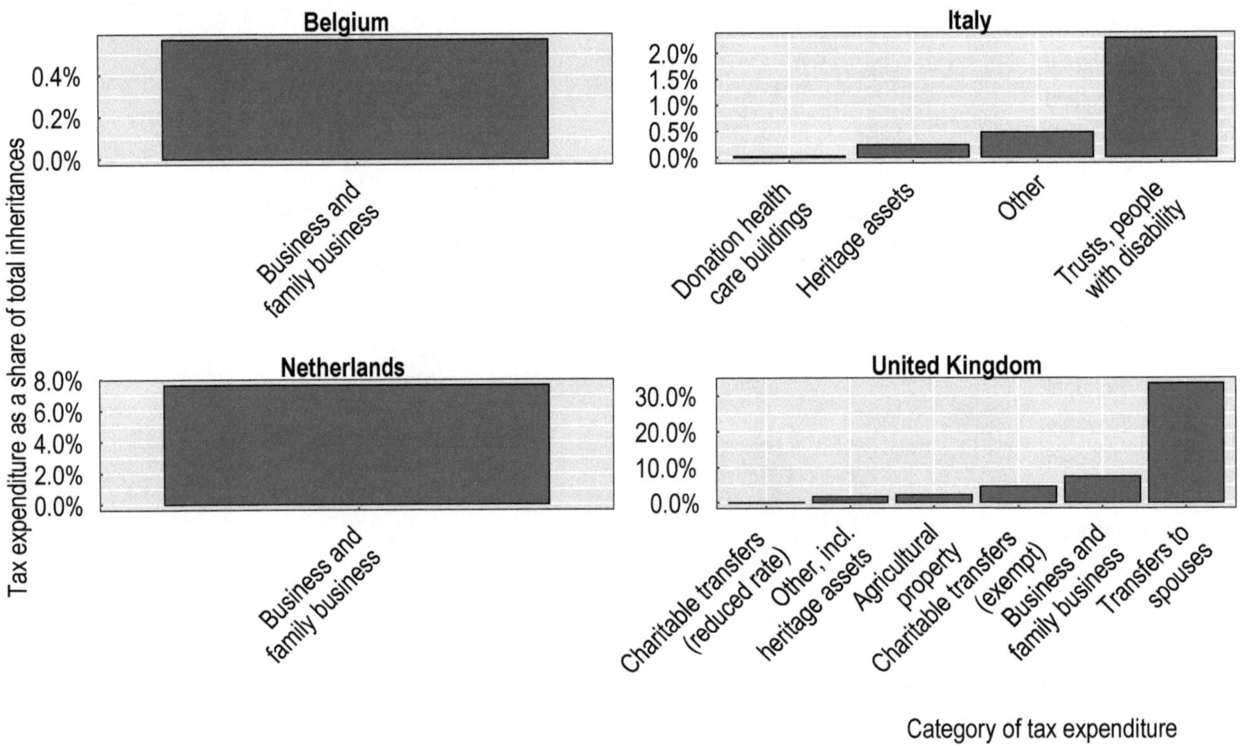

Note: Belgium: refers to the Brussels-Capital Region. Italy: no revenue foregone estimations are available for important exemptions (considered as part of the benchmark), such as the exemption for assets such as family businesses and control shares (if the business is carried on by the heirs), national and extra national government bonds, private pensions and life insurance plans, cars and other registered vehicles. For certain items, foregone revenue also refers to other taxes like stamp duties, registration tax or cadastral tax. United Kingdom: the denominator is the total value of inheritance transfers for estates above the nil-rate band.
Source: OECD Questionnaire on Inheritance, Estate, and Gift Taxes, 2020.

StatLink https://stat.link/8jieh9

3.8.2. Donors' main residence may benefit from special tax treatment

The main residence benefits from preferential treatment in twelve countries, but most apply conditions (Table 3.6). The main residence is fully or partially exempt in 11 countries and is valued at below-market values in one country. Two countries also apply lower than standard rates to housing; in

Belgium this is for specified heirs other than the spouse and in Portugal this is above the partial exemption. Most countries apply conditions, which include requiring the beneficiary to have lived with the donor prior to, at the time of, or following the donor's death. A minority of countries require that beneficiaries did not own other housing. Exemptions are only available for close family in most countries. Some countries relax conditions for beneficiaries aged over 65; Spain does not require older beneficiaries to be close relatives and Ireland does not require older beneficiaries to remain in the house following the donor's death. The value of preferential treatment for the main residence is uncapped in nine countries and is capped by size or by value in three countries. Countries may implicitly apply preferential tax treatment to housing if valuation methods generate below-market value estimates. This is discussed in section 3.10.

Table 3.6. Conditions for preferential treatment of the main residence

Countries	Preferential treatment	Beneficiary lives in the house before / after donor's death	Not own other housing	Beneficiaries
Belgium	Exempt	At time of death	..	Spouse
	Lower tax rates	..	..	Co-owners that are lineal heirs or cohabitants
France	Partial exemption (20%)	At time of death		Spouse, children
Germany	Full exemption	10 years after		Spouse, children
Greece	Additional tax-free threshold	..	Yes	Spouse, children
Ireland	Full exemption	3 years before & 6 years after	Yes	All beneficiaries
Japan	Partial exemption (80%)	..	..	All beneficiaries
Korea	Full exemption, capped at KRW 600 million	10 years before	Yes	Children, lineal descendants
Poland[1]	Full exemption, capped at 110 m^2	5 years after	Yes	Extended family, carers[2]
Portugal	Partial exemption, then lower tax rates	..	..	All beneficiaries
Spain	Partial exemption (95%), capped at EUR 122 606	10 years after	..	Spouse, ascendants, descendants
Switzerland	Valued slightly below market value	..	..	All beneficiaries
United Kingdom	Partial exemption	..	..	Lineal descendants

1. Refers to all residential property, not just the donor's main residence.
2. Non-related persons who have taken care of the donor for at least two years, where a written and signed agreement has been attested by a notary, receive an exemption on inherited residential property.
Source: OECD Questionnaire on Inheritance, Estate, and Gift Taxes, 2020

Special treatment for beneficiaries that continue to live in the main residence may reduce distortions and hardship but could create lock-in effects. Beneficiaries may face liquidity problems when the main residence is subject to inheritance or estate taxes and may be forced to sell the residence if they have not inherited other assets that they could use to pay the tax. Forced sale could result in hardship, as housing provides an essential service to households, and may require heirs to incur other costs, such as transaction taxes to purchase another residence. However, lock-in effects may arise where the favourable treatment is conditional on continuing to live in the residence. This creates problems when heirs could relocate to access family support, more appropriate housing or better labour market opportunities.

Countries may consider alternate preferential treatment for the main residence, which may address liquidity issues while reducing tax avoidance. Wealth held in housing is illiquid, raising the possibility that it would need to be sold to pay inheritance or estate taxes. Wealth held in real estate is more equally distributed among the population than other assets (Chapter 1), so levying inheritance and estate taxes on the main residence may be less effective for breaking up wealth concentrations. Favourable treatment of the main residence may create avoidance opportunities, where households maximise the wealth they hold in the main residence or, depending on the rules regarding debt deductibility, borrow against assets that are subject to inheritance and estate taxes in order to invest in the tax-exempt main residence. Countries may reduce avoidance by capping the value of preferential treatment for the main residence and restricting the deductibility of debt for tax-exempt assets. As an alternative, countries may consider applying a standard deferral period for tax on the main residence, followed by payment of inheritance or estate taxes by instalments over a number of years. This would minimise avoidance opportunities, while addressing liquidity issues and allowing taxpayers the flexibility to sell the residence if they need to relocate.

3.8.3. Family businesses benefit from generous concessions

Most countries apply preferential treatment to business assets to support family business successions and allow businesses to survive after the death of their founders (Table 3.7). The preferential tax treatment of business assets may include exemptions or reductions in the taxable value of transferred assets, as well as special valuation rules and lower tax rates. As discussed below, countries may apply conditions, including to ownership share, the location of business assets within the country or economic zone, or the continuation of the business by heirs. Countries may explicitly target preferential treatment of business assets to family businesses or implicitly target family businesses through, for example, requirements for the heirs to continue management of the business. Countries may instead apply special treatment to a broad range of businesses, including all small and medium enterprises (SMEs).

Full or partial exemption of business assets are the most common type of preferential treatment, while lower tax rates, preferential valuation rules and deferrals may also apply (Table 3.7). In the ten countries that provide an exemption for business assets, these may be fully exempt in five countries and partially exempt in seven. One country (Germany) allows businesses to choose between a full or partial exemption, with more conditions applying to businesses claiming a full exemption. One country (the Netherlands) provides an additional tax-free threshold for business assets, in addition to a partial exemption. Businesses in several countries are valued at below-market levels for tax purposes and in one country (Belgium) are taxed at lower rates. A few countries may grant extensions for the tax payment or the option to pay by instalments, and interest may or may not apply. One country (Germany) allows heirs receiving privileged business assets apply for tax abatement if they are not capable of paying the inheritance and gift tax. Tax relief for businesses is typically uncapped.

To be eligible for preferential treatment, countries typically set a range of conditions, including a minimum duration and share of ownership of the business (Table 3.7). In order to ensure that preferential treatment of businesses genuinely supports business continuity, some countries require donors to have owned the business for a minimum period and/or to have owned a minimum share of the business. As with other assets, close family members may benefit from the most favourable treatment.

Heirs may be required to maintain ownership for a specified time (Table 3.7). Following the donor's death, beneficiaries are required to maintain ownership of the business or shares in the business for a defined number of years. Some countries apply further conditions on beneficiaries to receive preferential treatment. In addition to maintaining ownership, businesses must also maintain a share of the wage bill, the number of employees, and/or the assets invested in the company. Several countries require beneficiaries to run the business, which may constitute carrying out paid work and/or being a member of the managerial team.

Some countries require the business or management to be located in the country or, for European countries, in the European Economic Area (Table 3.7). Businesses must be located or headquartered in the country or – in some European countries – located or headquartered in the European Union or the European Economic Area.

Certain types of businesses are excluded from preferential treatment and some countries restrict eligibility for preferential treatment to Small and Medium Enterprises (SMEs) (Table 3.7). Only small businesses or SMEs are eligible for preferential treatment in a few countries, while one country (United Kingdom) applies different treatment to unlisted companies than to listed companies. Businesses must carry out approved activities, including real economic activity, to qualify for preferential treatment in most countries with preferential treatment of business assets.

Some countries apply preferential treatment to agricultural and forestry property, in addition to preferential tax treatment for businesses. Preferential tax treatment for businesses explicitly excludes agriculture in Switzerland and forestry in Finland. However, privately-owned agricultural land and farms may be fully (Germany, Italy, Poland, and the United Kingdom[16]) or partially (France and Ireland) exempt from inheritance and estate taxes. In Luxembourg, agricultural land benefits from generous valuation rules and in Japan, tax deferrals are available for agricultural and forestry properties. Countries impose conditions on this tax treatment, restricting the exemption to professional farmers (Ireland), young farmers that are close relatives of the donor (Italy), or to farms of a specific size (Poland), and specifying minimum holding periods after inheriting the farm (Italy). Forestry is also exempt from inheritance and estate taxes when inherited by close relatives (Italy). In the United States, privately held land that is protected by a qualified conservation easement, which restricts the use of the land for reasons such as protecting wildlife and forestry, is partly exempt up to a cap.

Clawback provisions may apply where taxpayers do not respect the conditions, but most countries do not apply penalties. If certain conditions are not met, preferential treatment is reduced or withdrawn in Belgium, Finland, Germany, Ireland, Italy, Japan, Korea, the Netherlands, Poland, Spain, Switzerland, and the United States. Interest is charged on the tax in Italy and Spain. Italy and Finland are the only countries to apply penalties when the conditions for preferential treatment for businesses are not met.

Table 3.7. Non-exhaustive summary of inheritance or estate tax preferential treatment of business assets and applicable conditions

	Preferential treatment type		Conditions			
	Exemption or tax-free threshold	Other	Minimum time of ownership	Businesses types excluded	Heir involved in business	Other
Belgium		Reduced tax rates[1]	3 years (heir)	Investment		Local management; maintain capital; rate depends on beneficiary type
Finland		Preferential valuation (40% of tax value); 10-year interest-free deferral	5 years (heir)	Forestry, real estate	Management	Minimum ownership 10%
France	75%		4 years (heir)	All firms except industrial, commercial, craft, agricultural or liberal activity	Management	Signed commitment to conserve shares[2]
Germany	85% or 100%[3]	Abatement assets over EUR 26 million	5 to 7 years (heir)			Local management; maintain wage bill[4], minimum ownership 25%
Hungary	25% capped at HUF 2.5 million					Small business only

Ireland	90%		2 years (donor)[5] 6 years (heir)[6]	Finance, real estate, investments		Minimum ownership 25%[7]
Italy	100%		5 years (heir)			Specified heirs[8]
Japan		Payment deferral	5 years (heir)[9]	Asset holding or management	Management, receive salary, majority vote[10]	Local management; maintain employees; SMEs only
Korea	100%, capped at KRW 20 to 50 billion[11]	Taxable value capped at KRW 1.5 billion (agriculture)[12]	10 years (donor) 5 to 7 years (heir)[13]	Finance, insurance, real estate (excl. housing rental management)	Employed	Maintain 80% ownership; maintain employees and wage bill; resident taxpayers only; SMEs only
Luxembourg		Preferential valuation		Non-agriculture		
Netherlands	Partial exemption (83%) above additional tax-free threshold (EUR 1 million)		1 year (donor) 5 years (heir)	Investments		
Poland	100%		2 to 5 years (heir)[14]	All firms except unincorporated businesses and agricultural activity		Between 11 and 300 hectares for agricultural land
Spain	95%		10 years (heir)		Management, receive salary	Carry out economic activity; exempt from wealth tax; minimum ownership share 5% individually or 20% family
Switzerland		Preferential valuation, 80% reduction of tax liability	10 years (heir)	Agriculture	Management, self-employed	Local management, minimum ownership 51%
United Kingdom	50% or 100%	Pay by instalments over 10 years interest-free	2 years (donor)	Investments, real estate, securities		Exemption for listed company (50%) or for privately-held or unlisted company (100%)
United States		Preferential valuation, capped at USD1.18 million	5 years (donor) 10 years (heir)			Business is minimum share of donor's estate; specified heirs

1. One set of preferential rates apply to the spouse and lineal descendants and another, higher set of preferential rates apply to other heirs.
2. A collective commitment to conservation has to be signed on at least 10% of the shares for a listed company and 17% of the shares for a non-listed company. One of the heirs or associates of the collective commitment to conservation is required to assume management of the firm for at least three years.
3. Taxpayers may choose between the two exemptions. Heir should maintain the business for 5 years for 85% exemption and for 7 years for the 100% exemption. If the heir chooses the 85% exemption and the remaining tax base does not exceed EUR 150 000, it is also tax exempt. This tax-exempt amount is reduced by half of the amount that exceeds it. That is, starting with an asset value of EUR 450 000 the exemption is reduced to zero.
4. The share of the wage bill to maintain depends on the number of employees and whether the heirs opt for the 85% or 100% exemption.
5. This condition may be partially met if the property was owned by either the spouse or civil partner or a trustee.
6. If the property is sold within six years and replaced within one year, relief may not be withdrawn.
7. This applies to unquoted shares only and may be reduced to 10% if the heir has worked for the company full-time for 5 years preceding the inheritance.
8. Spouse and direct descendants.
9. After 5 years, heirs must continue holding the shares and receiving an income.
10. Heirs and related persons in the family must take the majority of the voting rights of the company and the heir must have the largest number of voting rights among the family.

11. The tax exemption depends on the time the donor has operated the business; KRW 20 billion for 10-20 years, KRW 30 billion for 20-30 years, and KRW 50 billion for 30+ years.
12. Agriculture businesses may either benefit from exemption or capped value. Only the ongoing ownership (5 years) condition applies to agricultural businesses.
13. Heirs must maintain agricultural activities for 5 years or other business activities for 7 years.
14. Heirs must maintain business activities for 2 years or agricultural activities for 5 years.
Note: Countries may apply different treatment to different taxpayers depending on their characteristics. As such, not all preferential treatment will apply to all business assets; similarly, not all conditions will apply to all taxpayers.
Source: OECD Questionnaire on Inheritance, Estate, and Gift Taxes 2020

While providing some relief for business assets may be justified, such provisions pose a number of issues. In addition to reducing revenue, concessionary treatment for businesses may be regressive, as ownership of business assets is concentrated among the wealthiest households. Recent studies in Germany and the United Kingdom show that relief for business and agricultural assets predominantly benefit the wealthiest households, significantly reducing the effective tax burden on some of the largest estates (Office of Tax Simplification, 2018[7]; Dao, 2019[9]). Figure 3.18 shows that in the United Kingdom the amount of revenue forgone from business asset relief can be substantial and that the majority of the benefit accrues to the wealthiest estates. Without adequate eligibility requirements, preferential treatment for business assets may also create significant avoidance opportunities, where taxpayers may use business structures to obtain preferential treatment. Finally, the macroeconomic benefit of relief for family-business assets is unclear. Liquidity risks tend to be confined to a small number of businesses, and evidence shows that heirs who inherit a business tend to perform less well than their parents (see Chapter 2).

Figure 3.18. Value of preferential tax treatment in the United Kingdom

2019 or latest available year

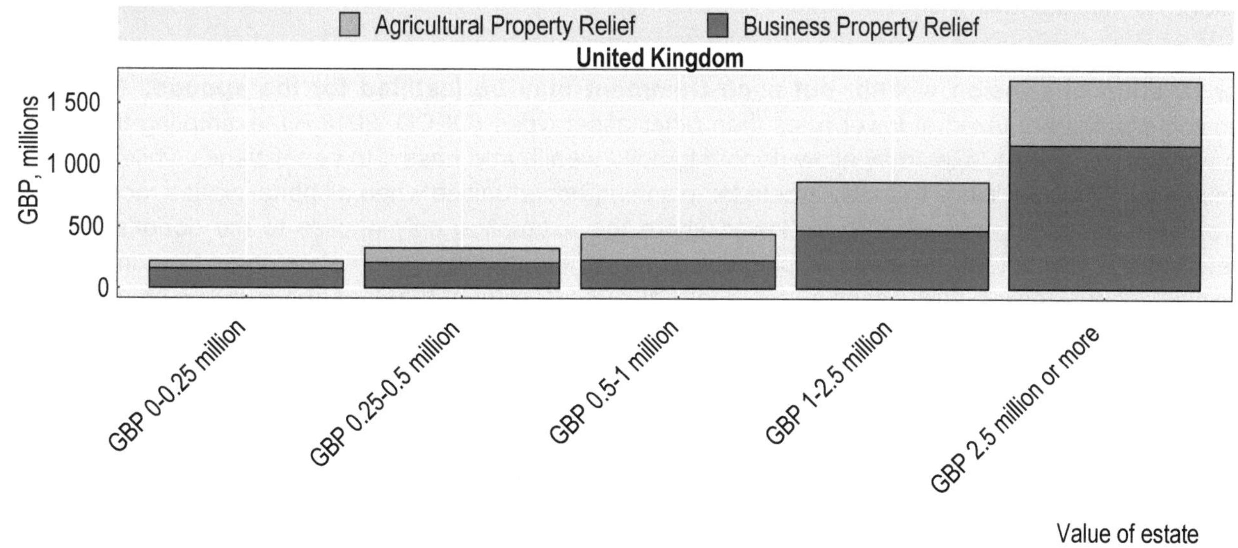

Source: OECD Questionnaire on Inheritance, Estate, and Gift Taxes

StatLink https://stat.link/ubthzv

Overall, exemptions or reliefs for business assets should be carefully designed and alternative policy options could be considered. At a minimum, if exemptions or reliefs are provided for business assets, there should be strict eligibility requirements (e.g. minimum ownership, real economic activity requirements) and relief clawback if conditions are not met. Countries could also consider restricting eligibility to businesses below a certain size, capping the amount of available relief (e.g. capping the value of business assets that can benefit from inheritance or estate tax relief) or introducing some form of means-testing (e.g. based on profitability). There may also be cases where alternative reforms could be considered. For instance, a low rate inheritance tax allowing tax payments in instalments (e.g. over ten years) would significantly reduce the need to exempt or provide significant relief for business assets. For agricultural property, reliefs should also be conditional to ensure that agricultural land does not become an attractive investment for tax purposes, potentially raising the cost of agricultural land for farmers.

3.8.4. Private pension savings can pass tax-free to beneficiaries in some countries

Private pension savings are typically an optional pillar of pension systems in OECD countries and may benefit from preferential inheritance or estate tax treatment. Unlike occupational pensions and universal minimum pensions, which typically provide income to the donor or their spouse only, private pension savings are owned by or held in trust for the taxpayers, who can bequest the balance of their individual account upon death. Several countries exclude private pensions from their inheritance and estate taxes.

Private pensions benefit from preferential inheritance and estate tax treatment in around one third of countries. In nine countries, private pensions are fully exempt (Ireland, Italy, the Netherlands, Poland, Portugal, Switzerland, and the United Kingdom) or benefit from an additional tax-free threshold (Chile and Japan). In Spain and Denmark, private pension savings are subject to personal income tax but exempt from inheritance taxes. In the Netherlands, inherited pension wealth is not taxed but counts towards the spouse's tax-free thresholds. Preferential treatment typically applies to all beneficiaries, but in Italy, only applies when the pension savings are inherited by the donor's nominated beneficiary. In the United Kingdom, private pensions are subject to estate taxes if the pension reverts to the donor's estate but are exempt if the pension fund trustees retain discretion as to who to pay the pension or death benefits to (the donor may indicate their wishes but this is not binding).

Favourable tax treatment for the accumulation and transfer of private pensions may lead to very low taxation of pension wealth, but such treatment may be justified for the spouse. As private pension savings are taxed at lower rates than other asset types (OECD, 2018[10]), exempting them from inheritance and estate taxes may allow donors to build wealth and pass it to beneficiaries while incurring minimal tax liabilities. While this may create tax planning opportunities when all beneficiaries receive such favourable treatment, the risk may be lower where the exemption only applies to the donor's spouse. Preferential treatment for the donor's spouse may prevent inheritance and estate taxes from influencing decisions about lifecycle savings, as partners may plan for retirement together and organise time in formal employment around the expectation of a shared retirement. On the other hand, exemptions for beneficiaries other than the spouse may not be necessary to encourage retirement savings.

3.8.5. Life insurance and accidental death insurance may act as additional savings vehicles not subject to inheritance and estate taxes

A minority of countries provide concessionary treatment for payments received from life insurance and accidental death insurance. Life insurance and accidental death insurance pay a sum of money to beneficiaries when the policyholder passes away. Some forms of life insurance also have an investment component, allowing policyholders to increase the savings that they can access themselves or pass to heirs. The majority of countries include life and accidental death insurance in the inheritance or estate tax base, but insurance benefits are fully exempt in Chile, Greece, Hungary, Ireland, Italy, and Poland,[17] Portugal, Spain, and the United Kingdom and benefit from an additional tax-free threshold in Japan. In France, instead of being subject to inheritance taxes, life insurance benefits are taxed under a separate and more generous tax with higher exemption thresholds and lower marginal rates (depending on the age at which contributions were made and the date the account was opened). The exemption is capped in Spain. Countries may apply conditions, including that the beneficiary be a close relative or direct descendant of the donor (Italy and Spain), that beneficiaries be nominated by the donor in the life insurance contract (Greece and Italy), that the insurance be intended to pay the tax liability (Ireland; minimum holding period applies), or that insurance be held through a trust (the United Kingdom; a relatively simple opt-in process offered by insurers). In Denmark and Finland, beneficiaries are liable under personal income tax for insurance benefits received, but are exempt from inheritance taxes.

Exempting life insurance pay-outs creates tax planning opportunities. Preferential treatment for life and accidental death insurance policies, particularly where policies serve as “wrapper products” that contain the same savings products as those that individuals can hold directly, create opportunities to minimise inheritance and estate tax liabilities. This allows donors to ensure a tax-exempt or tax-favoured payment is made to family members who would otherwise face a higher tax liability.

3.8.6. Charitable giving is almost always exempt from inheritance and estate taxes

Across the OECD, bequests to institutions that act in the public good are typically tax exempt. In most countries, transfers to certified organisations that undertake educational, scientific, religious, or other charitable activities are exempt from inheritance and estate taxes (Chile, Denmark, Finland, France, Germany, Hungary, Ireland, Italy, Japan, Korea, Lithuania, the Netherlands, Portugal, Slovenia, Spain, Switzerland, the United Kingdom, and the United States). Organisations that pursue other activities may be taxed as corporations or as other beneficiaries; for example, associations in France that do not fulfil the criteria for a full exemption may receive the same tax treatment that is provided for inheritances between the donor’s siblings or (if they fulfil none of the criteria) are subject to a flat 60% rate. Some countries instead tax charitable bequests at a lower rate than transfers to natural persons (Belgium), allowing taxpayers to reduce but not eliminate the inheritance tax liability by donating to philanthropic organisations. In some countries, transfers to governments are also tax-free.

Belgium and the United Kingdom offer additional special treatment for wealth passed to non-charity beneficiaries where donors make donations of a particular type or size. Taxpayers in Belgium may leave a “legs en duo”, where the donor leaves their wealth to a charitable institution (taxed at low rates) which then pays a sum to the donor’s heir, remits the total inheritance tax due, and keeps the remainder.[18] This is a particularly attractive strategy if the donor wishes to leave their wealth to an heir that is taxed at high rates. The United Kingdom, in addition to exempting charitable bequests from inheritance taxation, reduces the inheritance tax rate on the donor’s remaining wealth from 40% to 36% if 10% or more of their estate is donated.

Empirical evidence suggests that exemptions for charitable donations increase giving, but care should be taken to minimise avoidance opportunities and revenue losses. Wealth given to charitable institutions reduces the wealth that passes to heirs and may thereby reduce wealth concentration. While tax reductions for charitable giving present a cost for government budgets, charitable activities are expected to benefit the public through their educational, social, and scientific works. Where philanthropic entities are required to obtain certification in order to benefit from the tax exemption, the risks for abuse of such exemptions are reduced. However, there might be cases where special structures with some charitable or philanthropic component may be set up primarily to minimise the inheritance or estate tax burdens faced by non-charity heirs. This may require stricter eligibility rules in order to benefit from exemptions or relief for charitable giving or in some cases revisions in valuation rules (see Section 3.10).

3.8.7. *Favourable tax treatment applies to items of historical or cultural value in some countries, on the condition of being accessible to the broader public*

Buildings or objects such as manuscripts, artworks, or scientific collections that are part of the national or regional heritage are granted preferential treatment in a minority of countries. A partial exemption applies in Spain and a full exemption applies in Germany, Ireland, France, Poland, Slovenia, Switzerland, and the United Kingdom. Conditions may apply to ensure that the broader society can benefit from the preservation of these buildings and objects and to prevent that such exemptions allow families to pass down wealth in the form of historical and cultural artefacts. The exemptions are conditional on the objects or buildings being accessible to the public (France, Ireland, Slovenia, and the United Kingdom), used for the exercise of cultural activities (Slovenia), registered and maintained in line with government regulations (Poland), or held by the State (Ireland). Tax relief may be clawed back where these conditions are not met.

Conditional tax relief can help pursue cultural objectives and preserve historical heritage for the benefit of society. Exemptions for objects and buildings of historic or cultural value may allow households to preserve the heritage of their country or region across generations, but requiring that they be accessible to the public and monitoring this access is key to fulfilling this goal and limiting avoidance opportunities.

3.9. Tax filing and payment

3.9.1. *Tax filing and payment procedures vary, but many countries allow tax payment in instalments and conditional tax deferrals*

Taxpayers are typically required to file declarations with the tax authority (Table 3.8). Among the documents required, countries may request an inventory of the donor's assets, an inheritance or estate tax return, a declaration of acceptance or refusal of the inheritance by beneficiaries, and a declaration of transfer of assets to beneficiaries. These requirements may depend on whether the country operates a system of universal succession, where the full estate passes immediately to heirs upon the donor's death, or a system of probate, where the executor (the donor's appointed legal representative) applies for probate in order to recognise the validity of the will and proceed to settle the donor's estate.

Table 3.8. Taxpayer declarations to submit during a succession

Documents	Countries
Inventory of the donor's assets	Belgium, Chile, Denmark, Finland, France, Hungary, Ireland, Italy, Japan, Korea, Luxembourg, Portugal, Spain, Switzerland, United States
Inheritance or estate tax return	Belgium, Denmark, Spain, Finland, Greece, Ireland, Italy, Japan, Korea, Luxembourg, Netherlands, Poland, Portugal, United Kingdom, United States
Declaration of acceptance or refusal of the inheritance	Belgium, Denmark, France[1], Greece, Ireland, Italy, Korea, Lithuania, Poland, Spain, Switzerland
Declaration of transfer of assets to beneficiaries	Denmark, France, Italy, Korea, Spain, Switzerland, United States

1. The declaration of acceptance of the succession may be implicit, expressed by taking actions that reveal the intention to accept the succession.
Source: OECD Questionnaire on Inheritance, Estate, and Gift Taxes.

The deadline for paying inheritance and estate taxes ranges from a few months to several years, but some countries require heirs to pay the tax before receiving the assets. Countries require beneficiaries or estates to pay the required tax within a specified time following the donor's death (6 to 48 months) or shortly after receiving the tax assessment (up to two months). In countries that apply universal succession, heirs are collectively responsible for paying taxes and debts, while responsibility falls to the executor in countries that operate a system of probate. Some countries do not allow heirs to receive ownership of inherited assets until they have paid inheritance or estate taxes (e.g. the United Kingdom). While this may reduce non-payment or late payment, it may also create significant difficulties for taxpayers who do not have immediate access to the liquidity necessary to pay the tax. Where inheritance and estate taxes are not paid on time, most countries apply a penalty. This can range from as little as EUR 25 per month late in Belgium to a maximum of 200% of the tax owed in Portugal.

Around half of the countries require inheritance or estate taxes be paid in a lump sum, while the remainder allow taxpayers to pay in instalments. Unless the assets benefit from extensions or instalment plans, as outlined in Section 3.8, inheritance and estate taxes must be paid in a single payment in Chile, Denmark, Hungary, Ireland, Japan, Lithuania, Luxembourg, Poland, and the United Kingdom. Thirteen countries instead allow the taxes to be paid in instalments (Belgium, Finland, France, Germany, Greece, Italy, Korea, Netherlands, Portugal, Slovenia, Spain, Switzerland, and the United States); in some cases without conditions (Finland, Greece, Korea, Netherlands, Slovenia, and Spain). Countries may instead require that taxpayers do not have other tax liabilities or other repayment plans (Belgium), that they undergo an income and expenditure review (Belgium, if other criteria are not fulfilled), or that they agree to a repayment plan (Switzerland). Two countries allow payment in instalments only where the taxpayer is inheriting a family-owned business (Germany and the United States). France requires taxpayers to offer a guarantee and Italy requires taxpayers to pay a portion of the tax by the original due date, in order to benefit from payment by instalments. Interest on payment by instalment applies in Italy, the Netherlands, Spain, and the United States.

Most countries allow conditional inheritance or estate tax payment deferral. Countries may allow taxpayers to apply for a deferral of the tax payment under certain conditions, such as proving that paying the tax would cause financial distress or where it cannot be paid as a lump sum (Ireland, Japan, Slovenia, Switzerland, the United Kingdom, and the United States). Deferral may also be available upon application by the taxpayer and subject to the tax office's approval (Belgium, Finland, Korea, and Poland). Extensions may instead depend on the type of assets inherited, such as immovable property (Germany, Ireland, the Netherlands, and the United Kingdom), agricultural property (Ireland), and business assets (Denmark, France, Germany, Ireland, the Netherlands, and the United Kingdom), and be limited to the share of the tax that is due on these assets. Deferral may be conditional on not disposing of the asset (the Netherlands and the United Kingdom), on having no outstanding tax liabilities (the Netherlands) or on offering a guarantee (France). The tax authority may impose additional criteria on taxpayers requesting an extension, such as an income and expenditure review (Belgium), and extensions may only be available for tax liabilities that exceed a threshold (Japan and Korea). Interest charges typically apply when taxpayers are granted longer extensions (Belgium, Finland, Ireland, Japan, the Netherlands, Poland, Slovenia, United Kingdom, and the United States).

3.9.2. Flexible payment options and taxpayer-friendly administration can improve compliance and efficiency

Allowing payment in instalments and payment deferrals where demonstrably necessary may help ease liquidity issues. Flexible payment options, including payment in instalments and extensions of the payment deadline can help taxpayers fulfil their tax obligations while avoiding hardship or inefficient forced asset sales. Countries may wish to offer a range of flexible options, including short extensions or payment plans on request – requiring minimal assessment by the tax administration – and extensions or longer extensions for larger tax liabilities – where the tax administration may need to review requests.

Digitalisation, third party reporting, and information exchange between government agencies represent significant opportunities to enhance tax compliance and administration. Exchanging information between government agencies, cooperating with foreign tax administrations on cross-border inheritances, and third-party reporting (e.g. from banks) could allow tax administrations to partially pre-fill tax returns, and to form a more complete picture of taxpayers' assets and wealth transfers. Digitalisation also presents an opportunity for tax administrations to facilitate tax compliance and ensure that reporting is efficient and taxpayer-friendly. Digitalisation may also allow tax authorities to strengthen reporting requirements, particularly for low-value transfers that are not taxable and not currently reported. For example, countries could introduce reporting obligations for transfers above a certain low-value threshold, even if these are not subject to tax, and make such reporting simple and available online. In addition to strengthening tax authorities' efforts to monitor tax compliance and detect high-risk taxpayers, additional and higher quality data on wealth transfers and wealth transfer tax payments could strengthen countries' capacities to measure wealth inequality, and to assess the distributional impacts of inheritance, estate, and gift taxes and potential reforms.

Tax administrations could allow donors to pre-lodge inheritance tax returns, to strengthen the culture of compliance and reduce the administrative burden on their family. Donors could elect to pre-lodge inheritance tax returns, which would be updated by executors or heirs upon the donor's death. Allowing donors to choose to pre-lodge would bring tax compliance into the scope of their estate preparation. Pre-lodging could reduce the impact of the administrative process on the family and lower the overall administrative burden by allowing donors, who are familiar with the detail of their estate, to choose to pre-lodge.

3.10. Valuation methods

3.10.1. The most common valuation method is fair market value, but this may be complex to apply to some asset types

Across countries, fair market value (FMV) is the most common valuation method (Table 3.9). Most OECD countries specify which method should be used to value different assets, although taxpayers may be able to choose between valuation methods for some asset classes. The FMV approach measures the price a willing buyer would pay a willing seller in a transaction on the open market,[19] assuming neither is under any compulsion to buy or to sell and both having reasonable knowledge of relevant facts. Listed equities are a notable exception to this rule, as they are usually valued according to the market price at the date of valuation (MP). Immovable property is typically valued according to the value established by the tax authority for the purposes of taxes (e.g. property taxes) other than inheritance or estate taxes (VTP). Rarer methods include the value established by a government authority for non-tax purposes (VNTP), sometimes used to value immovable property, and capitalised earnings or profits (CEP), sometimes used to value family-owned businesses. Hard-to-value goods, such as artwork and jewellery, and low-value consumer goods, such as furniture and other household goods, are typically valued at FMV or as a specified portion of the value of the estate or the residential property (PO).

There might be challenges associated with estimating fair market value for some assets, particularly for unlisted shares and closely held businesses. Fair market value can be determined based on different approaches: an income-based approach (i.e. the value of the business is equal to the present value of the net income expected to be generated), an asset-based approach (i.e. the valuation of the business is based on the fair market value of its total assets after deducting liabilities) and a market-based or comparability approach (i.e. the value is established based on sales of comparable businesses or business interests). It may be easier to use a market-based approach in the case of large private businesses, which have the advantage of centrally-registered stock transactions and are typically valued on secondary markets (Saez and Zucman, 2019[11]). For smaller private businesses, valuation may be significantly more difficult, particularly in the case of a start-up with large growth potential that does not yet generate significant income. Issues also arise with respect to valuing particular business assets, including intellectual property (Daly and Loutzenhiser, 2020[12]). This reveals that, even if asset valuation is typically undertaken by qualified appraisers, there may be some scope for discretion when it comes to determining asset values. Recent research in the United States points to the fact that the gaps between the wealth values reported for estate tax purposes and those estimated by Forbes are highest when portfolios mainly consist of assets for which valuation is difficult to observe or involves some subjectivity and when individuals hold relatively more debt (see Chapter 2 for a discussion of Raub, Johnson and Newcomb, 2010[120]). Issues may also arise with valuation discounts, which may apply to account for lack of control (i.e. when heirs inherit a minority stake in a business) or lack of marketability.

Asset valuations are also often viewed as difficult for artwork and high-value jewellery, although the issue may be overstated. For artwork or high-value jewellery, it has sometimes been recommended to use insurance values, on the basis that establishing market values for infrequently traded assets is difficult. Insurance values would be readily available and are independently verified by third parties, namely insurance firms (Daly and Loutzenhiser, 2020[12]). However, insurance values may be significantly higher than actual values, particularly where valuations take into account the costs associated with replacing the original item. As there is a fairly transparent market for artwork and high-value jewellery and information about auctions is widely reported, establishing appropriate market values may be less difficult than commonly assumed (Daly and Loutzenhiser, 2020[12]).

Table 3.9. Principal valuation method for selected asset classes

	Main residence	Other residential property	Buildings of historical value	Land and immovable property used for agriculture or forestry	Other immovable property, including commercial property and vacant land	Bank deposits in national currency	Bank deposits in foreign currency	Government or corporate bonds	Listed equities	Unlisted equities, excluding shared held in family-owned businesses	Family-owned businesses, including shares held in family-owned businesses	Artwork	Jewellery	Vehicles	Furniture and other household goods	Intangible property, including goodwill and patents
Belgium	FMV	FMV	FMV	FMV	FMV	FMV	FMV	FMV	FMV	FMV	BV	FMV	FMV	FMV	FMV	FMV
Chile	VTP	VTP	VTP	VTP	VTP	FMV	FMV	MP	MP	FMV	BV	FMV	FMV	VTP	PO	FMV
Denmark	FMV	FMV	NA	FMV	FMV	FMV	FMV	FMV	FMV	FMV	FMV	FMV	FMV	FMV	FMV	FMV
Finland	FMV	FMV	FMV	FMV	FMV	FMV	FMV	FMV	FMV	FMV	FMV	FMV	FMV	FMV	FMV	FMV
France	FMV	FMV	FMV	FMV	FMV	FMV	FMV	MP	MP	FMV	FMV	FMV	FMV	FMV	FMV	FMV
Germany	FMV	FMV	VA	CEP	VNTP	FMV	FMV	FMV	FMV	FMV	CEP	FMV	FMV	FMV	FMV	FMV
Greece	VTP	VTP	VTP	VTP	VTP	VA	VA	Oth	Oth	Oth	Oth	FMV	FMV	FMV	PO	FMV
Hungary	Oth	Oth	Oth	Oth	Oth	Oth	Oth	Oth	Oth	Oth	Oth	Oth	Oth	Oth	Oth	NA
Ireland	MP	MP	MP	MP	MP	VA	VA	MP	MP	MP	MP	MP	MP	MP	MP	MP
Italy	VTP	VTP	NA	FMV	VTP	MP	MP	VCA	MP	BV	BV	PO	PO	VCA	PO	FMV
Japan	FMV	FMV	FMV	Oth	Oth	MP	MP	Oth	MP	BV	BV	FMV	FMV	FMV	FMV	CEP
Korea	FMV	FMV	FMV	FMV	FMV	FMV	FMV	FMV	MP	FMV	FMV	FMV	FMV	FMV	FMV	FMV
Lithuania	FMV	FMV	FMV	FMV	FMV	Oth	VNTP	MP	MP	FMV	FMV	VTP	VTP	FMV	FMV	NA
Luxembourg	FMV	FMV	FMV	FMV	FMV	FMV	FMV	FMV	FMV	FMV	FMV	FMV	FMV	FMV	FMV	FMV
Netherlands	VTP	VTP	VTP	FMV	FMV	FMV	FMV	FMV	FMV	FMV	FMV	FMV	FMV	FMV	FMV	FMV
Poland	FMV	FMV	FMV	FMV	FMV	Oth	Oth	FMV	FMV	FMV	FMV	FMV	FMV	FMV	FMV	FMV
Portugal	VTP	VTP	VTP	VTP	VTP	MP	MP	MP	MP	FMV	FMV	FMV	NA	FMV	NA	FMV
Slovenia	FMV	FMV	FMV	NA	FMV	FMV	FMV	FMV	FMV	FMV	FMV	FMV	FMV	FMV	FMV	FMV
Spain	FMV	FMV	FMV	FMV	FMV	FMV	FMV	FMV	FMV	FMV	FMV	FMV	FMV	FMV	FMV	FMV
Switzerland	Oth	Oth	Oth	Oth	CEP	MP	MP	MP	MP	BV	BV	IV	VCA	VCA	NA	BV

United Kingdom	FMV	FMV	FMV	Oth	FMV	FMV	FMV	FMV	MP	FMV	FMV	FMV	FMV	FMV	FMV	VTP
United States	FMV	FMV	FMV	FMV	FMV	FMV	FMV	FMV	FMV	FMV	FMV	FMV	FMV	FMV	FMV	FMV

Note: **BV**: Book value on the basis of tangible and intangible assets, annual sales, equity, employment etc.; **CEP**: Capitalised earnings or profits, on the basis of sales, earnings prospects, imputed income etc.; **FMV**: Fair market value; **IV**: Insured value; **MP**: Market price at the date of valuation or an average of prices over a specified time preceding the date of valuation; **Oth**: Other; **PO**: A specified portion of the value of the estate or a specified portion of the value of the residential property in the case of furniture and other household goods; **VA**: Value at acquisition or last market transaction; **VCA**: Value of comparative assets; **VNTP**: Value established by a government authority for non-tax purposes (e.g. exchange rate for foreign currencies); **VTP**: Value established by tax authority for purposes other than inheritance or estate taxes (e.g. recurrent taxes on immovable property, net wealth taxes etc.)
Source: OECD Questionnaire on Inheritance, Estate, and Gift Taxes

As cadastral values are typically below market values, using the VTP for residential property may result in substantial undervaluation. The VTP may draw on different tax estimates, such as transaction taxes (stamp duty), recurrent taxes on immovable property, and net wealth taxes. The base for these taxes may in turn draw on cadastral values, which are rarely updated in many OECD countries. As the VTP may underestimate the property value, this method could lead to implicit preferential treatment.

3.10.2. Accurate and consistent valuation is key to efficient and equitable inheritance and estate taxes

Taxable values should, as much as possible, be based on fair market value, and different approaches could be combined where such an approach to valuation is difficult. As discussed above, establishing FMV can be straightforward for many assets, but assets such as unlisted shares and closely held businesses pose particular challenges. In these cases, the type of business will be an important factor in determining the best approach to valuation. The comparability/market approach may be appropriate for large private businesses for which comparable listed companies exist. The book/asset approach may be more appropriate for small closely held or private businesses, although this will likely need to be combined with the income or market approach, as book values may understate the value of a business. Intangible assets are also challenging to value, given the lack of observable arm's length transactions of identical or substantially similar assets. Where the intangible asset is income producing or when it allows an asset to generate cash flow, income-based approaches may be the most appropriate. Transparent and consistent approaches to valuation are essential to ensure the fairness of inheritance or estate taxes.

Additional measures can be taken to address valuation issues. Allowing the tax authority to independently verify valuations can prevent taxpayers from artificially reducing their tax liability through undervaluation and there should be penalties associated with clear cases of undervaluation. Valuation discounts for family businesses due to minority holding or lack of marketability could also be carefully scrutinised.

3.11. The design of gift taxes

3.11.1. The design of gift taxes and their integration with inheritance and estate taxes varies widely across countries

Most countries that levy an inheritance or an estate tax also levy a gift tax. 23 of the 24 OECD countries that levy an estate or inheritance tax also levy a gift tax on inter vivos transfers. Latvia and Lithuania tax gifts through the personal income tax (Latvia taxes gifts only while Lithuania also levies an inheritance tax), and one country (Denmark) applies gift taxes to close relatives but applies income taxes to gifts to extended family and non-relatives.

However, the degree of alignment between gift taxes and inheritance or estate taxes varies (Table 3.10). Gift taxes and inheritance or estate taxes may be very similar in some countries, with identical rate structures and asset treatment, for example, while these operate as separate, but complementary, taxes in other countries. One aspect of the integration between gift taxes and inheritance and estate taxes is the tax exemption threshold. In a few countries, the inheritance tax exemption threshold is reduced by the value of gifts received during the donor's life (e.g. Chile, Italy, and Switzerland). Countries may instead have a small tax-free threshold for gifts renewed each year (e.g. Denmark, Lithuania, Slovenia, and the United States), or a larger thresholds renewed every few years (e.g. France and Germany). Another aspect of integration between gift taxes and inheritance or estate taxes is the tax base; for example, the United States applies gift taxes on a tax-exclusive basis, while applying estate taxes on a tax-inclusive basis.[20]

Gifts made shortly before the donor's death are re-characterised as inheritances in several countries (Table 3.10). In Finland, France, Japan, Korea, and the Netherlands, gifts received before the donor's death are included in the inheritance tax base, and any previously paid gift tax is deducted from the inheritance tax liability. In Belgium and Luxembourg, gifts are reinstated for the calculation of the inheritance tax unless gift taxes were paid at the time. Note that gift taxes are optional in Belgium for moveable and foreign immovable property, allowing donors to pay lower gift taxes or risk paying higher inheritance taxes if the donor dies within three years. In Ireland, gifts made before the donor's death are characterised as inheritances, but this does not affect the final tax liability as all gifts and inheritances are taxed under the single lifetime wealth transfer tax. The United Kingdom exempts all gifts that are made more than seven years before the donor's death, but adds gifts made within those seven years to the inheritance tax base. Gifts above the exemption threshold are taxed on a sliding scale, with older gifts taxed at lower rates than more recent gifts. In the United States, gifts over the annual tax-exempt threshold reduce the estate tax exemption that applies upon death.

Several countries provide a tax advantage where bare ownership and usufruct are separated for gift purposes, while others actively discourage this arrangement. Taxpayers may separate the full ownership of an asset into bare ownership (legal ownership of property without the right to use or derive income from it) and usufruct (the right to use or derive income from property). This strategy may be employed, for example, by parents who wish to give ownership of their main residence to their children, while retaining the right to live in the home until they die. There may be a significant tax advantage to such an arrangement, where gift taxes apply only to the bare ownership (that is, the value of the full ownership minus the value of the usufruct) and no further tax applies when the donor passes away and beneficiaries receive full ownership (Finland, France, Germany, Greece, Hungary, Italy, Luxembourg, Slovenia, Spain, and the United States). In contrast, Belgium, Denmark, and Switzerland tax the value of full ownership when bare ownership is gifted, to eliminate the tax advantage described above. Other approaches exist in a minority of countries. Ireland applies an annual charge on usufruct through its capital acquisition tax and the United Kingdom discourages gifts with reservation of benefit through anti-avoidance rules.

A minority of countries have special provisions for gifts to young people. As discussed in Chapter 1, the age at which people receive inheritances is increasing with the rise in life expectancy. To encourage wealth transmissions to people earlier in life, some countries may apply reliefs to gifts to younger generations, such as tapered relief for transmissions to recipients below a certain age. For example, the Netherlands allows parents to make a once-in-a-lifetime tax-free gift of around EUR 55 000 to children for their study and around EUR 100 000 to a young person aged 18 to 40 to purchase their own home. In Italy, transfers of agricultural land and farms to farmers under 40 years old are exempt if the heir is a descendant or ascendant up to the third degree of kinship.

A minority of countries tax in-kind gifts and some apply special exemptions to certain types of gifts. Rather than making direct transfers to beneficiaries, which may be subject to gift taxes, taxpayers can instead pay for expenses such as private education, health bills, and weddings. Five countries tax donations in kind like regular gifts (Greece, Lithuania, Slovenia, Spain, and Switzerland), while six countries also tax donations in kind but apply special exemptions in cases involving specified expenses, such as medical, education, weddings or maintenance costs (Finland, Ireland, Latvia, Netherlands, the United Kingdom, and the United States). Some conditions may apply to this exemption, including that the value of the gifts in kind be reasonable (Ireland and the Netherlands) and that the recipient be the donor's child, a young person, or unable to maintain themselves due to disability (Ireland, the Netherlands, and the United States). In Finland, beneficiaries should not be able to use the funds for purposes other than education and maintenance and in Latvia, the exemption is conditional on retaining documentation of the nature of the expense. The United Kingdom does not tax gifts in kind, such as paying life insurance for a spouse, on the condition that these are regular gifts made from income.

Table 3.10. Gift tax exemption thresholds and threshold renewal

Country	Tax-free threshold for gifts		Renewal of tax-free thresholds	Gifts made before death are re-characterised as inheritances
	Children	Non-relatives		
Belgium	No exemption[1]	No exemption[1]	NA	3 years prior to death
Chile	USD 44 352	No exemption	Lifetime	No
Denmark	USD 10 257	Income tax[2]	Annual	No
Finland	USD 5 711	USD 5 711	3 years	3 years prior to death
France	USD 114 220	USD 1 821	15 years	1 year prior to death
Germany	USD 456 879	USD 22 844	10 years	No
Greece	USD 171 329	USD 6 853	Lifetime	No
Hungary	Exempt	USD 487	Every transaction separate	No
Ireland	USD 382 636	USD 18 561	Lifetime	2 years prior to death
Italy	USD 1 142 197	No exemption	Lifetime	No
Japan	USD 10 302	USD 10 302	Annual	3 years prior to death
Korea	USD 42 363	No exemption	10 years	10 years
Latvia[3]	Exempt	Income tax	Annual	No
Lithuania[3]	Exempt	USD 2 855	Annual	No
Luxembourg	No exemption	No exemption	NA	1 year prior to death
Netherlands	USD 6 299	USD 2 522	Annual	180 days prior to death
Poland	Exempt	USD 1 257	5 years	No
Portugal	Exempt	No exemption	Lifetime	No
Slovenia	Exempt	USD 5 711	Annual	No
Spain	USD 18 225	No exemption	3 years	No
Switzerland	Exempt		Lifetime	No
United Kingdom	Exempt[4]	Exempt[4]	NA	7 years prior to death
United States	USD 15 000	USD 15 000	Annual	Lifetime (amounts over annual threshold)

1. Taxpayers may opt to register the donation before a Belgian notary and pay gift taxes, which have no tax-free threshold but which are levied at lower rates than inheritance taxes. Registration is compulsory for domestic immovable property but is optional for moveable property and foreign immovable property.
2. Gifts between close relatives are subject to the gift tax (spouse, children, grandchildren, parents, grandparents, great-grandparents). Gifts to other recipient are subject to income tax (siblings, nieces, nephews, aunts, uncles, cousins and more distant relatives, parents-in-law, children-in-law, non-related parties).
3. Gifts are taxed under the personal income tax.
4. Gift is made more than seven years before the donor's death.
Note: Exemption thresholds are reported in USD 2020. This table assumes that beneficiaries are adults and do not have a disability.
Source: OECD Questionnaire on Inheritance, Estate, and Gift Taxes

Box 3.3. Illustrative simulations: impact of tax exemption thresholds on final tax liabilities

The stylised examples in Table 3.11 demonstrate the impact of tax design features, in particular of gift tax exemption thresholds, on the final tax liability. In each of the four scenarios, a donor transfers EUR 375 000 each to two beneficiaries, for a total transfer of EUR 750 000. In all scenarios, the transfers are taxed at 10% and the tax-free threshold is EUR 12 500. However, the frequency of the wealth transfers and the application of tax-free threshold varies for each case. In scenarios (1) and (2), the donor gifts EUR 25 000 to each beneficiary every year for 15 years. In scenario (1), both heirs benefit from the EUR 12 500 exemption every year and in scenario (2), both heirs benefit from the EUR 12 500 exemption once every five years. In scenarios (3) and (4), the donor bequeaths EUR 375 000 to each beneficiary upon the donor's death. In scenario (3), heirs are taxed on the wealth they receive and therefore both receive a EUR 12 500 exemption. In scenario (4), the estate is taxed and therefore the EUR 12 500 exemption applies only once.

The lowest tax liability arises in the scenario with annual gifts and annual tax exemption thresholds. These stylised examples lead to varying tax liabilities, with the lowest tax liability for gifts with annual exemptions (scenario 1), followed by scenarios with some renewal of tax-exempt thresholds for gifts (2) and tax-exempt thresholds for multiple heirs under an inheritance tax (3). Scenario 1 leads to the lowest effective tax rate of 5.0%, as half of the annual wealth transfer falls under the annual exemption threshold, while Scenario 4 leads to the highest effective tax rate of 9.8%, as the full estate is taxed and the tax-free threshold applies only once. This stylised example demonstrates how the level and frequency of gift tax exemption thresholds can have a significant impact on the tax liability.

Table 3.11. Stylised example of inheritance, estate, and gift taxation, with different tax design assumptions

	Gift tax with annual exemption (1)	Gift tax with 5-year exemption (2)	Inheritance tax levied on beneficiaries (3)	Estate tax levied on donor (4)
Total amount transferred	750 000	750 000	750 000	750 000
Number of beneficiaries, receiving equal shares	2 beneficiaries	2 beneficiaries	2 beneficiaries	2 beneficiaries
Amount transferred	50 000 annually	50 000 annually	750 000 at end of life	750 000 at end of life
Number of gifts or inheritances	15 gifts (one per year for 15 years)	15 gifts (one per year for 15 years)	1 inheritance (end of life)	1 inheritance (end of life)
Amount received by each beneficiary, per transfer	25 000 annually	25 000 annually	375 000 at end of life	375 000 at end of life
Amount received by each beneficiary, total	375 000	375 000	375 000	375 000
Tax-free threshold	12 500 annually	12 500 every 5 years	12 500 per beneficiary	12 500 per estate
Total amount taxable	187 500 per beneficiary	337 500 per beneficiary	362 500 per beneficiary	737 500 per estate
Tax rate	10%	10%	10%	10%
Total tax due, per beneficiary	18 750	33 750	36 250	..
Total tax due	37 500	67 500	72 400	73 750
Effective tax rate (Total tax / total transfer)	5.0%	9.0%	9.7%	9.8%

Source: Authors' calculations.

3.11.2. Gift taxes should be carefully designed, in particular to avoid significant tax minimisation opportunities

The provision of renewable gift tax exemption thresholds can allow taxpayers to significantly minimise their tax liability. Where taxpayers are able to transfer assets under a specified value tax-free each year they can decrease their gift tax and inheritance or estate tax liabilities by transferring wealth early. Wealthy families who hold a greater portion of wealth in liquid assets and whose wealth exceeds their needs for retirement are the best placed to take advantage of these opportunities. In contrast, middle-class families who hold most of their wealth in their main residence and poorer households who rely on their savings to fund their retirement may not be able to gift their wealth during their lifetime.

Revising gift tax exemptions may improve equity and efficiency of inheritance and estate taxes. The provision of renewable gift tax exemptions should be carefully assessed and reviewed, as these can lead to tax-driven decisions to transfer wealth early and can allow wealth transfers to go largely untaxed. To combat tax avoidance through inter vivos gifts, one option would be to have a lifetime wealth transfer tax, allowing a certain amount of wealth to be received free of tax during the recipient's lifetime. Where that is not possible, countries could seek to approximate as much as possible a reasonable lifetime exemption threshold. The shorter the periods between gift tax exemption renewals, the smaller the exempt amounts should be. For more generous tax exemption thresholds, the time before tax-free thresholds are renewed could be lengthened to reduce tax planning and increase fairness, although that may increase tax administration and compliance costs. Full exemptions for gifts that have been made a certain number of years before death should be removed.

There could also be a careful examination of other tax-minimisation opportunities, such as separating bare ownership from usufruct or making significant gifts in kind. Gifts of bare ownership (while donor retains usufruct) may enable households in the middle of the wealth distribution – whose wealth is typically tied up in their (illiquid) home – to take advantage of inter vivos giving, which may be easier for wealthier families who typically hold more (liquid) financial wealth. Countries may wish to issue a preliminary tax assessment where the value of usufruct is discounted according to mortality tables, and then adjust the assessment when the donor passes away and the beneficiary receives full ownership. Countries may also set limits to the value of gifts in kind, beyond which they would be considered direct transfers.

Countries may focus their compliance and reporting efforts on inter vivos gifts, where non-compliance risks are greater. Unlike wealth transfers upon death, where non-compliance risks may be comparatively lower due to the requirement for probate or notarial acts, gifts are more prone to underreporting. To ensure that tax authorities have a full view of gifts, the thresholds for reporting requirements could be lower than the taxable threshold. Where undeclared gifts are discovered at a later date, tax authorities could use part of the appreciated present value, rather than the value of the gift at the time of the transfer, to determine the basis for taxation.

Favouring gifts to young people may have positive multiplier effects, but risks increasing intra-generational inequality. Wealth transfers may help young people make investments in their education and mobility, which could improve their productivity and earning capacity. Wealth transfers may also help kick-start savings and spur further investments, for example allowing the recipient to purchase a home or start a business. Gifts may therefore have positive multiplier effects, including for productivity and investment. Wealth transfers to younger generations could also decrease intergenerational wealth inequality. However, as wealth transfers are unequally distributed across the wealth distribution, young people receiving a gift may come from wealthy households, so favouring gifts to young people could reinforce unequal opportunities and intra-generational inequality. Countries wishing to apply tax relief to gifts to young people should carefully assess this relief to ensure that it generates additional transfers of wealth; otherwise the relief may generate a windfall for households who were already intending to make the transfers.

3.12. Tax treatment of unrealised capital gains at death

3.12.1. Most countries that levy inheritance or estate taxes do not tax unrealised capital gains at death

Three broad approaches apply to the transfer of assets with unrealised capital gains. First, countries may consider that when assets are transferred, either as a gift or as a bequest, a capital gain is realised. In this transfer-as-realisation basis, capital gains taxes will apply to non-exempt assets. Second, countries may pass the liability for unrealised capital gains to the beneficiary, known as the carry-over basis. In this case, capital gains taxes are levied only when the beneficiary sells the asset, but are levied on the total increase in value since the donor acquired the asset. Third, assets may be stepped-up to market value when assets are transferred as a gift or at death. Under the step-up in basis, the capital gain that accrues to the donor is not subject to capital gains taxes and the heir acquires the asset at market value. When the heir sells the asset, only the capital gains accrued since they received the inheritance or gift are subject to capital gains taxes. This section does not consider ordinary exemptions, such as those applying to certain asset classes, low-value capital gains, or capital gains on long-held assets.

The step-up in basis is the most common approach among countries that levy inheritance, estate, and gift taxes (Table 3.12). The step-up in basis is the most common approach in countries that levy inheritance, estate, and gift taxes, applied in 12 countries, followed by the carry-over basis in eight countries, and the transfer-as-realisation basis in two countries. Three countries apply different rules depending on the assets received. The transfer-as-realisation approach applies to most assets in Denmark (except artwork, jewellery, vehicles, and household goods, which are taxed on the step-up in basis and family-owned businesses, which are taxed on the carry-over basis) and Hungary (except intangible property, which is taxed under the step-up in basis). The step-up in basis applies to all assets in Finland, except to business property, where the carry-over basis is partially applied.

The carry-over basis is the most common approach for countries that do not levy inheritance or estate taxes. In countries that do not levy an inheritance or estate tax, the carry-over basis is the most common approach for unrealised capital gains, applied in seven countries. The step-up in basis applies in Latvia, while Canada is the only country that applies the transfer-as-realisation approach, levying capital gains taxes upon the donor's death.

The tax treatment of unrealised capital gains may depend on whether assets were transferred as a gift or inheritance. A few countries apply a more favourable tax treatment to inherited assets with unrealised capital gains than to gifted assets. For example, the United Kingdom and the United States apply the step-up in basis to unrealised capital gains at death, but the United Kingdom taxes unrealised capital gains when gifted and the United States applies the carry-over basis to gifts.[21] Inconsistent interactions between inheritance, estate, and gift taxes and capital gains taxes can distort behaviour and give rise to incoherent outcomes.

Table 3.12. Treatment of unrealised capital gains at death

	Countries where treatment applies to most assets	
	Country levies inheritance or estate taxes	Country does not levy inheritance or estate taxes
Unrealised capital gains are taxed at death	Denmark, Hungary	Canada
Unrealised capital gains pass to heirs on a carry-over basis	Denmark, Finland, Germany, Ireland, Italy, Japan, Luxembourg, Switzerland,	Australia, Austria, Estonia, Israel, Mexico, Norway, Sweden
Unrealised capital gains are exempt upon death and transferred with a step-up in basis	Chile[1], Denmark, Finland, France, Hungary, Korea, Lithuania, Portugal, Slovenia, Spain, United Kingdom, United States	Latvia[2]

1. This is considered a non-taxed event, not an exemption.
2. Taxes gifts through personal income taxes, does not levy a separate gift tax or an inheritance tax.
Note: Countries may appear multiple times in the table if different treatment applies to different assets. Missing information from Poland and, the Slovak Republic. This table does not consider ordinary exemptions for certain asset classes, low-value capital gains, or capital gains on long-held assets. There is no capital gains tax in Belgium, Greece, and the Netherlands (levy inheritance or estate taxes) or in Czech Republic and New Zealand (do not levy inheritance or estate taxes). There is no capital gains tax on privately held movable property in Switzerland, except when individuals are judged to be traders.
Source: OECD Questionnaire on Inheritance, Estate, and Gift Taxes.

3.12.2. Allowing unrealised capital gains at death to partially or fully escape taxation reduces equity and efficiency

The step-up in basis creates significant distortions and avoidance opportunities, particularly where inheritance or estate taxes are not levied, or where inheritance or estate tax exemption thresholds are very high (Table 3.13). The step-up in basis allows taxpayers to reduce their total tax liability by passing on their wealth in the form of unrealised gains, and these gains will go fully untaxed where there is no inheritance or estate tax. In addition to generating distortive lock-in effects, this may have significant distributional implications, as unrealised capital gains make up a large portion of the richest taxpayers' wealth. The step-up in basis also creates distortions where an inheritance or estate tax is levied because it discourages people from realising capital gains. Indeed, a taxpayer that sells appreciated property while alive may pay capital gains taxes, and then, if they transfer the net proceeds of the sale to their heirs when they die, they will also pay inheritance or estate taxes. The step-up in basis therefore creates horizontal inequity between taxpayers who realise gains during their lifetime and those who transfer wealth in the form of unrealised gains at death. Thus, there is a strong case for removing the step-up in basis for unrealised capital gains at death, especially where inheritance taxes are not levied. Unrealised capital gains may also very largely escape any form of taxation where the inheritance or estate tax threshold is very high. In such cases, countries could either reconsider the step-up in basis or lower the inheritance or estate tax exemption threshold.

Taxing unrealised gains at death may be the most efficient and equitable approach, especially where some payment flexibility is provided, such as deferral, in cases where this is demonstrably necessary. Compared to the step-up in basis, the carry-over basis reduces distortions by taxing unrealised capital gains when heirs sell the assets. This ensures taxpayers have the necessary liquidity when capital gains taxes are due, however, as this allows heirs to postpone liability for capital gains taxes until realisation, taxpayers may defer liability for an indefinite and potentially long period. Lock-in effects may be strong if there is a large tax liability due to long deferral of capital gains taxes. The carry-over basis would also require recipients to track the original cost basis of the donor, although this may become less difficult with digitalisation. On the other hand, taxing capital gains upon the donor's death ensures that gains made during the donor's life are taxed, preventing taxpayers from deferring capital gains taxes indefinitely or avoiding them altogether by holding assets until death. However, this may create liquidity problems for beneficiaries who could be forced to sell assets to pay capital gains taxes. In addition, taxing both capital gains and inheritances upon death may generate a high tax burden. Overall, levying capital gains and inheritances at death at reasonable tax rates, combined with deferral options when payment of tax may create hardships, may address some of the difficulties associated with existing approaches to taxing unrealised capital gains.

Countries should apply consistent tax treatment to gifted and bequeathed unrealised capital gains. Applying more favourable treatment to inherited unrealised capital gains, compared to gifted unrealised capital gains, incentivises taxpayers to retain assets until their death. There is no clear justification for differing treatment between inheritances and gifts, and the inconsistent treatment creates avoidance opportunities and unfair outcomes.[22] These distortions could also have wider economic impacts, as taxpayers could retain underperforming assets to benefit from the capital gains uplift at death (step-up in basis).

Table 3.13. Defining and assessing capital gains tax treatment at death

	Transfer-as-realisation basis	Carry-over basis	Step-up in basis
Definition	A capital gain is realised upon death and non-exempt assets are taxed	Liability passes to the beneficiary; gains since the donor acquired the asset are taxed when beneficiary disposes of the asset	Assets are stepped-up to market value and the capital gains that have accrued since the donor acquired the asset are exempt
Advantages	• Ensures capital gains are taxed • Removes tax incentive to hold assets until death or defer realisation	• Ensures capital gains are taxed • Liability occurs when taxpayers have liquidity	• Prevents liquidity issues
Disadvantages	• Liquidity issues • Potential for high tax burden (capital gains taxes + wealth transfer taxes)	• Heirs may postpone realisation indefinitely • Bookkeeping	• Avoidance opportunities • Lock-in effects • Negative distributional effects

3.13. Tax planning, avoidance and evasion

Tax avoidance and evasion can undermine the fairness and efficiency of inheritance and estate taxes. Avoidance and evasion opportunities can significantly reduce the revenue potential of taxes on wealth transfers. They may also reduce efficiency by distorting taxpayers' savings behaviours. In addition, tax planning and tax evasion opportunities may contribute to lowering the tax burden on those at the top of the distribution, potentially making inheritance taxes less progressive or even potentially regressive. This section finds that the design of inheritance, estate, and gift taxes can reduce opportunities for avoidance. Effective enforcement and tax transparency can address tax evasion.

3.13.1. Opportunities for tax planning and avoidance exist across OECD countries

Tax planning and tax avoidance allow taxpayers to reduce their inheritance or estate tax liability. The term "avoidance" may be used to describe the arrangement of a taxpayer's affairs in a way that is intended to reduce their tax liability.[23] Although the arrangement could be strictly legal, it may be in contradiction with the intent of the law it purports to follow. Alternately, governments may seek to encourage certain taxpayer behaviours through preferential tax provisions. This section examines some of the common techniques that taxpayers use to reduce their inheritance or estate tax liabilities, drawing on responses to the OECD Questionnaire on Inheritance, Estate, and Gift Taxes, as well as existing literature.

Opportunities for tax planning and avoidance should be carefully examined and addressed where they contradict the intended purpose of the tax code. Countries may wish to retain certain aspects of their inheritance, estate, or gift taxes even though they may give rise to risks of tax planning and avoidance, particularly where there is a strong justification for tax relief. However, in cases where the justification is weaker or a policy has unintentionally created planning and avoidance opportunities, these measures should be revised.

Bequests to certain heirs and bequests of certain assets

Taxpayers may spread their wealth among several heirs or leave bequests to heirs that are exempt. Where a single, large bequest to one heir would exceed the tax exemption threshold, several smaller bequests to multiple heirs may instead fall under the threshold. Similarly, several smaller bequests may be taxed at lower rates in countries that apply progressive inheritance tax rates, compared to one large bequest that may be taxed at higher rates. This tax planning strategy would not apply in countries that levy estate taxes on the donor's wealth and apply one tax exemption threshold. Donors may also reduce inheritance taxes by concentrating bequests among heirs that are exempt or benefit from the most generous inheritance or estate tax treatment, such as the spouse or children. As most countries apply the most favourable treatment to the spouse and few extend this treatment to co-habiting couples, there may be an incentive for couples to marry or enter a civil union.

Taxpayers may orient their portfolios toward assets that receive preferential tax treatment, in order to reduce their inheritance or estate tax liabilities. Preferential tax treatment may encourage taxpayers to hold assets that countries consider socially and economically desirable, such as businesses and owner-occupier homes, but it may also create tax planning opportunities for taxpayers who eschew other assets in favour of those that receive special treatment. These tax planning opportunities may have broader economic effects, where investment decisions are overly influenced by tax considerations or where taxpayers retain assets that are misaligned with their needs in order to benefit from the preferential treatment.

Emigrating to a location with lower or no inheritance or estate taxes

Taxpayers may relocate to a region or country with lower or no inheritance or estate taxes. Empirical studies have generally found limited evidence of tax-induced migration in response to inheritance or estate taxes, with super wealthy households being the exception, as recent research has found that billionaires' tax residency is sensitive to inheritance taxes, and that this sensitivity increases with age (Moretti and Wilson, 2020[13]) (see also Chapter 2 for a more detailed discussion). This is consistent with more anecdotal evidence of high-profile examples of fiscal expatriations, particularly among well-known business owners (Henrekson and Waldenström, 2016[1]). Fiscal expatriation may be a more serious concern for countries with close geographical neighbours where their citizens have residency rights, such as in many European countries. Tail provisions, where emigrants remain subject to their home country's inheritance, estate, and gift taxes for a number of years, are one option to address this form of avoidance.

Holding private assets through businesses or taking advantage of valuation rules

Preferential treatment for business assets may enable taxpayers to hold private assets through their business, though anti-abuse provisions can limit this type of avoidance. To avoid inheritance, estate, and gift taxes, taxpayers may also artificially cloak private wealth in the guise of tax-favoured assets by, for example, holding business assets or agricultural land without undertaking genuine economic activities. This strategy can be limited through anti-abuse provisions, such as restricting preferential treatment to assets used for business activities, but this may be more difficult for some asset classes, such as vehicles.

There may also be some scope for asset undervaluation where assets are hard to value. This may be particularly relevant for taxpayers whose portfolios mainly consist of assets for which valuation is difficult to observe or involves some subjectivity in choosing the most adequate valuation method (e.g. closely-held businesses, intellectual property assets).

There may be cases where taxpayers may claim significant valuation discounts on transferred assets by setting up specific structures. For example, donors in the United States may establish a Family Limited Partnership (FLP) and transfer assets to a limited partnership whose limited partners are typically family members. The tax advantage lies in the fact that valuation discounts may be available, based on a presumed lack of marketability and control because individual beneficiaries receive a minority interest in the partnership, even though family members might together hold the totality of the partnership interests (Schmalbeck, 2001[69], and US Senate Finance Committee, 2017). To prevent such avoidance, the federal government in 1990 restricted the use of valuation discounts for certain transfers among family members, but changes in partnership law at the state level have largely made the regulations implementing these anti-abuse rules ineffective (US Senate Finance Committee, 2017).

Gifting bare ownership of an asset, while retaining usufruct until death

In some countries, taxpayers may minimise their inheritance and estate tax liabilities by separating full ownership of assets into bare ownership and usufruct. Taxpayers may retain the usufruct of an asset, continuing to receive the income and benefits that an asset confers, while passing the bare ownership of the asset to their heirs. For example, taxpayers may transfer ownership of their main residence but continue living in it, or transfer control of a company but retain the income that the company produces. Inheritance and estate taxes are levied on a lower value than if the full ownership had been transferred where countries tax the transfer of bare ownership (i.e. the value of full ownership less the value of the usufruct) and do not levy further taxes when the usufruct ceases to apply and beneficiaries receive full ownership on the donor's death. In the countries that tax the full ownership of assets, even when taxpayers pass on bare ownership while retaining usufruct, this strategy may still reduce indirectly the tax liability by allowing donors to make earlier property transfers, taking advantage of lower property values than if the asset were transferred upon death.

Interactions between inheritance or estate taxes and gift taxes or capital gains taxes

Taxpayers may avoid inheritance taxes by transferring their wealth during their life. In countries where gifts are only taxed where they occur shortly before the donor's death and in countries where tax-free thresholds are renewed yearly or every few years, taxpayers may avoid inheritance and estate taxes by giving (regular) gifts during their life. As discussed in Chapter 2, there is empirical evidence that taxpayers use gifts as a tax-minimising strategy to some extent. As discussed in Section 3.11, revising the design of gift taxes or implementing a tax on lifetime wealth transfers would be a way to reduce avoidance by limiting the importance of timing for gifts and inheritances.

The difference in tax treatment of unrealised capital gains between inheritances and gifts opens opportunities for avoidance. For instance, some countries apply a carry-over basis for unrealised capital gains on gifted assets but apply a step-up in basis for unrealised capital gains on bequeathed assets. This creates an incentive to retain assets until death, when capital gains are "forgiven", rather than being subject to capital gains taxes when the donor or the beneficiary of the gift sells the asset.

Preferential tax treatment for charitable giving

Charitable giving may allow taxpayers to reduce their tax liability while also creating a benefit for society. As discussed previously, most countries fully exempt transfers to charitable organisations, which have typically received certification allowing them to receive tax-free gifts and bequests. There is evidence that exemptions increase charitable bequests (Bakija, Gale and Slemrod, 2003[14]), which may generate a benefit for society. However, the tax treatment of charitable giving creates tax planning and avoidance opportunities (OECD, 2020[15]). Countries reported that common strategies include overvaluation of nonmonetary donations, donations of assets in which the donor retains an interest, and payments for goods and services disguised as donations.

There may be cases where wealth is transferred partially or entirely free of tax, using special structures that take advantage of the preferential tax treatment for charitable giving. The structures typically involve partial or time-limited transfers to charities. In the United States, for instance, a donor may set up a "charitable lead trust", whereby they transfer property to a trust with instructions to make payments to a charity on a fixed schedule for the term of the trust, with remaining assets in the trust being distributed at the end of the trust term to non-charitable beneficiaries. The gift and estate tax benefit lies in the fact that assets are transferred to ultimate beneficiaries at reduced values (Schmalbeck, 2001[16]). When the charitable lead trust is created, estate or gift taxes are levied on the amount that is left in the trust at the end of its fixed term, discounted using "hurdle" rates set by the Internal Revenue Service (IRS).[24] Most donors structure their trusts so that the estimated value of the reportable gift (i.e. the remaining assets for distribution to beneficiaries) is (close to) zero. A "charitable remainder trust", where the beneficiary receives income for a certain time and then assets are passed to the charity, can be used to achieve similar goals.

The use of trusts

Trusts may also be used to minimise inheritance or estate tax liabilities in some countries. Trusts typically involve a "settlor" or "grantor": the person who puts the assets into a trust; a "trustee": the person who manages the trust; and the "beneficiary": the person who benefits from the trust. Typically, trusts are used to separate the entitlement to the income that the property generates from the entitlement to the property itself, or to ensure that capital and income are distributed on a discretionary basis at infrequent intervals. While they may be used for legitimate succession or other non-tax reasons, the fact that ownership and access to benefits is split in some way means they can also potentially be used to avoid taxes on wealth transfers. Whether trusts are treated as separate entities or are transparent for tax purposes (i.e. tax authorities can "look through" trusts to assign assets to a taxpayer) may affect whether trusts can be used to minimise inheritance or estate taxes. Trusts have been a particularly significant challenge in Common Law countries. There may also be cases where trusts may be used to evade taxes, by concealing asset ownership, in particular through opaque offshore structures, although this has become much more difficult with the recent progress on international tax transparency (see section on tax evasion).

There are various types of trusts and their tax treatment differs. A common distinction between trusts is whether they are revocable or not. A revocable trust is a trust that can be changed or terminated at any point during the lifetime of the person who established the trust. An irrevocable trust, on the other hand, is essentially permanent, as the terms of the trust cannot be amended or revoked without the permission of the beneficiaries. Revocable trusts offer limited tax benefits and irrevocable trusts are typically those used for inheritance or estate tax planning. In the United Kingdom, trusts can also be divided into discretionary and interest in possession trusts. Discretionary trusts may give trustees complete discretion over income and sometimes over capital, while interest in possession trusts refer to trusts where beneficiaries have the right to receive trust income (although there may be discretion over capital). However, these simple trust categories group together more complex arrangements. For instance, the powers of the trustees may be restricted in some discretionary trusts, and interest in possession trusts may in practice devolve significant discretionary powers to the trustees (Chamberlain, 2020[17]).

In the United Kingdom, inheritance tax rules applying to trusts were tightened in 2006. Significant changes to the inheritance tax treatment of trusts were introduced in 2006 in the United Kingdom. Most lifetime transfers into trusts (whether discretionary or interest in possession) set up by a UK domiciled settlor are now subject to a 20% entry charge over the GBR 325 000 threshold, with an additional 20% tax if the settlor dies within seven years (Chamberlain, 2020[17]). This differs from the "potentially exempt transfer" (PET) system, which provides that inter vivos gifts between individuals (not through a trust) are free of inheritance tax if the donor survives seven years. In addition, a ten-year anniversary charge of up to 6% is levied every ten years from the start of the trust on the net value of any relevant property in the trust and an exit tax of up to 6% (although they tend to be much lower in practice) is levied on assets transferred out of the trust. Nowadays, trusts set up by UK domiciled settlors tend to be limited to "nil rate band" trusts settling GBR 325 000 every seven years or property that qualifies for business or agricultural property relief, or trusts settled by will, which are subject to a different tax regime (Chamberlain, 2020[17]). However, there are still considerable tax advantages for the foreign domiciled person that sets up non-UK resident trusts (Chamberlain, 2020[17]).

In the United States, inheritance tax planning and avoidance through trusts remains common. In the United States, a common type of trust to avoid estate taxes is the grantor retained annuity trust (GRAT). A GRAT is an irrevocable trust, where the grantor retains the right to receive a fixed periodic payment during the trust term, and if the grantor survives the trust term, remaining assets pass to "remainder" beneficiaries. When the grantor transfers wealth to the GRAT, the wealth transfer is considered as a taxable gift to beneficiaries, but the value of the gift is discounted because of the interest that the grantor retains, i.e. the annuity payments. The discount is calculated using IRS valuation tables, which assume that during the term of the GRAT trust assets will generate a modest rate of return – significantly below common stock market or private business rates of return. If the assets in the trust appreciate more than the IRS's so-called "hurdle" rate, the excess growth in asset values passes to "remainder" beneficiaries free of estate or gift tax (The United States Senate Finance Committee, 2017). These types of trusts are particularly beneficial to grantors who expect their assets to appreciate significantly. Special trusts, called irrevocable life insurance trusts (ILITs) can also be used to avoid estate taxes on life insurance proceeds. The trust purchases an insurance policy on the life of the grantor, or the grantor transfers a policy to the trust. To fund the trust's premium obligations with respect to the insurance policy, the grantor makes periodic payments to the trust, which are treated as gifts to the trust beneficiaries, but may qualify, under certain conditions, for the USD 14 000 gift tax annual exclusion. The value of the life insurance policy grows tax free, and when the grantor dies, the life insurance proceeds are distributed to the trust, and ultimately the trust beneficiaries, free of gift or estate tax (The United States Senate Finance Committee, 2017).[25]

Overall, the possibilities for tax planning through trusts or similar structures should be carefully assessed, and their tax treatment possibly revised. Whether trusts are treated as separate entities for tax purposes or as transparent entities (i.e. where the assets settled on trust are included in the taxable estate of the settlor or the beneficiaries on the basis that trusts can be 'looked through'), the rules should not allow the use of trusts to significantly reduce the tax burden on wealth transfers. The tax treatment of other structures, such as foundations, should also be carefully examined.

3.13.2. Common forms of tax evasion range from simple cash gifts to sophisticated cross-border structures

Taxpayers can illegally reduce their inheritance or estate tax liability through tax evasion. The term "tax evasion" may be used to describe arrangements where taxpayers pay less tax than they are legally obligated to pay by hiding income or information from the tax authorities.[26] The following sub-section examines some of the techniques that taxpayers use to evade inheritance and estate taxes, drawing on various sources including responses to the OECD Questionnaire on Inheritance, Estate, and Gift Taxes.

Undeclared wealth transfers and incomplete inventories

A simple evasion technique is to pass on undeclared cash to heirs. It is difficult for tax authorities to trace transfers of cash, particularly when beneficiaries do not deposit it in a bank account. Such transfers may take place at any time, and could occur in anticipation of the donor's death or over the months and years prior to their death. As keeping large amounts of cash carries the risk of theft, this technique is likely limited to small to moderate amounts and may be more attractive for regular gifts over the annual tax-free threshold than a (larger) bequest.

Taxpayers may also exclude assets from the inventory or not declare transfers of wealth. Heirs may receive some of the donor's assets following their death, without the heirs notifying the tax authority of the act. Failing to declare an asset or the transfer of an asset may be easier for assets that are difficult to trace, such as low- or moderate-value jewellery, compared to assets where ownership is certified by a public body, such as housing. Alternately, taxpayers may falsely declare that the total value of the donor's assets is below the threshold for the requirement to declare or pay tax on an inheritance. To reduce the administrative burden of declaring all transfers while preventing evasion of inheritance and estate taxes on low-value goods, some countries value household goods as a percentage of the value of the estate's housing assets.

Abuse of deduction provisions

Taxpayers may make excessive deductions for expenses and debts, by inflating their value or deducting ineligible expenses and debts. Debts are deductible in most countries that levy an inheritance or estate tax, but several countries apply conditions. Such conditions prevent abuses, such as disallowing deductions for debts that were contracted to purchase tax-exempt assets or debts that are to heirs or close family. Taxpayers may deduct fraudulent or inflated deductible expenses to reduce the inheritance or estate tax due. Tax authorities may require taxpayers to retain proof of expenses and cap the deduction of certain expenses, such as funeral costs.

Wealth held offshore

Taxpayers may attempt to hide assets offshore. Undeclared assets held in low-tax jurisdictions have traditionally posed a challenge to tax administrations, particularly when these jurisdictions practised banking secrecy. While taxpayers may hold wealth in low-tax jurisdictions for non-tax reasons, such arrangements limit countries' information about taxpayer wealth and enable taxpayers to evade taxes.

Exchange of Information (EOI) promotes tax transparency and helps tax administrations address tax evasion. Under the Exchange of Information on Request (EOIR) standard, tax authorities in one jurisdiction can request information about a particular taxpayer from tax authorities in another jurisdiction. Authorities can request a broad range of information, including accounting records, bank statements and information on the ownership of real and financial assets. Under the Automatic Exchange of Information (AEOI) standard, participating jurisdictions exchange information automatically and on a periodic basis. The Common Reporting Standard (CRS) is the global standard for reciprocal annual exchanges on financial accounts held by non-resident taxpayers and defines the type and format of information to be shared. This includes details about the account holder (e.g. their name, address, and date of birth) and the financial account (e.g. the account number and the account balance). The CRS is designed to capture information about commonly held assets and financial accounts, which tax authorities can then compare with other sources and, if necessary, pursue further investigation. This could include submitting a request for information under the EOIR standard, which allows for a broader type of information to be exchanged on a pre-identified taxpayer. EOI networks have expanded dramatically and have been increasingly relying on multilateral approaches (O'Reilly, Parra Ramirez and Stemmer, 2019[18]), especially since 2014 when countries were invited to commit to the AEOI standard to exchange information by 2017 or 2018. In 2019, 97 jurisdictions carried out automatic exchange of financial information, covering 84 million accounts and EUR 10 trillion of total assets (OECD, 2020[19]). The global exchange on request is also wide, with about 30 000 requests having been received in 2019[27].

However, taxpayers may seek to circumvent the Common Reporting Standard (CRS). Assets such as real estate and art are not included in the CRS. While taxpayers may hold these assets for legitimate reasons, they do provide one avenue for circumventing the CRS (see e.g. (De Simone, Lester and Markle,

2020[20]), for the impact of FATCA). As financial accounts are typically reported on by third parties, such as banks, taxpayers may establish an entity, such as a family-managed trust, that has the responsibility to report on its own assets and then fail to report. Taxpayers may also establish entities to hold financial assets and fracture ownership of these entities in order to fall below the relevant threshold at which reporting institutions should look-through to find the controlling person. In cases where taxpayers are subject to third party reporting, they may hold assets in non-participating jurisdictions. Certain residence and citizenship by investment (RBI/CBI) schemes, which allow individuals to obtain citizenship or residence rights through local investment or for a fee, can also be misused to circumvent the CRS.

There is a need for continued progress on international tax transparency and efforts to ensure that taxpayers do not circumvent the CRS. To address the risks posed by RBI/CBI schemes, the OECD has assessed and identified schemes that pose a high-risk to the integrity of the CRS. Financial institutions are recommended to take the outcome of the OECD's analysis into account when carrying out their CRS due diligence obligations. The OECD's Global Forum also assesses whether jurisdictions continue to effectively participate in EOIR and assesses the effectiveness of the implementation of the AEOI standard through peer review processes to ensure that all implementing jurisdictions are dedicating adequate resources, including by ensuring compliance by financial institutions with the requirements. While it has become increasingly difficult to circumvent EOI as the treaty network has densified and the culture of tax transparency has strengthened, it will also be critical to ensure that persons, assets, and institutions not covered under existing EOI standards do not offer opportunities for continued tax evasion.

As is the case for avoidance techniques, sophisticated evasion techniques will be more accessible to higher-wealth taxpayers. While low-wealth households may find it easier to engage in simple evasion techniques, such as undeclared transfers of cash and low- to moderate-value household goods, leveraging tax-exempt assets to invest in taxed assets or concealing assets abroad, for example, require some forethought and professional advice, and will incur costs.

3.14. Political economy of inheritance tax reforms

3.14.1. Inheritance and estate taxes tend to be unpopular and poorly understood

In many countries, inheritance or estate taxes are (among) the least popular taxes. In the United Kingdom, a 2015 YouGov Poll revealed that the inheritance tax was viewed as "fair" by only 22% of the respondents, making it the least popular tax among eleven major taxes.[28] In France, aversion to taxation is particularly strong when it comes to wealth transfers, on par with labour income taxation, and 87% of the French population said they were favourable to a reduction in inheritance tax to allow parents to transfer as much wealth as possible to their children. This opinion has seen an 8-percentage point increase since 2011 (Grégoire-Marchand, 2018[21]). In Sweden, where the inheritance tax was eventually repealed, a survey of attitudes towards taxes conducted in 2004 showed that almost two thirds of the respondents, including a majority of left-leaning individuals, wanted inheritance and gift taxes to be either reduced or altogether repealed (survey cited in Henrekson and Waldenström, (2016[1]). Similar unpopularity was reported in many other OECD countries.

Evidence also shows that inheritance or estate taxes are not well understood. In the United States, Kuziemko et al. (2015[22]) found that providing information on the incidence of the estate tax significantly increases support for it. This largely reflects misinformation, as many respondents believed a majority of families were subject to the estate tax, when the actual share was 0.1%. In France, where inheritance and gift taxes are levied on much lower wealth transfers, a recent study also shows that inheritance and gift taxation is misunderstood, with respondents significantly overestimating tax levels (Grégoire-Marchand, 2018[21]). For instance, on average, respondents estimated the average tax rate on transmissions to spouses to be 22%, when those wealth transfers are actually exempt. Respondents were also asked to estimate the average effective tax rate on wealth transfers. Since the 1980s, this rate has remained relatively stable: between 4% and 7% for all assets transferred, and between 2% and 3.5% for assets transferred to direct descendants. However, a majority of respondents thought that this rate was greater than 10% and more than 36% of respondents estimated it to be greater than 20%. A Tax Policy Survey conducted by Stantcheva (2020[23]) also found that the French had a poor understanding of the progressive nature of the tax: 42% of respondents wrongly believe that inheritances are taxed at a flat rate. Respondents who correctly answered that there are several rates were also asked to give their best guess on the lowest marginal tax rate on estates transmitted by direct transmission. The average estimation was 20%, 15 percentage points higher than the actual lowest rate of 5%.

The rest of this section considers ways in which governments may enhance the public acceptability of inheritance tax reform, starting with tax design. Indeed, some of the popular rejection directly stems from the way inheritance, estate, and gift taxes are designed and operate. There is for instance a strong sense of injustice in reaction to the fact that wealthy households have largely been able to avoid inheritance taxation in some countries. A better-designed tax, limiting the preferential tax treatment provided to certain assets and other tax-minimising opportunities, would contribute to reducing the unpopularity of inheritance taxation. In addition to limiting tax planning opportunities and increasing progressivity, broader tax bases could potentially allow lowering statutory tax rates, which may also enhance the public acceptability of inheritance taxation. There is evidence that in some countries, higher tax exemption thresholds would make taxes on wealth transfers more acceptable (Bastani and Waldenström, 2021[5]). Finally, a frequent popular concern is related to asset-rich but income-poor taxpayers who might be forced to sell their assets to pay the tax. Such concerns should be addressed through improved tax design, in particular by allowing tax payments in instalments and tax payment deferrals under certain conditions. In addition to having these measures in place, there should be clear communication highlighting their availability.

3.14.2. Information and policy framing are important to increase the public acceptability of inheritance tax reforms

Evidence also shows the importance of narratives and policy framing. The repeal of the estate tax in the United States,[29] and how it gained widespread popular support, provides an interesting example of the role of narratives and policy framing. Indeed, in the United States, many polls in the late 1990s and early 2000s showed widespread public support for repeal of the estate tax, in the range of 60% to 80%. Part of the popular rejection of the estate tax was the result of misperceptions of self-interest (only the wealthiest 2% of Americans paid the estate tax at the time, but the share of estate taxpayers tends to be vastly overestimated) but also of carefully framed narratives, particularly around the notion of "fairness". For instance, references to the "death tax" and double taxation have helped frame the estate tax as an unfair tax. Emphasising the estate tax burden on family farms and businesses has also helped shape public opinions, particularly as entrepreneurship and family businesses form part of the "American dream" but also because many people have close family members who are small business owners (Birney, Graetz and Shapiro, 2006[24]). In reality, however, most of the estate tax burden does not fall on family–owned businesses or farms. Birney, Graetz and Shapiro (2006[24]) argue that these findings about public opinion were then used by interest groups in campaigns and building coalitions for the repeal of the tax. This highlights the importance of the way inheritance tax reform is framed. Reframing reforms aiming to raise more revenue from inheritance taxation around notions of equality of opportunity and inequality reduction may help increase their public acceptability. Such changes in narratives and policy framing may be easier with inequality becoming a more prominent topic in recent years (Perret, 2020[25]). Such reframing may also be more effective if, as mentioned above, it goes hand-in-hand with real changes in tax design that address popular concerns, particularly in relation to tax avoidance.

Providing information can play an important role in enhancing the acceptability of inheritance tax reform. There is evidence that people's attitudes and public perceptions of capital and inheritance taxation change when they are given information on inequality. For instance, Bastani and Waldenström (2021[5]) find that exposing people to facts about inherited wealth significantly increases support for inheritance taxation through a randomised survey of 12 000 Swedish adults, linked to administrative register data, in which they expose different parts of the target population to different information treatments. They find that average support for inheritance taxation in the control group (which did not receive information) is 24.5% and that receiving information about inherited wealth increases support by about eight percentage points. This result holds true after controlling for various individual characteristics. These effects appear to be driven by changes in perceptions about inherited wealth and whether luck is considered to matter most for economic success. In addition to information about wealth inequality and inheritances, the perceptions and acceptability of inheritance taxation may change when people are better informed about the design and functioning of these taxes, in particular who they apply to. In the United States, a poll asking whether the estate tax should be abolished found very different results depending on whether respondents had received information about which estates were affected by the tax. Among the group told that the tax only affected estates worth more than USD 5 million, support for maintaining the tax was close to 20 percentage points higher than in the group that had not received the information (46% compared to 27%).[30] Stantcheva (2020[26]) also finds that showing people instructional videos about the workings and consequences of the estate tax in the United States strengthens the view that increasing the estate tax is a good way to reduce inequality.

Policy packaging may also be helpful. Inheritance tax reform may be more acceptable if it is accompanied by other reforms. If the introduction of an inheritance tax or an increase in existing inheritance or estate taxes is part of a more comprehensive tax reform and goes hand-in-hand with a decrease in other taxes, especially in labour taxes, which a majority of people are subject to, it may be more acceptable politically. Packaging an inheritance tax reform as part of a broader reform aiming at tax mix shifts rather than overall tax burden increases may increase the chances of the reform being adopted.

Finally, earmarking part of the revenues raised from inheritance or estate taxes may help increase popular support, although this should be considered very carefully. Part of the revenues collected from inheritance, estate, and gift taxes could for instance be earmarked for the financing of old-age care. Alternatively, revenues could partly be earmarked for education, particularly if inheritance tax reforms are framed as aiming to enhance equality of opportunity. Taxpayers may perceive inheritance or estate taxes as more legitimate if they know what part of the revenues are used for. The fact that the revenues raised from inheritance or estate taxes tend to be low compared to other taxes may reduce the potential inefficiencies arising from earmarking large amounts of public revenues, but earmarking still needs to be considered with caution.

References

Acciari, P. and S. Morelli (2020), *Wealth Transfers and Net Wealth at Death: Evidence from the Italian Inheritance Tax Records 1995–2016*, National Bureau of Economic Research, Cambridge, MA, http://dx.doi.org/10.3386/w27899. [8]

Bakija, J., W. Gale and J. Slemrod (2003), *Charitable bequests and taxes on inheritances and estates: Aggregate evidence from across states and time*, http://dx.doi.org/10.1257/000282803321947362. [14]

Bastani, S. and D. Waldenström (2021), "Perceptions of Inherited Wealth and the Support for Inheritance Taxation", *Economica*, pp. -, http://dx.doi.org/10.1111/ecca.12359. [5]

Batchelder, L. (2020), *Leveling the Playing Field between Inherited Income and Income from Work through an Inheritance Tax*. [3]

Birney, M., M. Graetz and I. Shapiro (2006), "Public Opinion and the Push to Repeal the Estate Tax", *National Tax Journal*, Vol. 59/3, pp. 439-61, https://EconPapers.repec.org/RePEc:ntj:journl:v:59:y:2006:i:3:p:439-61 (accessed on 9 November 2020). [24]

Boadway, R., E. Chamberlain and C. Emmerson (2010), "Taxation of Wealth and Wealth Transfers", in *Dimensions of Tax Design; The Mirrlees Review*, Oxford University Press, Oxford. [6]

Chamberlain, E. (2020), *Defining the tax base – design issues. Wealth Tax Commission Evidence Paper, 8.* [17]

Daly, S. and G. Loutzenhiser (2020), *Valuation. Wealth Tax Commission Evidence Paper, 9.* [12]

Dao, M. (2019), *Wealth Inequality and Private Savings in Germany*, IMF. [9]

De Simone, L., R. Lester and K. Markle (2020), "Transparency and Tax Evasion: Evidence from the Foreign Account Tax Compliance Act (FATCA)", *Journal of Accounting Research*, Vol. 58/1, pp. 105-153, http://dx.doi.org/10.1111/1475-679X.12293. [20]

European Commission (2011), *Commission Recommendation regarding relief for double taxation of inheritances*, Office for Official Publications of the European Communities, Luxembourg. [4]

Grégoire-Marchand, P. (2018), *La fiscalité des héritages: connaissances et opinions des Français*, France Stratégie, http://www.strategie.gouv.fr (accessed on 14 December 2020). [21]

Henrekson, M. and D. Waldenström (2016), "Inheritance taxation in Sweden, 1885–2004: the role of ideology, family firms, and tax avoidance", *Economic History Review*, Vol. 69/4, pp. 1228–1254, http://dx.doi.org/doi.org/10.1111/ehr.12280. [1]

Kuziemko, I. et al. (2015), *How elastic are preferences for redistribution? Evidence from randomized survey experiments*, American Economic Association, http://dx.doi.org/10.1257/aer.20130360. [22]

Moretti, E. and D. Wilson (2020), *Taxing Billionaires: Estate Taxes and the Geographical Location of the Ultra-Wealthy*, National Bureau of Economic Research, Cambridge, MA, http://dx.doi.org/10.3386/w26387. [13]

Nolan B., J. C. Palomino, P. Van Kerm, and S. Morelli (2020), *The Wealth of Families: The Intergenerational Transmission of Wealth in Britain in Comparative Perspective*. Nuffield Foundation and INET at the Oxford Martin School [2]

O'Reilly, P., K. Parra Ramirez and M. Stemmer (2019), "Exchange of information and bank deposits in international financial centres", *OECD Taxation Working Papers*, No. 46, OECD Publishing, Paris, https://dx.doi.org/10.1787/025bfebe-en. [18]

OECD (2020), *International community continues making progress against offshore tax evasion.* [19]

OECD (2020), *Taxation and Philanthropy*, OECD Publishing, Paris. [15]

OECD (2018), *Taxation of household savings*, OECD Publishing, Paris, http://dx.doi.org/doi.org/10.1787/19900538. [10]

Office of Tax Simplification (2018), *Inheritance Tax Review - first report: Overview of the tax and dealing with administration*, Office of Tax Simplification, London. [7]

Perret, S. (2020), *Why did other wealth taxes fail and is this time different?, UK Wealth Tax Commission, Evidence Paper n. 6.* [25]

Saez, E. and G. Zucman (2019), *Progressive wealth taxation. BPEA Conference Draft, Fall.* [11]

Schmalbeck, R. (2001), "Avoiding Federal Wealth Transfer Taxes", in Gale, W., J. Hines Jr. and J. Slemrod (eds.), *Rethinking Estate and Gift Taxation*, Brookings Institution Press, Washington, D. C. [16]

Stantcheva, S. (2020), *2020 Taxes and Policy Survey*, https://www.stefanie-stantcheva.com/research/Taxes_and_Policy_Survey_France.pdf. [23]

Stantcheva, S. (2020), "Understanding Economic Policies: What do people know and learn?", Harvard University Working Paper, Cambridge. [26]

Notes

[1] The report presents information for 2020 and covers all 37 OECD countries except Colombia (which became a member of the OECD after the data collection exercise was completed), Iceland and Turkey.

[2] The chapter reports dollar values in USD 2020, using 2020 average exchange rates from the OECD National Accounts. The conversion series can be found at http://dotstat.oecd.org/restsdmx/sdmx.ashx/GetDataStructure/SNA_TABLE4.

[3] Portugal abolished the Inheritance and Gift Tax in 2004, replacing it with a stamp duty that is levied on transactions, including deemed transactions such as the transfer of assets when the donor passes away and the assets are passed on to the beneficiaries. The revenues from the stamp duty are no longer

recorded in category 4300 (Inheritance, estate, and gift taxes) of Revenue Statistics, which is the source for Figure 3.1.

[4] Further analysis has found identical trends when measuring inheritance, estate, and gift tax revenues as a share of GDP.

[5] Taxpayers who are tax residents in the United Kingdom but are domiciled abroad (i.e. their permanent home is outside the United Kingdom) are deemed tax domicile if they were tax resident in the United Kingdom for 15 of the past 20 years.

[6] These rules apply to donors who are former tax residents of France, Ireland; to donors who are citizens and former tax residents of Germany, Greece, and the Netherlands; and to donors who are deemed domicile or former actual tax-domicile of the United Kingdom. These rules apply where both donors and beneficiaries are citizens and former tax residents of Japan. In all countries, these provisions expire after a number of years.

[7] If the donor spouse is domiciled or deemed domiciled in the United Kingdom and the beneficiary spouse is not, the exemption is limited. However, the beneficiary spouse can elect to be deemed domiciled for inheritance tax purposes.

[8] If co-habiting partners have signed a notarial cohabitation agreement, this period is six months (inheritance) or two years (gift).

[9] Of the 24 countries that levy an inheritance or estate tax, marriage equality exists in 13 and same-sex civil unions exist in 20. Four countries do not recognise same-sex relationships and so restrict spousal treatment to different-sex married couples only (Japan, Korea, Lithuania, and Poland). Switzerland, which does not recognise same-sex marriage, provides more generous treatment to married couples than couples in a civil union.

[10] The tax-free threshold rises with the donor's wealth in Luxembourg, as the donor's children are exempt on the portion they would have received under an intestate succession (which is largest for children, compared to other heirs).

[11] The United Kingdom provides a residence nil-rate band (RNRB), which is an additional tax-free threshold for bequests of a "qualifying residence" to lineal descendants. The donor may have held the residence at death or held the residence in the past, allowing taxpayers to downsize or dispose of their residence and still qualify for the RNRB. Like the standard nil-rate band, any unused RNRB can be passed from a donor to their surviving spouse, regardless of whether the first spouse held a qualifying residence. The RNRB is tapered once the estate exceeds GBP 2 million. Only transfers at death qualify for the relief.

[12] Estates can choose between a standard deduction per donor and an itemised deduction, though most taxpayers claim the standard deduction. In both cases, estates can also claim a spousal deduction. Standard deduction: KRW 500 million. Itemised deduction: KRW 200 million basic deduction, KRW 50 million per child, KRW 10 million per minor for each year until they reach 20 years of age, KRW 50 million per heir 65 years or older, KRW 10 million per heir with a disability for each year until the reach their expected remaining years (as determined by Statistics Korea), and a housing allowance.

[13] In the United Kingdom, gifts are tax-exempt if the donor survives more than seven years. If a donor bequeaths assets to their spouse at death and the surviving spouse immediately gifts those assets to the couple's children, no inheritance tax will be due if the surviving spouse lives seven or more years. However, if the donor bequeathed their wealth directly to their children upon death, estate taxes would be due on

wealth over the exemption threshold. This avoidance opportunity would be eliminated if all inter vivos gifts were taxed, without needing to alter spouse exemption.

[14] In addition to the statutory rate of 1%, a surcharge of 20% of the tax liability applies to siblings and other 2nd rank relatives, resulting in a final tax rate of 1.2%.

[15] Backward-looking tax rates draw on data of actual inheritances and tax paid on these transfers to develop a single indicator of the tax burden on past inheritances.

[16] Agricultural Property Relief (APR) is available only up to the agricultural value of the property and can apply to rented land owned for more than 7 years.

[17] These benefits are not considered part of the inheritance and so are exempt from inheritance taxation.

[18] For example, a donor living in Brussels wants to bequeath EUR 1 000 000 to a friend. Under a classic scenario, the donor bequeaths their estate to their friend, who pays EUR 758 750 in inheritance taxes and receives EUR 241 250 net. Under a legs en duo scenario, the donor bequeaths their estate to a charitable institution, who agrees to pay the inheritance taxes due and to pay half the donor's wealth to the friend, keeping the remainder. The charitable institution pays EUR 393 750 in inheritance taxes (the taxes due on the wealth received by the friend and by the charitable institution), pays EUR 500 000 to the donor's friend, and retains EUR 106 250. Simulations made on the 3rd August 2020 using the calculator at https://www.amnesty.be/donnez/legs-duo-testament.

[19] https://www.oecd.org/ctp/glossaryoftaxterms.htm#F.

[20] The estate tax applies to the full amount bequeathed by the donor and the gift tax applies to the amount received by beneficiaries after tax. For an estate tax rate of t=40%, the effective gift tax rate is $t/(1+t) = 28.6\%$.

[21] While gifts are taxed at a lower effective rate than bequests (see footnote 20), the (more favourable) step-up in basis applying to bequests may offset the (less favourable) carry-over basis applying to gifts, for transfers of assets with unrealised capital gains.

[22] The favourable tax treatment of unrealised capital gains at death may offset the lower effective tax rate on gifts, meaning the overall distortion is ambiguous in the case of transfers of appreciated assets (see footnotes 20 and 21).

[23] https://www.oecd.org/fr/ctp/glossaryoftaxterms.htm.

[24] For example, a donor transfers USD 500 000 to a charitable lead trust and mandates it to pay 5% of the initial transfer (USD 25 000) to a chosen charity for 20 years. The initial value of the transfer (USD 500 000 = USD 25 000 x 20 years) is discounted according to IRS tables. Assuming an interest rate of 0.4%, the annuity rate is 19.1841 (IRS 1457, Table B). The present value of the annuity is USD 479 603 (USD 25 000 x 19.1841) and the taxable transfer is therefore USD 20 397 (= USD 500 000 - USD 479 603).

[25] https://www.finance.senate.gov/imo/media/doc/101217%20Estate%20Tax%20Whitepaper%20FINAL1.pdf.

[26] https://www.oecd.org/fr/ctp/glossaryoftaxterms.htm.

[27] http://www.oecd.org/tax/transparency/documents/global-forum-annual-report-2020.pdf.

[28] https://yougov.co.uk/topics/politics/articles-reports/2015/03/19/inheritance-tax-most-unfair.

[29] Legislation enacted in 2001 gradually phased out the estate tax by raising the tax exemption level and reducing the tax rate, leading to the tax's temporary repeal in 2010. The estate tax was re-instated in 2011.

[30] http://big.assets.huffingtonpost.com/tabsHPEstateTax20170929.pdf.

4 Summary and recommendations

Chapter 4 summarises the key findings and recommendations of the report. The chapter begins with a review of the key trends in inheritance taxation across OECD countries, and then presents the main recommendations and policy options that countries could consider to enhance the design and functioning of inheritance, estate, and gift taxes.

4.1. Key trends in OECD countries

Household wealth is unevenly distributed. Household wealth is highly concentrated at the top of the wealth distribution. The wealthiest ten percent of households own half of all household wealth on average across 27 OECD countries, while the top one percent of the wealth distribution own 18% of household wealth. The composition of assets also varies across households, with financial assets being particularly unevenly distributed and accounting for a large portion of wealth among the richest households.

Wealth transfers also appear to favour wealthy households. Wealthy households are more likely to receive gifts and inheritances. In addition, the average value of wealth transfers is consistently higher for wealthier households. Across 16 OECD countries, the average inheritance received by households in the bottom wealth quintile ranged from around USD 300 to USD 11,000. For households in the top wealth quintile, the average inheritance ranged from around USD 30 000 to USD 526 000. Wealth transfers may have an equalising effect for some poor households, whose inheritance receipts tend to be larger relative to their overall wealth, but the effect may be short-lived because poorer households are more likely to consume their inheritances.

Wealth accumulation dynamics and wealth transfers are likely to exacerbate wealth inequality in the future. Over time, the level of household wealth has increased, due in particular to increases in asset prices and savings rates. There is also some evidence that the share of inheritances in private wealth has increased in some countries over the past few decades. Inheritances are also expected to increase in value, if recent trends in asset prices continue, and in number, with the baby-boom generation getting older. Moreover, as a result of longer life expectancies, the age at which people inherit and wealth concentration among older cohorts, which is already high, are expected to rise. There is also a risk that recent highly expansionary monetary policies could potentially contribute to the formation of asset bubbles, which could further increase wealth inequality and widen the gap between the older asset-owning generations and younger generations who might face barriers to asset ownership, such as increasingly high housing prices.

Wealth transfer taxes are levied in 24 OECD countries. Most countries levy recipient-based inheritance taxes. Denmark, Korea, the United Kingdom and the United States, on the other hand, levy estate taxes on donors' overall estates. Ireland levies a specific type of recipient-based inheritance and gift tax on lifetime wealth transfers. Ten OECD countries have abolished their taxes on wealth transfers since the early 1970s, citing a lack of political support, tax minimisation opportunities and high administrative burdens for relatively small amounts of revenue as the main justifications for their repeal.

The design of inheritance, estate, and gift taxes varies widely across countries. Significant differences include the levels of tax exemption thresholds. While they tend to favour close relatives, they vary considerably across countries, ranging from around USD 17 000 in Belgium to USD 11.6 million in the United States for transfers to direct descendants. There is also significant variation in tax rates across countries. Most countries have progressive rates but their levels vary widely, and some countries tax transfers to distant relatives at much higher rates than others do. The tax treatment of gifts also varies widely depending on the country, even if in-life giving often benefits from a preferential tax treatment compared to wealth transfers at death through the renewal of tax-free thresholds.

Across OECD countries, however, inheritance, estate, and gift tax bases have often been narrowed, reducing their revenue potential, efficiency and fairness. Today, only 0.5% of total tax revenues are sourced from these taxes on average across the countries that levy them and revenues from inheritance, estate, and gift taxes exceed 1% of total taxation in only four OECD countries (Belgium, France, Japan, and Korea). Low revenues largely reflect narrow tax bases. A majority of estates go untaxed in a number of countries, in large part due to highly preferential tax treatment for transfers to close relatives and relief provided for specific assets (e.g. main residence, business and farm assets, pension assets, and life insurance policies). In a number of countries, inheritance and estate taxes can also largely be avoided through inter vivos gifts, due to their preferential tax treatment. Other tax planning opportunities have also allowed taxpayers to minimise their inheritance or estate tax burdens (e.g. separating bare ownership from usufruct, use of preferential valuation rules). In addition to significantly reducing potential revenue and generating distortions, tax reliefs, tax planning and tax evasion opportunities have contributed to lowering the tax burden on those at the top of the distribution in some countries.

4.2. Policy options and recommendations

Overall, the report finds that there is a good case for making greater use of well-designed inheritance and gift taxation, based on equity, efficiency and administrative considerations. There are strong equity arguments in favour of inheritance taxation, in particular of a recipient-based inheritance tax with an exemption for low-value inheritances. The case might be strongest where the effective taxation of personal capital income and wealth tends to be low. From an efficiency perspective, while the number of studies is limited, the empirical literature generally suggests that inheritance taxes tend to have more limited effects on savings than other taxes levied on wealthy taxpayers, and confirms their positive effects on heirs' labour supply and donors' charitable giving. In addition, while inheritance taxes might negatively affect family business successions (depending on tax design), they might at the same time reduce risks of misallocating capital. The report also shows that there is evidence of tax planning and migration among the very wealthy in response to inheritance taxation, but that these behaviours could largely be addressed through better tax design. Finally, inheritance taxes have a number of administrative advantages compared to other forms of wealth taxation and recent progress on international tax transparency enhances the ability of countries to tax capital effectively.

However, taking into account country context is critical. The appropriate choice of tax instruments will depend on country-specific circumstances, including the level of wealth inequality and the level of administrative capacity. In addition, policy choices regarding inheritance taxation should take into consideration the rest of the tax system, especially the other taxes that countries may be levying on personal wealth and capital income. As discussed in Chapter 2, while inheritance taxes in combination with taxes on personal capital income can be powerful tools to reduce the pace of wealth accumulation over generations, other tools can be used to achieve this objective. For instance, a significant reduction in the pace of wealth accumulation over generations could be achieved through taxes on personal capital income, but these may need to be levied at high and progressive rates in order to have a significant effect. From an efficiency point of view, the combination of more moderate progressive taxes on personal capital income with a progressive inheritance tax may be preferable.

It is also important to mention that inheritance taxation is not a silver bullet. Even well designed inheritance, estate, and gift taxes may remain relatively limited sources of revenue, compared to taxes on labour income or consumption for instance. That should not be interpreted as a sign that inheritance, estate, and gift taxes cannot play an important role in strengthening equality of opportunity and reducing wealth gaps. However, it does highlight that they are not a silver bullet and that complementary reforms may be necessary to raise revenue and address inequality. In fact, the simulations discussed in Chapter 2 show that inheritance taxes need to be combined with strengthened taxation of personal capital income if countries wish to significantly reduce the pace of wealth accumulation over generations. Having well-designed taxes on personal capital income, including capital gains, should also be a priority.

4.2.1. Type of wealth transfer tax

There are different ways of taxing wealth transfers, often involving trade-offs between simplicity and equity. As discussed below, there are good arguments for having a separate tax on wealth transfers rather than taxing them through the income tax. However, different types of wealth transfer taxes may be implemented and these involve some trade-offs. An estate tax can be considered to be the simplest form of wealth transfer taxation, but will likely be less equitable because it does not take into consideration the wealth received by each beneficiary. An inheritance tax levied on recipients may be more equitable, but it will not be as easy to administer. Finally, a tax on lifetime wealth transfers has the potential to be the most progressive form of wealth transfer taxation, but will likely involve additional tax compliance and administration costs. The choice between these different types of wealth transfer taxes should take into account country-specific circumstances, including the level of inequality, the capacities of tax administrations, preferences for redistribution, as well as the existence of other taxes on personal wealth and capital income and the overall progressivity of countries' tax systems.

There are good arguments for taxing wealth transfers under a separate tax rather than through the income tax. Some have proposed treating inheritances as taxable personal income in the hands of recipients on horizontal equity grounds. Integrating inheritance and gift taxation with income taxation would require the inclusion of the market value of the assets transferred to recipients as taxable income under the personal income tax (PIT). The tax liability would depend on the recipients' personal characteristics, the amount of their other income and other factors affecting their PIT liability. However, the lumpiness of inheritances could make their inclusion as income problematic in the absence of income averaging. Another disadvantage of taxing inheritances through the PIT is that different heirs would face different tax liabilities depending on their level of taxable income. Further, taxing inheritances under the income tax could lead to very high marginal effective tax rates for recipients who have other sources of income (e.g. labour income) and receive inheritances, which could have strong disincentive effects (e.g. on labour supply). More generally, taxing inheritances under the PIT would significantly increase the complexity of the PIT system. If inheritances were redefined as personal income, there would also be important implications regarding the allocation of taxing rights between countries in the case of cross-border inheritances. Such effects can be avoided by having a separate tax on inheritances.

An inheritance tax levied on recipients is more equitable than a tax levied on donors' estates. If the objective is to promote equality of opportunity, there is a strong case for a recipient-based inheritance tax rather than an estate tax levied on donors, as it is the amount of wealth received by each recipient and their personal circumstances that should matter rather than the overall amount of wealth left by the donor. This approach allows for progressive tax rates to be levied on the amount of wealth received by beneficiaries. Another advantage of a recipient-based inheritance tax, as opposed to an estate tax levied on donors' estates, is that it may encourage the division of estates and further reduce concentrations of wealth as splitting bequests among multiple beneficiaries reduces tax liabilities. Evidence of this behavioural response is sparse, however. Arguments against wealth transfer taxes, based on double taxation concerns, are also weaker in the case of inheritance taxes that are levied on recipients as there is no double taxation of the donor as the wealth transfer is only taxed once in the hands of the recipient upon receipt of the inheritance. On the other hand, an advantage of estate taxes over inheritance taxes is that they may be easier to collect given that they are levied on overall estates and involve a smaller number of taxing points.

A particularly fair and efficient approach would consist of taxing beneficiaries on the gifts and bequests they receive over their life through a tax on lifetime wealth transfers. The tax liability for each wealth transfer would be determined by taking into account the amount of wealth previously received by the beneficiary. Such a tax could be levied above a lifetime tax exemption threshold, i.e. above an amount of wealth that beneficiaries would be entitled to receive tax-free during the course of their life (i.e. both in-life gifts and end-of-life inheritances). The lifetime exemption threshold could either be a standard amount applicable regardless of the relationship between the donor and the beneficiary, or could provide for additional tax-free amounts for transfers to direct descendants. Such a tax levied on lifetime wealth transfers would ensure that individuals who receive more wealth over their lifetime pay more inheritance tax than individuals who receive less, particularly if tax rates are progressive. It would also ensure that beneficiaries receiving the same amounts of wealth, regardless of whether it is through multiple small transfers or one large transfer, face similar tax labilities. It would also limit the importance of timing for gifts and inheritances, reducing avoidance opportunities. Moreover, a tax on lifetime wealth transfers encourages donors to pass their wealth to individuals who have received less over their lifetime.

However, a tax levied on lifetime wealth transfers may involve a number of practical difficulties that should be carefully assessed. A tax on lifetime wealth transfers may increase administrative and compliance costs, though these costs and the extent to which they fall on taxpayers or the tax administration will depend on whether the tax is based on self-assessment or whether the tax administration tracks and records the history of wealth transfers received by beneficiaries. Such a reform may be easier to implement thanks to digitalisation, albeit still with considerable implementation costs. On the other hand, the requirement for lifetime record keeping would allow for valuable information on wealth transfers to be collected. Taxing lifetime wealth transfers may also give rise to difficulties in relation to the application of international tax rules in determining where transferred assets are taxable in the case of cross-border wealth transfers. These issues are important, but the many advantages of taxing recipients on the wealth they receive during the course of their lifetime make further exploration of these possibilities worthwhile.

Where a tax on lifetime wealth transfers may not be feasible, it could still serve as a useful guide for exploring other wealth transfer tax reform options. For instance, where such a reform may not be possible, countries could consider first better aligning the tax treatment of in-life gifts and end-of-life inheritances. Additionally, under the purest form of a tax on lifetime wealth transfers, it is the cumulative amount of wealth received by beneficiaries over their lifetime that matters with no distinction depending on who it was received from, i.e. there is no preference given to wealth received from close relatives. Even if such a tax is not adopted, countries may reform their existing taxes by reducing tax treatment differentials between transfers to close and distant relatives.

In addition to the type of tax that is levied, more specific tax design considerations discussed below are key to well-functioning inheritance, estate, and gift taxes. Whether considering incremental changes or a comprehensive reform such as the tax on lifetime wealth transfers outlined above, countries could improve the design of their taxes on wealth transfers through careful analysis and adherence to the principles of good tax policy. The rest of this chapter suggests a number of more specific reforms that countries could consider to improve the design and implementation of inheritance, estate, and gift taxes.

4.2.2. Tax rate schedules

Tax exemption thresholds, whether they are lifetime-based or not, should allow recipients to receive a small amount of wealth tax-free. There is some evidence that inheritances have an equalising effect, i.e. they reduce relative inequality, which justifies exempting small inheritances from an equity perspective. There is also evidence showing that an inheritance tax with a higher tax exemption threshold would receive more popular support.

Progressive tax rates enhance the vertical equity and redistributive effects of inheritance taxes. Progressive rates increase vertical equity by ensuring that those who receive more wealth are taxed more, and ultimately strengthen the redistributive function of inheritance, estate, and gift taxes. Chapter 2 also showed that progressive inheritance taxes, in combination with taxes on personal capital income, can be powerful tools to prevent the build-up of excessive wealth over generations. Moreover, progressive inheritance tax rates can encourage giving to those who have less. If a tax is levied on lifetime wealth transfers, progressive rates would be an even more powerful instrument to reduce inequality as they would not be applied to each wealth transfer separately but to the accumulated gifts and inheritances received by beneficiaries during their lifetime. Progressive inheritance or estate tax rates may also help avoid significant increases in marginal effective tax rates if tax rates increase gradually with the value of the inheritance. Chapter 3 showed that progressive rates are often applied to relatively low-value wealth transfers, with top marginal tax rates kicking in at relatively low levels of transferred wealth. Countries may consider strengthening progressivity by applying higher tax rates to high-value inheritances. However, this requires finding a balance so that tax rate levels are not excessively high, as high tax rates may strengthen the case for tax reliefs that undermine the redistributive and revenue raising potential of the tax, and could encourage greater tax avoidance or evasion. The level and degree of progressivity of inheritance and estate taxes should also take into account the level and degree of progressivity of other taxes on personal capital income and assets.

Excessive gaps between the tax treatment of direct descendants and distant relatives or non-related heirs should be avoided. Some have argued that wealth transfers to distant relatives or non-related heirs should be taxed more heavily than wealth transferred to direct descendants or closer relatives, on the basis the former are more akin to a windfall. However, in some cases, very high tax rates (and low tax exemption thresholds) on transfers to more distant relatives and non-family members may be questionable, for instance in cases where recipients have not received much from their parents. The rise of blended families also raises the question of the tax treatment of transfers to stepchildren and the extent to which it should differ from the tax treatment of transfers to children. Applying higher tax rates to more distant family members also incentivises donors to concentrate their wealth transfers among closer family members. Thus, reducing the difference in the tax treatment between closer and more distantly-related heirs may encourage donors to spread their wealth among more heirs and thereby reduce concentrations of wealth. It may also be worth taking into account some beneficiary-specific characteristics in determining the tax liability of beneficiaries receiving wealth transfers from distant relatives or non-related donors (e.g. income/wealth testing of beneficiaries or whether they have received wealth from their parents).

4.2.3. Exemptions and reliefs for specific assets

Countries should consider scaling back tax exemptions and reliefs for which there is no strong rationale and which tend to be regressive. Some countries provide exemptions for private pension savings. As private pension savings are typically taxed at lower rates under income tax systems than other asset types (see section 3.8.4), exempting them from inheritance and estate taxes may allow donors to build wealth and pass it on to beneficiaries while incurring minimal tax liabilities. Some countries also provide concessionary treatment for payments received from life insurance policies. The justification for these exemptions appears limited, as in many countries life insurance policies are simply tax-efficient investment vehicles that contain the same investments and savings products as those that people can hold directly. These types of exemptions or preferential tax treatments also tend to be regressive, primarily benefitting wealthy households. In cases where there may be more justification for maintaining relief (e.g. for a house that remains occupied by a cohabitee), the value of tax relief could be capped (e.g. capping the value of residential property that can benefit from such relief).

Exemptions or reliefs for business assets should be carefully designed and alternatives could be considered. Most countries provide very generous relief for business assets to ensure business continuity after the donor's death. However, evidence shows that these reliefs predominantly benefit the very wealthy and that they have sometimes been unnecessarily generous, with the rationale for providing such generosity being the need to prevent liquidity issues. The goal itself of promoting business transmissions to descendants has also sometimes been questioned given evidence that heirs tend to underperform when they inherit a business. At a minimum, if exemptions or reliefs are provided for business assets, there should be strict eligibility requirements (e.g. minimum ownership) and conditionality (e.g. business continuity after the business is transferred), with clawback relief if the business is sold before a certain number of years. Countries could also consider targeting relief at businesses below a certain size, capping the amount of available relief (e.g. capping the value of business assets that can benefit from inheritance or estate tax relief) or introducing some form of means-testing (e.g. based on firm profitability). There may also be cases where alternative reforms could be considered. For instance, a relatively low-rate inheritance tax allowing tax payments in instalments (e.g. over ten years) would significantly reduce the need for and political pressure to exempt or provide significant relief for family businesses.

4.2.4. Tax treatment of inter vivos gifts

The provision of renewable gift tax exemptions should be carefully assessed and reviewed where they allow wealth transfers to largely go untaxed. Where taxpayers are able to transfer assets under a specified value tax-free each year, they can effectively avoid inheritance and estate taxes by transferring wealth early. Wealthy families who hold a greater portion of wealth in liquid assets and whose wealth exceeds their needs for retirement are the best placed to take advantage of these opportunities. On the other hand, middle class families who hold most of their wealth in their main residence and poorer households who rely on their savings to finance their consumption in retirement may not be able to engage in such tax planning. To combat tax avoidance through inter vivos giving, one option, as mentioned above, would be to have a lifetime wealth transfer tax, allowing a certain amount of wealth to be received free of tax during the recipient's lifetime. Another option is for gift tax exemption thresholds to approximate as much as possible a reasonable lifetime exemption threshold. The shorter the periods between gift tax exemption renewals, the smaller the exempt amounts should be. For more generous tax exemption thresholds, the time before tax-free thresholds are renewed could be lengthened to reduce tax planning and increase fairness, although that may increase tax administration and compliance costs.

Favouring wealth transfers to younger generations would decrease intergenerational wealth inequality but would increase intra-generational wealth inequality. As discussed in Chapter 1, the age at which people receive inheritances keeps increasing with the rise in life expectancy. To encourage earlier wealth transmissions, some countries may be considering reliefs for gifts to younger generations, e.g. tax breaks or tapered relief for transmissions to recipients below a certain age. Such measures would encourage the intergenerational circulation of capital, but create unequal opportunities among younger generations. Besides, transferring earlier in life will mostly be possible for the wealthiest households. One option would be to limit the tax advantage for large transfers.

Inter vivos gifts should be carefully monitored, given the greater risks of non-compliance. As opposed to wealth transfers upon death, which are usually linked to probate or notarial acts, thereby minimising non-tax compliance risks, gifts are much more prone to underreporting. Thus, tax authorities' compliance efforts should largely focus on gifts. If undeclared gifts are uncovered, governments could consider making tax-free thresholds unusable. For non-reported gifts of assets whose value has significantly appreciated since it was gifted, (part of) the appreciated value could be used to determine the tax base when the gift is uncovered. Reporting requirements could also be increased to minimise non-compliance risks (see below).

4.2.5. Asset valuation

Regarding asset valuation, taxable values should to the extent possible be based on fair market value. For many assets, it is fairly straightforward to establish fair market value. However, determining fair market value may be more difficult for some assets, including for unlisted shares and closely-held businesses. In these cases, the best valuation approach or combination of approaches will depend on the size and type of business. For large private businesses, it may be possible to use the comparability/market approach, i.e. to determine fair market value based on the share prices of comparable listed companies. For small closely-held or private businesses, the book/asset approach may be used, but in combination with another approach (i.e. the income or market approach). Determining the market value of intangible assets also poses significant challenges given the lack of observable arm's length transactions of identical or substantially similar assets. Where the intangible asset is income producing, income-based approaches may be the most appropriate. In addition to valuation methods, there may be cases where valuation discounts, e.g. for minority shareholdings or lower marketability, may be overly generous and could be revised. Finally, from a compliance perspective, there should be frequent tax audits, as well as penalties in cases of clear undervaluation.

4.2.6. Preventing liquidity issues

Payments in instalments and deferred payments under certain conditions should be allowed to overcome liquidity issues. Short-term payment extensions should be available, and be free of interest charges where certain conditions are met, to give taxpayers some flexibility. Countries may also consider the impacts of requiring beneficiaries to pay inheritance or estate taxes before receiving ownership of the inherited assets. While this may decrease late or non-payment, it can also create hardship for taxpayers without sufficient funds, although much will depend on the rate at which inheritance taxes are levied. Payments in instalments over longer periods of time could be restricted to certain assets, and could require taxpayers to prove that paying the tax as a lump-sum would cause hardship. For business and farm assets, below-market interest rates or no interest could apply to long-term payments in instalments. Tax payment deferral may also be provided in certain cases and under certain conditions, for instance a standard tax deferral period (e.g. five years), perhaps combined with payments in instalments after that period, may be provided for homes or other assets where immediate tax payments would demonstrably cause financial distress. Tax payment deferral could also require a deposit, where a portion of the tax is paid by the original due date.

4.2.7. Tax avoidance and evasion

Measures should prevent taxpayers from transferring private wealth in the guise of business assets to benefit from exemptions or preferential tax rules. Taxpayers may hold private wealth in closely-held businesses, that have been established for the purpose of transferring private wealth or that are mixed with other assets that generate genuine economic activity. Some countries already prevent this type of avoidance, by requiring assets to be linked to the businesses' economic purpose or by limiting the share of the business that can be dedicated to owning immovable property. Countries that do not have such rules in place should consider adopting or expanding them.

Possibilities for tax planning through trusts or similar structures should be carefully examined and tax rules could be revised to prevent tax avoidance. While trusts may be set up for legitimate succession and other non-tax reasons, the fact that ownership and access to benefits is split in some way means they can also potentially be used to avoid taxes on wealth transfers. Whether trusts are treated as separate entities for tax purposes or as transparent entities (i.e. where the assets settled on trust are included in the taxable estate of the settlor or the beneficiaries on the basis that trusts can be 'looked through'), tax systems should not allow the use of trusts to significantly reduce the tax burden on wealth transfers. The tax treatment of other structures, such as foundations, should also be carefully examined.

Countries concerned with the distributional impact of the preferential tax treatment granted to charitable giving could revise deductions and limit opportunities for tax-free wealth transfers through charitable structures. Countries may consider alternatives to tax deductions for charitable giving, as these provide a greater tax benefit for high-income or high-wealth taxpayers that can deduct donations at their marginal income tax rate (see section 3.13.1) or marginal inheritance or estate tax rate in countries with progressive rates. Countries may instead implement a tax credit, to ensure that all taxpayers receive the same tax benefit for equivalent donations. Some countries may also wish to restrict the use of charitable structures that allow donors to transfer wealth to heirs with a significantly lower tax burden than if the transfer was made directly between the donor and the ultimate beneficiary.

There is a need for continued progress on international tax transparency to prevent offshore tax evasion. It is important to ensure that jurisdictions continue to effectively participate in exchange of information on request (EOIR) and to assess the effectiveness of the implementation of the automatic exchange of Information (AEOI), including by dedicating adequate resources to the analysis of the data collected and by ensuring compliance by financial institutions. Going forward, it will also be critical to ensure that persons, assets, and institutions not covered under existing exchange of information standards do not offer opportunities for continued tax evasion.

4.2.8. Reporting requirements and data collection

Reporting requirements could be strengthened and tax administrations are encouraged to collect more data. In a number of countries, there is limited available data on inherited and gifted wealth. In particular, there is a lack of available data on untaxed gifts, on transfers of assets that are exempt, and on the costs and distributional effects of such exemptions. Countries may wish to introduce reporting obligations for transfers above a certain low-value threshold, even if these are not subject to tax. Such reporting should be simple, available online, and able to be completed by the taxpayer without needing professional advice. Digitalisation represents a significant opportunity, in terms of both collecting and analysing data. For instance, this may allow governments to track lifetime wealth transfers in ways that were previously impossible at a reasonable cost.

4.2.9. Tax treatment of unrealised capital gains at death

The step-up in basis should be reconsidered, particularly where inheritance or estate taxes are not levied, or where inheritance or estate tax exemption thresholds are very high. Under the step-up in basis, which a number of countries provide for, the cost basis of the assets transferred at death is "stepped up" for capital gains tax purposes to their fair market value at the time of the bequest. When the heir sells the asset, only the capital gains accrued since they received the inheritance are subject to capital gains taxes. The step-up in basis allows taxpayers to reduce their total tax liability by passing on their wealth in the form of unrealised gains, and these gains will go fully untaxed where there is no inheritance or estate tax. In addition to generating distortive lock-in effects, this may have significant distributional implications, as unrealised capital gains make up a large portion of the richest taxpayers' wealth. Thus, there is a strong case for removing the step-up in basis for unrealised capital gains at death, especially where inheritance taxes are not levied. Unrealised capital gains may also largely escape any form of taxation where the inheritance or estate tax threshold is very high. In such cases, countries should either reconsider the step-up in basis or lower the inheritance or estate tax exemption threshold. The step-up in basis also creates distortions where an inheritance or estate tax is levied because it still discourages people from realising capital gains. Indeed, if taxpayers sell appreciated property while alive, the gains are subject to capital gains tax, and if they transfer the proceeds of the sale (reduced by the income tax paid) to their heirs when they die, the inheritance or estate tax will also be levied. The step-up in basis therefore creates inequity between taxpayers who realise gains during their lifetime and those who transfer wealth in the form of unrealised gains at death.

The most equitable and efficient alternative to the step-up in basis may be to tax unrealised gains at death but allow for some flexibility in terms of payment arrangements, such as deferral, where necessary. Levying capital gains taxes and inheritance taxes on the same event could result in high tax burdens. In addition, even where the donor bears the capital gains tax and the recipient pays the inheritance tax, it may still be perceived as double taxation. An alternative may be to carry over the accrued gain on transferred assets (whether through in-life gifts or bequests) to the recipients. This would mean that the capital gains accrued during the donor's lifetime would eventually be subject to tax when recipients sell the assets, but would avoid the concomitant levy of the capital gains tax and the inheritance or estate tax. A downside would be that it would require recipients to track the original cost basis of the donor, although this may become less difficult with digitalisation. Another more significant issue is that the capital gains tax liability might become disproportionately large, in particular for businesses and farms that continue operating for several generations, and provide significant lock-in incentives. Thus, the most appropriate approach may be to tax unrealised gains at death, but allow for some flexibility in payment arrangements (i.e. deferral) where demonstrably necessary.

4.2.10. Cross-border inheritances and migration

Taxing rights in respect of cross-border inheritances should be better aligned across countries and adequate double taxation relief should be provided. Considering the differences across countries in rules determining liability for inheritance or estate taxation, non-taxation, double taxation, or even multiple taxation may arise in cross-border wealth transfers. A majority of countries levying inheritance or estate taxes provide unilateral relief for inheritance and gift tax paid abroad in respect of movable and immovable assets located abroad, but it is sometimes incomplete, and some countries do not provide such relief under their domestic legislation. Given that double tax treaty networks to prevent double taxation under inheritance or estate taxes are very limited, there might be merit in preventing risks of non-taxation or double taxation by first improving and harmonising unilateral inheritance or estate tax relief related to cross-border inheritances.

"Tail provisions" should be introduced to ensure that people remain subject to inheritance taxes for a number of years after they move abroad. In several jurisdictions, taxpayers continue to be liable for inheritance or estate taxes for a number of years after leaving the country. Such "tail provisions" limit the risk of inheritance or estate tax avoidance by emigrating shortly before the donor's death.

4.2.11. Political economy

Providing information on inequality as well as on the design and functioning of inheritance taxes can enhance the public acceptability and political feasibility of inheritance tax reforms. Chapter 3 discussed the fact that inheritance and estate taxes are often misunderstood, which contributes to their unpopularity. Evidence has shown that providing information on inherited wealth and inequality can play an important role in making inheritance taxes more acceptable (see section 3.14.1). Similarly, as the share of taxable wealth transfers and effective tax rates tend to be overestimated, sometimes considerably so, providing information on the way inheritance and estate taxes work, and who they apply to, can significantly increase support for them.

Policy framing and packaging can also play an important role in the acceptability and feasibility of reforms. Inheritance or estate tax reform has often suffered from unfavourable narratives and policy framing, notably through references to "death taxes" and "double taxation". Reframing inheritance tax reforms around issues of fairness, equality of opportunity and inequality reduction may play an important role. Such changes in narratives and policy framing may be easier with inequality becoming a more prominent topic in recent years. Such reframing may also be more effective if it goes hand-in-hand with real changes in tax design that address popular concerns, particularly in relation to tax avoidance. The use of policy packages may also be helpful. Indeed, inheritance tax reform may be more acceptable if it is accompanied by other reforms or if it is part of a broader reform aimed at shifting the tax mix rather than increasing the overall tax burden.

Printed by Libri Plureos GmbH in Hamburg,
Germany